CARL FRAMPTON

MY AUTOBIOGRAPHY

with

PAUL D. GIBSON

MERRION
PRESS

First published in 2023 by
Merrion Press
10 George's Street
Newbridge
Co. Kildare
Ireland
www.merrionpress.ie

9781785374692 (Hardback)
9781785374708 (Ebook)

A CIP catalogue record for this book is
available from the British Library.

Typeset in Minion Pro 12/17 pt

Cover design by Fiachra McCarthy.

Front cover image courtesy of Mark Robinson.
Back cover image © Charles McQuillan/Stringer, Getty Images.
Unless otherwise stated, all images courtesy of the author.

Merrion Press is a member of Publishing Ireland.

CONTENTS

To my wife Christine and my children Carla,
Rossa and Mila. The loves of my life.

FOREWORD

Patrick Kielty

All too often in a comedian's life someone will utter the following words with genuine sincerity – 'I think what you do is the hardest job in the world. I don't know how you get up there.'

It's tricky enough to keep a straight face when the person saying it has a job that's way harder and far more important, like a doctor or a teacher. But when the words fall out of Carl Frampton's mouth, you can't help breaking your bum laughing. To his face.

When I realised he was actually serious, I had to go home, lie down in a dark room and try to work it out. What the hell was he thinking? Surely any eejit knows getting punched in the face is the hardest job in the world. Let alone someone who did it for a living. How did he not know that?

Then the penny dropped. He didn't think his job was the hardest in the world because he usually didn't get punched in the face. He spent most of his time in the ring ducking and diving and punching someone else in the face. Closing them down, breaking their will, then their hearts, until they realised that fighting Carl Frampton was the hardest job in the world.

It's why he became the champion he is and why the whole of Northern Ireland came to a standstill every time he climbed through the ropes. It's why he won three world titles at two different weights. And became arguably the greatest Irish boxer of all time. It's why, when he won his first war with Leo Santa Cruz and turned Brooklyn green for a night, I cried so hard the missus asked me if the dog had died. And it's why he's taken his place in the pantheon of boxing greats.

It goes without saying that boxing is the opposite of stand-up comedy. In boxing all talk is cheap. Backing it up is the hard part. But it's what Carl has always done. Both in and out of the ring.

I'll always remember where I was when he told me he thought stand-up was the hardest job in the world. We were beside the bags in Midland Boxing Club in his native north Belfast – a club he knew well but had no business being in, just a few short months after he hung up his gloves.

It was in the midst of the Protocol protests that had flared on the streets of loyalist Belfast, and I was making a documentary for the BBC. Carl was there helping to train some of the kids who could easily have been drawn into the riots that were making the news. Except they weren't. Because he was there alongside the other trainers in the club, not just showing them how to box but how to live their lives.

When you grow up in Northern Ireland, it's all too easy to see the world through a binary prism. Them and Us is a lesson that sticks and it's hard to shake off. But Carl Frampton lives his life by a different set of values. At the heart of it is the idea that we are all different but more similar than we think.

When it comes to looking to the future, Carl doesn't just talk the talk but walks the walk. And for a new generation in Northern Ireland, he is the future. Someone not afraid to play his part to make it happen. It's why he's loved out of the ring as much as he was in it.

Before you read on, it's confession time from me. I sadly never got to see Carl fight in the flesh. I was living in the US when he was fighting back home, and working back home when he fought in the US. The secret of comedy is timing, eh?

But I can't count the amount of times he had me on the edge of my sofa willing him on. There'll be plenty of you reading this who know the exact same purgatory of excitement and pride I'm talking about. And we all fooled ourselves thinking we helped him get the job done.

Maybe it's just as well I never got to any of his fights. Jimmy Nesbitt was at most of them and I'm not sure there would have been enough beer for both of us.

I'M A BOXER

I'm in the back seat of Billy's blue Ford Mondeo as we drive up the M2 and I'm absolutely shitting myself. Billy drives me everywhere these days. Anywhere I have to go where it is possible to get from A to B on four wheels, Billy drives. But this is our first trip together, our maiden voyage. Joe is in the passenger seat and they're arguing about something or other like they always do. About what, I've no clue. I'm listening to them, but I don't hear anything. The butterflies that awoke in my stomach a few hours before have now fluttered all through my body. Even my head and ears feel full of them. The state I'm in, it would be a struggle to confirm my full name and date of birth never mind take part in a coherent conversation. But I'm Carl Frampton. Born on the 21st of February 1987. That makes me seven years old and on my way to make my ring debut.

The fight had only been made a couple of days prior. Late notice even by the chaotic standards of matching kids in no-decision amateur boxing matches in Ireland. Billy had received a call from Scorpion Boxing Club in Ballymoney. They were looking for a kid to fight one of their lads at the Causeway Coast Hotel in Portstewart on Friday evening. This age, this size, this weight, this experience. Aye, Billy would have said, we have someone.

The late notice may have been a blessing in disguise. It didn't give me much time to actually think about what was happening. No time for the nerves to fester and swell and explode inside of me. It felt like I'd been told I was fighting one minute and the next I was in the car on my way to the venue. Only now was the reality of my situation dawning on me. What am I doing? I've only been going to the boxing club a couple of months. I have a sense I'm decent but sparring your mates isn't the same. First off, it's only sparring. And second, maybe my mates are all shit.

I can look back now and appreciate that Billy and Joe saw my potential. They knew what they were doing. They knew how good I was even then and that I, more than any other kid in the club, could handle this. How many other times have the pair of them done a three-hour round trip just to bring one solitary seven-year-old boxer to make his debut? That tells you the faith they had in my ability. But as I say, sat in the back of car as the north coast approaches, I don't know any of that yet.

The atmosphere around the ring was like so many others in those days. A rowdy crowd in a smoke-filled room. All men, drinking and looking forward to young fellas battering each other. I'm clearly the away fighter here and by the insular standards of my north Belfast upbringing I'm a long way from home. Overseas internationals aside, my da would rarely miss another one of my fights as an amateur and never as a professional throughout my twenty-seven-year career, but the two-day notice wasn't enough for him to arrange time off work. So it's just me, Billy and Joe versus the rest for this one.

That's not to say anyone from my opponent's side tried to intimidate me. It wasn't like that. It was never really like that while boxing in Northern Ireland. It wasn't like that when later I, a wee Prod from Tiger's Bay, walked into Provie drinking dens in west Belfast to fight, so certainly no one in Portstewart that night was being deliberately menacing. But it was all very daunting, nevertheless. When you really sit back and think about it from the view of a seven-year-old kid, how could it not be?

I was seven, but few who met me back then believed it. Most

would have guessed five. I was basically a midget, a full head shorter than my peers. My arms must have been in proportion because the gloves we used to spar in at the club came up to my elbow when laced. Huge, 14oz jobs that I'm sure had been in circulation for at least fifteen years before I had my turn with them. The size and heft of them meant it took all my effort just to throw a punch, and that punch was invariably a big straight-arm swing as I couldn't bend my elbow.

On this night, however, the gloves were different: 10oz. Four ounces may not sound a lot, and in most walks of life it isn't, but when it comes to boxing gloves it's a substantial weight. Now we're talking, I thought as they were laced up and my elbow could still breathe. I threw a few punches at the air around me. Wow. So this is what it's supposed to feel like.

They say when you fight the increased adrenaline pumping through your body prevents you feeling the majority of the physical pain being inflicted upon you by your opponent. I was so full of adrenaline when I clambered into the ring that I was numb to not only pain but every other emotion or sensation, physical or psychological. I'm not even sure I could see, hear or think.

You soon get used to it of course. The processes and procedures that precede the fight. You know to get in and relax. Move around the ring and stay loose. Your rival still has to enter the arena. There'll be announcements and instructions. There'll be walks to the centre and back to your corner. There'll be last-minute advice from your coach. It's second nature by the second fight but on your debut you're too nervous and bewildered to function normally. It's a cliché but the comparison with a dog getting let off the leash is not too far off the mark. And when the bell goes, you're free.

I'd be lying if I said I remember much of the fight that night. The main recollection is simply a sense of victory afterwards. It is declared an honourable draw as all such contests are at that level of boxing, but in general everyone knows who got the better of it. Billy and Joe were certainly telling me I'd won but who knows, maybe the other fella's corner was telling him the exact same.

I get changed and we hang around for a while. The hosting club always put on a spread for the boys to tuck in to after their fight. Juice, crisps, sandwiches and the like. The bread has been cut into dainty finger shapes here. What the fuck, I think. I'll need about 500 to fill me up. I sit down somewhere to watch the rest of the fights. As the youngest there, I was the first on, so there is still hours of boxing to come. It's all new and exciting but in truth I don't pay much attention. I'm not even really there anymore. I'm already back in school telling my mates all about it. Telling them that I've had a fight. Telling them that I'm a boxer.

CHAPTER ONE

THE BOXER FROM THE BAY

I don't remember much before boxing. Actually, that's not a great opening line for a boxer's autobiography, is it? So, let's be clear before we go any further, I'm definitely not punchy. What I mean to say is, when you're already fighting by the age of seven there isn't a whole lot to remember before that.

I'm told I lived in Syringa Street at the top end of Tiger's Bay in north Belfast the first year of my life. Then we made the short move to Upper Canning Street, where I lived until I left home twenty-two years later. *We*, by the way, is my da Craig, my ma Flo, my big sister Valerie and my younger brother Craig. My da never really liked living in Tiger's Bay. He was from a few miles up along the Shore Road in Fairhill and a lot of his family were still there. The story goes that my ma, who was from Seaview Street off York Road, put the application for the house in behind his back and before he knew it, he was there.

Our house was basically the same as all the others in Tiger's Bay. A small, red-bricked terrace with a kitchen, living room, bathroom, box room and two bedrooms. The front door of most houses opened up onto the street but the two families to the right of us somehow ended up with a three-foot wide space between their wall and the footpath, which could loosely be described as a front yard.

I remember being jealous of that three foot and thinking of them as the yuppy families for having such a luxury. Opposite our house was nothing, just open waste ground where they'd light the bonfire on the Eleventh Night. There were three or four massive rocks or boulders there and one day messing around when I was five or six, I found a balaclava, a pair of gloves and a handgun. I ran home and told my da and he just said not to go near it. He never told me until much later that it probably belonged to our neighbour Mark Haddock, a notorious UVF (Ulster Volunteer Force) commander and RUC (Royal Ulster Constabulary) Special Branch informer believed to have been involved in over twenty murders.

No one had a garden out the back but there was a twelve-foot by twelve-foot concrete yard to enjoy. Beyond that was a narrow alleyway separating the backs of our houses from the backs of those in the parallel Greenmount Place. In writing this book I was asked for my earliest memory and two sprang to mind. The first is a story my da still likes telling when he found me and my wee pals Keith Ansley and Vicky Patterson riding our trikes up and down the alleyway with me and Keith buck naked. We were around three or four years old at the time. My da went ballistic and we said a man told us to take our clothes off. To this day I'm not sure if that really happened or we made it up. The second is of playing in that yard with my brother. Again, I reckon I was three or four and Craig is a year and one month younger. We've some sort of see-saw that we barely fit into, and we've already broken it so it doesn't go up and down as it should. Instead, we just spin round and round on it until we're dizzy and laughing. Anything before that I need to rely on what my ma and da tell me. Apparently, I was well behaved but very active from day one. As a baby you'd need to hold me tight when I was on your knee or I'd bounce right off and I was already walking about the house on my own at seven and a half months. The only real drama was the night I tumbled out of a baby chair in the living room and ended up with my face briefly stuck to the glass door of the fire. My da pulled me free from it, put a wet tea towel over my cheek and shouted for my ma, who was pregnant with Craig at the time. When my da went to pay the taxi that took us to the hospital the driver refused to take the money.

'Forget about that and get that child in there quick,' was all he said.

I was lucky enough in the end that there was no serious damage. For a long time one cheek always used to be redder than the other but it didn't stop me being the best-looking child to ever walk the streets of Tiger's Bay.

Being so close in age me and my brother played together a lot in those early days, but we are very different characters. As soon as I was introduced to the concept of organised sports that's all that mattered to me whereas Craig had no interest whatsoever. I'd be outside the house every day kicking a ball against a wall for hours while he was trying to knock it down with a hammer. So, as we grew older, I was hanging about more and more with whoever I was playing sport with while he had his own gang. That tended to be the renegades in the area, the headers and loose cannons with no direction. Craig himself was hot-headed and liked a tantrum as a kid. He's never been the most comfortable in social situations and takes his time around new people, which means he's maybe misunderstood a little. In reality he's a great guy. Generous to a fault and as hard a grafter as I know. He's a labourer now but when he's out of work he goes round collecting scrap metal. He's known as the scrap man. Or Ma Doo. He used to have big mad hair and they called him Hair Ma Doo until that got shortened to Ma Doo. You sometimes see him with copper pipes or whatever in his pocket. He picks up anything, like a magpie. He used to fill my ma and da's back yard until it looked like a scrap heap. Then he'd head down to Clearway's in the Docks to sell it all. They all love him down there, buy him a bottle of vodka at Christmas and all. They got their tickets for my fights off Craig, and I remember meeting one fella from the Markets who works there telling me a good story. Craig never sat ringside for any of my fights. He prefers to be in the cheap seats with his mates and the priority is always having a drink and a laugh. This fella told me at one fight he was busting for a piss and sprinted out between rounds to find the gents. On his way back he spots Craig at the bar with a pint in his hand.

'What the hell are you doing?' he says to my brother. 'Carl's on now!'

Craig just shrugged and replied, 'I couldn't give a fuck – what's the price of aluminium at the minute?'

We've always had that unspoken brotherly closeness, though. Nothing touchy feely but I know without any shadow of a doubt he'd always back me up in a fight if I ever needed it and so would I for him. He's proved that many times, his bravery and loyalty. As teenagers a group of lads led by a guy called Kirk McAllister attacked my mate, Darren Stirling. Darren's big brother Biffo asked me to point out who McAllister was, but I went a step further and hit him a dig. Biffo then followed up with his own retribution on McAllister. This all happened one Eleventh Night, and by the Twelfth McAllister and his brother were on the phone threatening to kill me and all the rest. I was sitting in a house party with Craig and when he heard he said to tell them we'll see them now at the Grove Primary School and sort it out. We went, me with plenty of nerves and Craig seemingly without a care in the world, but they never turned up.

My sister Valerie's not my da's kid but he raised her as his own. I don't know her biological father, but she's never wanted anything to do with him. Valerie always seemed so much older when we were growing up. Eight years is a lot at that age. She'd babysit me and Craig, and I liked it when she'd bring her boyfriend Michael

McGurk round. They had my niece Sophie pretty young and moved in together, so Valerie was out of our house when I was about nine. McGurk is a bit of a character and their house got petrol bombed not long after. Valerie had taken our toastie maker with her and that was one of the casualties of the attack. I was raging and went about a year without a toastie.

Valerie's Sophie then had her own child when she was only fifteen. That made Valerie a granny when she was thirty. I remember thinking it was like something off Jeremy Kyle. I was shouting at everyone asking how the fuck has this been allowed to happen. I was angry that everyone else except my da didn't seem to be as angry as me by it all. It embarrassed me and I never told anyone about it. But Sophie is still with the same lad Dean she had the baby with. They have three kids now and they are raising their family brilliantly. The pair of them really stepped up to the plate and it all worked out.

My da was in the army before I was born. He did five years' service mainly in Münster, Germany, at the big British army base there and was in charge of manning the ski slopes. He was also based closer to home in Fermanagh for a while and was down there in 1981 when Bobby Sands stood for election in the area. After he left the army, he started working in Loughside Recreation Centre on the Shore Road. My ma has always worked in supermarkets. I remember her being in Woolworths, then Morrisons, then Asda. She's now working in Asda Living at Yorkgate just outside Belfast city centre. She doesn't really need to anymore, but I think she likes the social aspect as much as anything. Plus, like most working-class people, her and my da expect to get up and do a day's work and would probably be lost without it. My da actually took early redundancy when he turned sixty, but he didn't know what to do with himself and was soon back at it, working as a caretaker at a special-needs school.

My grandparents were all still alive when I was young. Jimmy and Maggie on my ma's side. They had seven kids with my ma being second youngest out of Jimbo, Bobby, Geordie, Cecil, Isa, Lilly and her. Granda Jimmy always seemed very strict when I was a kid. We'd sometimes go to his house in Alexandra Park after school while we waited on my ma and da to finish work, and he'd always be shouting at us for something. Like most though, he mellowed over the years. He went to all my fights along with my uncle Bobby. Even towards the end of his life when he was almost blind and could barely walk, he somehow made it out to New York and all. Amazing really, and Bobby there at each one looking after him. Back when Granda Jimmy was always losing his patience with us kids, Granny Maggie was as nice as Jimmy was strict. When he shouted at us, she'd shout at him and tell him to wise up. We were very close to Granny Maggie and Valerie actually lived with her for a while, so when she was the first of our grandparents to pass away it hit us pretty hard. I remember she'd been in hospital for something but was scheduled to be released. It was a Thursday evening because I was coming back from football training. I knew she was coming out of hospital that night, but I suddenly got this horrible feeling in my stomach that something wasn't right. I sprinted the last 500 yards up to our front door which my da opened to tell me she'd just died.

On my da's side there was Hughie and Mary. Granny Mary was born in Birkenhead and arrived over to Belfast young. She worked in Gallagher's tobacco factory all her life on the site of what is now Yorkgate shopping complex. Granda Hughie was from the Shankill and spent his working life in Mackie's on the Springfield Road. Mackie's, or James Mackie & Sons, was a huge textile-machinery plant and foundry that employed thousands of people in Belfast. Hughie, or Shughie as he got called, was a massive boxing fan from long before I ever laced a glove. He knew all the history of boxing in Belfast and would tell me all the stories from back in the day. He was also the secretary of a loyalist club on the Shankill Road that hosted plenty of amateur boxing nights. He was there working the famous night when the Irish team boxed West Germany. Having green vests with shamrocks on them inside Shankill loyalist clubs at the height of the Troubles was not the norm. Gerry Storey was the manager of the Irish team and probably the only man on earth who could have pulled it off. Barry McGuigan fought that night, and his old man sang 'Danny Boy' ahead of the fights as he always did. This was a step too far for some, and apparently someone wanted to shoot him. Hughie told me an old-school UVF man named Trainor from the Mountainview Social Club gave the culprit a slap, told him to wise up and sent him home. Mad really, but that's how it was in those days. It's been said many times that boxing had a special status that somehow protected it from the worst of the Troubles. It's true to an extent but it's easy to romanticise the whole thing. They were very dangerous times even if you did have a pair of boxing gloves on, and what the likes of Gerry Storey were able to do was truly remarkable.

***

I went to Grove Primary School. Technically just outside Tiger's Bay in the direction of Mount Vernon but Tiger's Bay is small and the borders aren't always clear. Plenty of people get confused and others claim to be part of the area when they're not really. It was about three quarters of a mile from my house and by the age of eight I was walking that myself. We live next door to my son Rossa's school now and you couldn't let him go on his own without social services giving you a call. There was a mixture of kids at Grove Primary, and I don't think it was that rough. Not notoriously rough anyway like plenty of the schools in Belfast. My ma actually went there in her day, so it was an old building. A bit eerie as a kid. It was apparently used as a hospital during the war, which lent itself to plenty of stories – so you'd be spooked when you first went if you had to walk the quiet corridors to use the toilet or whatever.

I never minded school. Never said no to the odd day off but I enjoyed it okay when I was there. I always liked to get there early to play football before the first bell. Break and lunch were for football too. Jumpers on the tarmac for goalposts type stuff, my class against the year above me. The boredom of formal education in between matches seemed worth it if I could play football three times before the final bell rang. In P4 my teacher was the auntie of David Healy, the all-time leading goal scorer for Northern Ireland.

I was into every sport. Probably a bit obsessed to be honest. Any chance I had to try something I'd go for it full pelt. At places like the summer scheme at the local leisure centre you got to try all sorts. Badminton, pool, table tennis, trampolining, whatever. In school I even played rugby despite all the size of me. Scrum half was the natural position for the smallest member of the squad, and I threw myself into the role. I was feisty and got stuck in without hesitation but there's no real substitute for size in a lot of situations on the rugby field, so I ended up just getting out-muscled and pushed about. So, like most boys at that age, football was my first love. I never saw him play but my da claims to have been a half decent footballer in his day. Me and him would watch all the matches we could on TV, supporting Crusaders, Glasgow Rangers and Northern Ireland. The main club I played for was Loughside Boys on the Shore Road. Before that it was Glenfield in Ballysillan, where I won player of the year and that led to the move to Loughside. The transfer was sealed when Big Junior, one of the coaches who happened to work for C&C, the drinks company, threw in a crate of Pepsi to sweeten the deal. Through Loughside I got a season ticket for a fiver to watch Crusaders, our local Irish League team, play at Seaview. I rarely missed one of their home games, and when we could get tickets me and my da went to Windsor Park to watch Northern Ireland matches as well.

I was still very shy around this time. In Tiger's Bay you were expected to be kissing girls by your eighth birthday, but I was still terrified of them. I was so small as well, which never helped. Even though I was the big brother, Craig was already taller than me and probably looked older too. It annoyed me everyone thinking I was the younger one. Maybe I was looking to compensate by running around with the likes of Keith (of naked trike ride fame), Sam Sloan, Darren Stirling, Polo and Cowan. Sam was the cool kid and hard man of the school. He was a bit wild in those days and no one messed with him. I thought it was great hanging around with Sam. He was stealing fegs off his ma when he was seven or eight and we'd smoke them in an empty house beside school. I'd never nick my da's fegs as I was too scared of getting caught but I'd pick butts off the street and get a couple of draws from them. Completely embarrassing looking back but there were thousands of kids all over the city doing equally daft things.

It was normal, and normal is pretty much how I felt my life was. My ma and da worked hard to provide, my da often doing double shifts in the leisure centre from 9 a.m. to 9 p.m. Despite that I don't think we ever had much dough to spend. But at the same time, I don't remember ever wanting for anything other than the normal jealousy kids have when another kid gets something bigger and better for Christmas. You'd see some of them in Tiger's Bay raking about on quads or other crazily expensive presents around Christmas or birthdays. I'd be looking at those kids and wondering how the hell they were getting all the top-of-the-range gear when I knew their parents were on the dole while mine were knocking their pans in working all day. A little later I understood exactly how. To be honest, even if we did have the cash, we weren't the types to splash it. My da is a very sensible and understated guy. One Christmas I got a petrol scooter that got up to around 28mph and that was unreal. I was delighted and knew it must have been a lot for my ma and da to spare. And for every family in Tiger's Bay handing out quads to their kids for Christmas there was another with absolutely nothing to give theirs, so I knew enough to be grateful to lie somewhere in the middle. I went straight out for a spin on Christmas morning and rode it to my cousin Rab's house as I was told he'd got one too. Mine was yellow and his was blue but other than that they were supposedly the same. But when we went out his would only get up to around 5mph, so I was bombing around, circling him and pissing myself laughing. He was raging until he discovered he had the choke all the way out and that was what was stopping it going a proper speed.

We didn't really have big family holidays growing up. Nor caravans up the coast like some people I knew. Butlins was the first trip outside Northern Ireland. My ma was friendly with the McFarlane family, and once went away with them. We actually called the McFarlanes 'the Electrics', as anytime a domestic appliance was broken Maureen McFarlane thought she'd be able to fix it. She rarely could. When I was about nine years old our two families booked our first ever foreign holiday. Salou on the Catalan coast in Spain. I don't think my da fancied it much, so he made an excuse up about not being able to get that much time off work and I said I'd stay with him. He went to work every day and I went with him to go to the Loughside summer scheme. A day of raking about and playing different sports with my mates was far more attractive to me than lying beside a Spanish swimming pool with my ma and the Electrics.

The next year, I got picked to go to America as one of the Project Children kids. Project Children was set up by two Irish brothers in the New York Police Department. It started in the 1970s and was an opportunity for kids caught up in the Troubles to get away from the madness and spend a summer with a family in the US. There was always a cross-community element to it, so Protestant and Catholic kids went out there together and spent a bit of time with one another. For most it was the only time they'd mix with ones from the other side. I went to Marshall, Texas, birthplace of the great heavyweight George Foreman, and stayed with a couple called Cathy and David Carter. It was amazing. I absolutely loved it. I went to a soccer school every day, which had these English guys as coaches, and I felt like Maradona. If I was small in stature next to my peers back home, I was even smaller next to the average American kid my age – but I was a superstar compared with them at playing football. The Carters couldn't have been any nicer to me and the next year they paid out of their own money for me to go back and spend another summer with them. My bro got picked to go that year too. He went to a family in Dallas who had a kid his age and a dad who was an ex-professional English footballer then playing in a six-aside indoor league that got 3,000 people watching every match. I remember thinking how that's wasted on Craig who couldn't care less about football and being jealous thinking, he'd got luckier than me! That was nonsense obviously because I couldn't have done better than the Carters. They even offered once again in the third year to pay for everything out of their own pocket so I could go back. But this time I didn't want to go. The excuse we gave was that Craig hadn't been picked again and it wouldn't be fair for me to go without him. That wasn't true, though. It's embarrassing for me to admit it, but the real reason was that I didn't want to miss the Twelfth of July for the third year in a row.

***

For us in Tiger's Bay the Twelfth of July holiday was pretty much the highlight of the year. As kids it was as good as Christmas and definitely better than a birthday or Halloween or any other celebration you can think of. Anyone interested can look up the historical significance of the date for the Protestant community in Northern Ireland, but when you're young you don't really know much about any of that. You're aware of the general idea that this is something we Prods do and it's for us and the Catholics hate it. But like all the other pointless sectarianism, that's about the limit of your understanding. In the early days all I was worried about was helping build the biggest bonfire imaginable. I used to roam for hours covering miles and miles looking for wooden pallets and rubber tyres to pinch and haul back to the bonfire site. The main men in the area would be coordinating it all and they'd give you a pat on the head and make you feel a foot taller yourself. You felt part of something, and it was class watching your pallet get positioned in the structure as it grew bigger and bigger. On the Eleventh Night, they set it alight and that was the best buzz of all.

The bands and marches are the other big part of the Twelfth. It was exciting sitting by the side of the road watching them go by. Some of them are very impressive, properly talented musicians. People would join a band to learn the flute or whatever. You didn't actually need to be a member of the Orange Order but it's true most of the bands are linked to the local paramilitaries. In Tiger's Bay it was the 1st Flute Band. I knew plenty of people who went once a week to band practice. My twin cousins, Craig and David, and my other cousin Rab were all in the Pride of the Shore band. Rab was very gifted on the flute. He would hear a song on the radio, like a happy hardcore song, then pick up his flute and start playing it. I thought that was amazing and went through a phase of wanting to learn. I got Rab to teach me, and I think I learnt the first eight notes of 'Orange Wings' before I gave up. Seeing how hard it was probably made me more impressed watching the better ones perform as they marched past in their uniforms, playing their songs. These are the ones that are genuinely talented musicians and win the competitions they have. Those bands tended to lead the way to be followed by the more blood-and-thunder boys, a lot of them half cut and shouting UFF (Ulster Freedom Fighters) and UVF chants. That element was always there, and plenty looked forward to it. Maybe I unwittingly did before I had some sense too. But the Twelfth was for everyone in Tiger's Bay. Every family in the area turned out for it. It was a street-party atmosphere with everyone having a drink and a laugh. We got new clothes to wear, more often than not the new Glasgow Rangers FC top for the boys. Unfortunately, it's normal that the section of the community that don't do themselves any favours with their behaviour attract the negative attention. The burning of Irish flags and singing of certain songs and all that nonsense. And I don't think the unionist or loyalist politicians and community leaders are as clever as their nationalist or republican counterparts when it comes to PR. They often fail to portray the culture in the right way, and that allows the bitter element to dominate the headlines.

It's true as well that you remember childhood events a lot differently than the reality. Or maybe you remember them right but through the eyes of a kid everything is much more grand, much more exciting. At the end of the marches the bands all pass through Shaw's Bridge to arrive at the field in Edenderry on the outskirts of South Belfast. In my head that was like a massive funfair, so a few years ago when my kids Carla and Rossa were around eight and four, my wife Christine and I brought them along to experience it. Christine is Catholic so it was her first time too. We went with our close friend Stacey and their wee girl Gaby, who is the same age as Carla. Stacey's partner Rab would have been there, but he was away working on the oil rigs. They still live in Tiger's Bay, and I think it's good to get back there as much as possible so Carla and Rossa can run around with the local kids and learn to be a bit more streetwise. When we got to the field though it wasn't how I remembered it at all. All I saw was a load of people sat around drinking carry-outs, a few burger vans and a Christian group in the corner giving a sermon to a crowd of around ten people. I got recognised and posed for a few photos and then some balloon shouted, up the UFF. I just walked away with the kids a bit disappointed and underwhelmed with the whole thing. It was nothing like how I thought it was as a kid.

Growing up in Tiger's Bay, you are conscious you're a Prod from a very early age. I suppose you don't have any real understanding of what that means but you just know you are one and them ones over the other side of the fence aren't. You know they're called Fenians and although you don't know what a Fenian is you know you must hate them because everyone around you tells you so. For us in Tiger's Bay, the other side of the fence meant the New Lodge estate. They were the enemy. And they were so close, especially for us on Upper Canning Street, as there was only the waste ground and the so-called peace wall separating us from them. I could look out any of our front windows and see them. That could cause fear when you're a kid. You were taught they hated you even more than you hated them, so they're going to want to hurt you if they get a chance. My ma and da have never driven. My da drove tanks in the army but has never driven a car. That meant if it wasn't somewhere we could walk to we had to take a bus or taxi. To get to the Mater Hospital, for example, we had to take a taxi and it would go up Spamount Street through the New Lodge to get there. As a kid I'd be sat in the back looking out the window thinking, if this car breaks down here we're all fucking dead.

We weren't a paramilitary family. My da is far too sensible a guy to have gotten involved in any of that and I think part of the reason he joined the army in his late teens was to get away from any of the nonsense going on. But at the same time, when you grow up in an area like Tiger's Bay, the local paramilitaries are a pretty prominent feature of daily life. In our area the UDA (Ulster Defence Association) and the UFF were in charge. Along the road in Mount Vernon it was a UVF stronghold. Even though they're all loyalists, there was tension between the groups and the two areas. When there was a feud in full swing between the organisations we'd go as kids to watch them fighting. I remember seeing crowds clash outside the Grove Tavern on York Road and the UDA Brigadier Jimbo Simpson getting his head slashed open by a machete. It was an absolute war zone and a lot of my mates from the Bay wouldn't dare go near Mount Vernon. The same way I used to worry we'd break down in the New Lodge and the IRA (Irish Republican Army) would get us; they'd be wary of walking by Mount Vernon and the UVF attacking them. It was a bit different for me because through football I knocked around with guys from Mount Vernon. I was mates with boys like Willy Fearn, wee Homer, Colin McClure (universally known as Victor after my da called him that because he was always complaining like Victor Meldrew) and Paul Hamilton, who was good enough to go over to Nottingham Forest in England.

The presence of paramilitaries was nothing out of the ordinary and everyone knew who was who. I'm young enough to have missed the worst of it, but at certain points in recent history it would have been as easy and natural to drift into the local loyalist paramilitary group as it would the local sports team or youth club. My da has four brothers, all older than him. Two of them, uncle Clarke and uncle Joe, were born early enough to avoid those risks. Clarke married a lovely woman named Marie and he helps run a very good football team in Greenisland. The two Evans brothers, Jonny and Corry, who have both had long careers at the highest level came through from Greenisland FC. Clarke played in bands too, but not the marching type – he was more rock 'n' roll. Uncle Joe was apparently a bit of a hippy back in his day with long hair and flashing the peace sign to characters inside Shankill Road bars. He married Mary, a girl from Cork, where they still live now. They used to come up for a weekend every few months when I was young, and I'd have palpitations if his Free State licence plate was parked outside our house. They'd stay with my granny, Mary, and I remember once my granny wearing a King Billy apron while she was cooking and wondering what Mary from the Rebel County thought of that. I've no idea if it was a wind-up or if granny was just totally oblivious to it! Next came uncle Junior who married Maureen and uncle Robin who married Gina. Two proper hard men. Junior is a massive Glasgow Rangers fan and would travel over to a lot of games with a supporter's group that included a mate of mine, Darren Gill. Darren once told me about some obnoxious fella inside Ibrox Stadium, who kept standing up in front of him so he couldn't see the match. After asking him a few times to sit down, Junior lost patience and hit him a dig that sent him down about six rows. My da has told me stories about his brother having barneys with their da too after Junior would nail Granda's slippers to the shed roof or something for a laugh. I don't think Robin was as ever as crazy. He's a painter and decorator and well known in the area because of it. I was always hanging around with his son Rab, so I'd be in their house a lot. I loved going on a Saturday and getting my dinner there. I don't even remember what Robin made but I'd look forward to it every week.

It's nice now that fewer and fewer kids in Northern Ireland are being raised in that type of environment. Certainly, my own two live a million miles from those dangers. Carla is twelve now and she even asked me recently what the difference between a Catholic and a Protestant is. We played a wee game and called out names of people we know, and she had to guess which of the two religions they are. I liked the fact she'd never given it much thought before. She actually did okay in the game too although I don't know how many she guessed. A couple she got wrong was thinking my mate the boxer Paddy Barnes is Protestant and Ruth Gorman, the sports presenter, is Catholic. It shows how quickly things have changed as when I was a fair bit younger than Carla is now, I'd know straight away from their names who was the Catholic and who was the Protestant. We had lots of little tricks and tells to find that information out as quickly as possible, either for defensive or offensive reasons. We knew Catholics by their Berghaus coats, caps worn higher on their heads, bum-fluff taches and short hairstyles with longer fringes. Kids used to get grabbed and told to spell the word 'home' with the pronunciation of the letter H being another giveaway. I'm obviously raging Carla says it the Catholic way but I've Christine to blame for that! Thankfully Rossa pronounces it correctly in the King's English.

* * *

The Midland Amateur Boxing Club is about a two-minute walk from our house on Upper Canning Street. It's Billy McKee's club. Billy was born in York Street in the area of Belfast city centre known as Sailor Town. He grew up in the post-war 1940s and '50s, when families in that part of town had it pretty tough. As a boy he played a lot of sport. Football, table tennis and badminton in the Boy's Brigade before he joined the Henry Street Boy's Club, where he did a bit of boxing. He had a few amateur fights out of that club before, still in his teens, he joined the merchant navy and spent the next seventeen years seeing most of the world. He continued boxing on the ships and a little on shore while stationed in England. When the Troubles started in 1969, Billy's wife Eileen begged him to come home to be with her and their young family. It was a rough time and families from both sides of the community were being forced to move for their own safety. The McKees went first to Rathcoole and then on to Tiger's Bay, where Eileen was originally from. In 1973 Billy was approached and asked to set up some sort of a sporting or social club for people in the area to use as a distraction from the violence on the street. He was already working with the local pensioners, helping to get them out and about in between riots and setting up a place above a shop where they could meet up safely, so the people knew Billy was the man for the job. He soon had a football team on the go and an empty shell of a building where he put a table tennis table and a space to show movies. It wasn't long before he introduced boxing to the club despite the fact they had no real gear to speak of and, as the building had no electricity or running water, they had to use the toilet and shower of a house across the way.

Billy was the type of man who would have made it all work no matter what the conditions, but in 1976 he got a letter out of the blue that gave the club a huge boost. The Labour Party's Lord Melchett was appointed Minister of State for Northern Ireland and directed a sizeable portion of his department's spending towards sports. The money was all to be allocated evenly between the two communities, and despite Billy not having even applied for the grant he received a cheque for £68,000. The money was used for both the club and the pensioners' scheme, and before long Midland ABC was developed into the boxing gym it was when I walked through the doors two decades later. Billy was the main man, but he had other local men like Ken Rafferty, Norman Rafferty and Joe McMinn all giving their time and effort to building something that would last. After a few years the football team fell away. Billy was the only one who could drive and with public transport not safe to use there was no way to get the team to away games. It was a shame for the footballers, but it meant the focus was suddenly fully on the boxing.

By the time I came along, the Midland had merged with the nearby White City Amateur Boxing Club and Joe Farrell was taking the boxing alongside Billy. Joe was well-known in the area, an old-school hard man still getting into scraps when he was in his seventies. He chinned the coalman once when he thought the fella was stroking him and the police were called. They let him away with it because of the age of him but a younger man probably would have been locked up. He was famous for patrolling the area with his dogs. Always had about five of them. Small, yappy dogs, cocker spaniels and the like. He had a wee chihuahua called Bobo, who would nip the ankles off you if you weren't on your guard. They ruled his house too, the lot of them sat on the leather sofa while the humans made do with whatever the dogs weren't using. When you saw him on the street he'd put his hands up and start throwing punches at you, messing around like. The problem was at least one of his dogs would have invariably taken a shit by then and he'd have it collected in one of the wee green bags he took with him on the walks. So, as he's throwing these punches at you your main concern was actually dodging the bag of shit swinging all over the place. In fairness, it was a decent training technique to encourage a young boxer to keep on the move and avoid punches.

Joe was also famous for his faith in weird and wonderful cures for different physical ailments. The best was for a sore back. He basically took a few lengths of string, plaited them together and then tied them loosely around his midriff. Most times he pulled his top off in the gym, there the string would be. Some herbal-remedy-type doctor obviously told him about it and Joe swore by it. He insisted I did the same when I felt any twinge in my back, even calling into the house in the morning when he was walking his dogs to make sure I was wearing it under my school uniform. There were others, some involving brown paper and olive oil, but it's the string that always sticks in my mind.

It was actually my ma who sent me to the boxing club the first night. She had seen Joe in the street one day and asked him about it. Joe said no problem, send him along. My ma says I asked about boxing as early as the age of three, but I don't really remember. I'm not sure if I asked again and that's why she spoke to Joe, but I was definitely up for it and couldn't wait to get inside the club and see what it was all about. Seven is young enough to be starting boxing, and my da thought it was a year or two too early for me to be going, but when I went in with my mates, Billy and Joe didn't even believe I was that age. They looked at all the size of me and told me just to watch everything before deciding whether I really wanted to try it or not. So, on that first night I sat on a chair like a pleb while my mates got stuck in. It wasn't until the next night when someone must have verified my age that they let me join in!

They needn't have worried. I never had any fear in the gym. Billy always used to say it, how game I was, how I never thought twice before getting in the ring with another kid. Others asked a lot of questions before sparring and things like that. Who is the other kid? What age is he? What weight is he? How many fights has he had? I never cared. I was happy to get in with whoever and as it was tough to find anyone as small as me it always tended to be a bigger, older, stronger fella in the opposite corner. I wasn't a wee hard man on the street. If anything, I was too shy and at that age probably preferred to back down from physical confrontation rather than seek it out. I was never bullied or anything but like any other kid you got into scraps. And maybe being so small I could have become more of a target. I think that might have been part of my ma's thinking in sending me to the boxing. But in the club every Monday, Wednesday and Friday I'd move about the ring with all the lads in the area anywhere near my age and it only took a round or two before they realised they'd bite off more than they could chew if they started on me.

The other thing Billy said was that as well as having the heart and balls to get in the ring and get punched in the face without running away crying, he could see from the off I was an athlete. The reflexes, the agility, the flexibility, the coordination, they were all there. With a bit of natural strength as well they saw from the start that I had what was required to do well in a physical sport, and I was definitely a kid they could work with and develop. Because of all that they paid me more attention than the others from that first week.

Both Billy and Joe worked with me in those early days, although I was always closer to Billy. Joe was a very intimidating figure back then. I caught up with him in my teens just before he passed away and he'd calmed down a lot by then, but when I was first in the gym there was definitely a bit of a fear of Joe. He was an ex-army man, fought in Korea I think, and liked things very regimented. He didn't like music in the gym during training and I remember him smashing CD players off the wall. He didn't like us drinking water for some reason either. We weren't allowed to bring our own bottle and instead he filled an empty milk carton with water which we all had to share. He didn't even let us swallow the water but instead had us spit it out into a bucket. He was always very hard to please as well. He'd take me on the pads, his top off and his trunks pulled up high over one of those massive, hard, barrel bellies some guys get. He'd push me and push me and when I started to tire, he'd be hitting me with the pads. Hitting me so it hurt. Hitting me hard enough that I'd be back home in tears saying I'm not fucking going back there. Bullying is a very strong word, but it was an approach you certainly wouldn't get away with today. Tough love is the euphemism I suppose. It created a tension between us that was never there between me and Billy. As I grew older, I gained more respect for Joe and maybe an understanding that he was doing what in his head was the right thing to do to make a kid with obvious natural talent into a champion. And maybe it did play a part. I'm sure if he treated 100 kids the way he treated me, not many of them would have kept going back to the gym three days a week, so maybe the fact I did and came out the other side gave me an edge others didn't have.

Billy was always the one who would back me up or defend me or, I guess, protect me at times from Joe and his *Full Metal*

Jacket approach to training kids. The pair of them had a love–hate relationship, I think. That's how it seemed to me back then. Maybe there was a bit of ego from both sides as they'd been in charge of their own clubs before the amalgamation and now there were suddenly two bosses. Billy was also easy to wind up and Joe knew all the triggers. The key one was the fact Joe had more boxing experience. He'd fought more. In the army out in Asia he'd won some sort of Far East title he liked to remind everyone of. The story goes he held a record of nine consecutive victories by knockout. Billy hadn't fought much back in his day and Joe liked to rub his nose in it and try to pull rank in certain situations. What would you know, you never boxed properly in your life. That type of thing. Billy had a short fuse, was feisty and was quick to take the bait so they'd go at it arguing, sometimes coming close to digging each other before one of them walked away.

If Billy and Joe had a bit of a love–hate relationship, that probably reflected mine with the boxing club in those early days. I loved boxing but hated the hard, regimented, repetitive nature of the training. I was in there every Monday, Wednesday and Friday from 6:30 p.m. to 8:00 p.m. Same drills, same exercises, same constant bollockings from Joe. Being honest, I much preferred football back then. And if there was a timetable clash, like there sometimes was on a Wednesday evening, I'd always pick football. That never went down well with Joe as you can imagine. The training and bollockings were tougher the Friday after I'd skipped Wednesday to play football. And then when I got home that night, the desire to fuck the boxing off was stronger than ever. All my mates already had anyway. None of them stuck at it. They all came and went, drifted in and out. When you grow up in a housing estate in Belfast, I think most young boys at least give it a go. Everyone has done a bit of boxing. But very few see it through. In my case it was always my ma forcing me out the door and back to the club when I was having a wee moan about it all. It's a little strange because it wasn't like she came from a massive boxing family or anything like that. Both my grandas liked talking boxing and my ma's da apparently did a bit of bare-fisted fighting years ago, but we weren't one of those families that had trophies and medals all over the house so that you grew up just expected to carry on a tradition. I think she just knew I was decent at it.

That was the hate aspect, but there was always a little kernel of love at the heart of it all. Part of what I loved was watching the senior boxers in the gym. Watching them training, watching them sparring, even just being near while they were sitting around chatting. I looked up to them all so much. I don't think I was old enough to be doing it to learn or absorb information or copy what they were doing in the gym. It was more just an infatuation, a feeling like these guys are warriors and it is cool they give me the time of day. As a kid I never showered after training, but I'd go into the changing room to talk to all the older ones in there. They'd be showering and I'd be sat their fully clothed trying to talk to them. I brought it on myself, but it was Cooper McClure who soon nicknamed me the Willy Watcher. Oi Frampton, are you in here willy watching again? I was scundered but didn't even care. And them slagging me was their way of showing me I was accepted, that they didn't mind having me around. Cooper says my character changed once I got into the club. That outside on the street I was still shy and quiet, but I opened up in the Midland. I never shut up in fact, always on them like a wee Jack Russell pup, always talking and asking them things. He says I was cheeky too but in a good-natured way. I never answered back, never slabbered at them like some of the headers that would appear off and on, and that's why they all warmed to me.

They were my heroes but, without disrespecting anyone, our area hasn't produced many standout fighters over the years. Kenny

Beattie from the Shore Road was by far the best. He was from
the White City Club and won a welterweight silver at the 1978
Commonwealth Games in Canada as part of the team which saw
Barry McGuigan, Gerry Hamill and Hugh Russell all medal for
Northern Ireland. Kenny was a brilliant fighter. He still has a sixpack
today well into his sixties. The great Mike McCallum beat him in the
final in Edmonton in a close fight. McCallum went on to become
a legend as a professional, a three-weight world champion, but he
still asks about Kenny whenever he's speaking to anyone connected
to Irish boxing and can't believe he never turned pro. My da knew
Kenny because he worked in the neighbouring Grove Leisure Centre
while my da was in Loughside. I met him that way and was in awe of
him and the stories everyone tells about him fighting.

The guys I looked up to from Midland never reached those
heights. Cooper, who's now a close friend and has taken on the
running of the club, was one of the best. He got to an Ulster semi-
final and got knocked out by John Duddy. I did a thing recently
for the BBC about unsung heroes, and I talked about Cooper and
how he was the level of fighter I aspired to be when I first laced
up a glove. It was Cooper who gave me my first, and some would
say only, proper job too. For a tenner a shift plus tips he brought
me along on his Saturday lemonade run. Just a favour from him
to me really so I'd have a few quid in my pocket. His route was
in and around the Shankill, and the very first house he sent me
up to was on a street next to the Diamond Bar. He gave me four
bottles and told me just to walk into the house without knocking or
anything and the fella will be there waiting. This is around 8 a.m.
on a Saturday morning but I followed Cooper's instructions and
dandered straight into the living room of this house. And right
enough, there was a fella waiting for his four bottles of lemonade.
Two fellas actually, sat on the sofa, drinking cans of Steiger. But the
best part of it was, the guy waiting on his delivery was bald and had

drawn on a full head of hair with a black permanent marker. Right down to little sideburns and all. I just froze. Never seen anything like it before or since. I'm wondering what the fuck is going on and then he says cheers kid and gives me a pound tip! I wander back outside and ask Cooper what's going on with your man's hair and he's just killing himself laughing.

Mitchell Wells was another very good fighter at flyweight, who was unfortunate that his career coincided with that of Damaen Kelly. In 1995 Mitchell collected the Midland's first ever Ulster senior title when Kelly wasn't available to fight. Then there were a couple of big guys called John English and Roy Stewart. John, known as Flash, was studying Finance and Spanish at Queen's University and ended up in Spain where he married a Kenyan girl and settled down in Barcelona. I only found out Roy's real name in talking to people for this book. He was, and probably still is, universally known as Chizz. I remember him having a war with a well-known guy in Andytown. It was an absolute bloodbath and at the end all the local Provies were applauding both of them equally. It was like a scene out of *Gladiator* to me. Now I can see that Chizz wasn't a good boxer at all. He was just a nut who was hard as nails. But back then, to be there, for that guy in the ring covered in blood to know my name and acknowledge me on his way past, that made me feel six foot tall. You're so impressionable at that stage of your life and I was lucky that these type of guys were in my club each night I walked through the door. They were just sound guys and so good towards me when they had no obligation to be like that. Little things that make all the difference to a kid and have a lasting effect on you. Like calling me over to sit or stand on their feet when they were doing sit-ups. I loved that, thinking they picked me out of everyone else to do it.

Acknowledgement from non-boxers could have that effect as well. Andre Shoukri, the UDA Brigadier for north Belfast famous for the chains and the tan and the muscles, knew me. He actually bought me my first decent pair of boxing gloves. He'd come and watch me fight too. My good mate Paddy Barnes has a great story about Shoukri watching us in a tournament in the Crues Club fighting against a Dublin select team. The Crues Club was a UVF bar so the fact that a high-ranking UDA man was in there was strange enough, but it got even better when according to Paddy he roared out during the fight, 'get into the Fenian bastard Paddy'!

Everyone in the area would bow down to Shoukri, so you thought he's some kind of superstar. Well, nearly everyone bowed down to him. I remember being in the club one evening with Billy when a couple of UDA heavies came in and said Andre wants a set of keys so he can let himself in to train whenever he wants. Billy's succinct response was that Andre can go fuck himself. That the club is open on Mondays, Wednesdays and Fridays from 6:30 p.m. until 8:00 p.m. and if Andre wants to train, he can come down at those times like everyone else. The two big lads didn't know how to react so away they went and soon after Andre appeared himself. I held my breath, fearing the worst, but he actually apologised to Billy and said he'd be there at the allotted times like the rest of us. Billy was a hard wee man – you couldn't tell him what to do!

The four years from first entering the club until I was eleven and could compete properly as a junior flew by. I became known as 'The Boxer' pretty early on. I'd be walking down to the club and guys my da's age would call out to me, there's the boxer. Word spread fast throughout our area that there was a wee lad in the club who had something about him. On my first night proper, after the session spent sat on the chair in the corner watching eejits who were clearly never going to be boxers but just happened to look older than me, I showed I could keep my hands up and punch straight. That was enough for Billy and Joe to send me to Portstewart for that first exhibition fight. But within six months I was demonstrating a lot more than those basics. There is a video still floating about of me aged eight sparring with a local kid called Davey English, who was older and a lot bigger than me. I'm wearing these 16oz gloves so it's comical-looking in a way. But once you get past that, it's clear for everyone to see that I had real potential. I fight as a southpaw throughout the sparring. Being right-handed I just presumed you started with your right, and no one had corrected that yet. They were just letting me find my own way. I outclass Davey in the spar. I'm on my toes the whole time, moving in and out, using footwork far too quick for him to deal with. I'm circling to my left and to my right. He rushes in at times, but I never flinch, never panic, never turn my back or just cover up to survive like most eight-year-olds naturally do. I'm in complete control, throwing different shots from different angles. I even throw in a sneaky final punch just after Joe calls time and turn around with a cheeky grin on my face. It's clear I love everything about it. All the kids are on one side of the ring and a few seniors are on the other. As the camera zooms in you see me climbing out between the ropes where the seniors are, and Flash throws a few pretend digs into my stomach. You can see the older ones have watched and been impressed, and I love that feeling too.

The other thing I loved was the dough! There were plenty of other little exhibition fights in clubs around Belfast and beyond in those years, and I'd always get a few quid off my uncles after each one. There were days fighting on the Shankill Road, in the Blues Club, Rangers Club or the Loyalist Club, when I'd go home with my pockets full of coins. Big Trainor, who told the eejit to behave that time, would walk me round the room telling everyone, this is young Carl, Shughie's grandson, stick your hand in your pocket for him. There'd be these groups of old paramilitary types sat in the corner who'd dig deep, and I'd end up walking out of there with about fifteen quid. And as there was no manager or promoter to take their cut back in those days that made me loaded. Sometimes people who didn't even watch me fight chipped in. My ma was working in a grocery store on the Shore Road and one of her customers always asked how I was getting on. If I'd won anything recently, she'd ask my ma to bring the medal in to show her and then she'd slip her a fiver or tenner to give to me. Unbelievable really but people are like that in Belfast. The less they have the more generous they'll be, and I think they just like to know someone from the area is doing well at something. They're proud of that. I remember once after fighting in the Crues Club some old guy I didn't know asked me for an autograph. My ma was with me, and I got embarrassed.

'Why the hell do you want an autograph from me?' I asked him.

'Because you're going to be world champion one day,' he replied.

CHAPTER TWO

CHRISTINE

I got a 'C1' in my 11 Plus and joined Glengormley High School. To be honest, I was just delighted not to get a 'D'. I wasn't daft or anything, I just never worked hard in school. I don't ever remember sitting down to revise for a test or concentrate on something in a textbook. Most days I didn't even bring a schoolbag to school. Just a pen in my shirt pocket and a homework diary. I'm not sure what the point of the homework diary was as I rarely paid much attention to it. My da usually worked late and I was in bed before he got home. And my ma was a lot easier to manipulate so I'd just tell her I'd done it or I had none. Valerie was never a dedicated student, so she'd probably played similar tricks. And Craig was even worse than both of us as he got himself suspended a couple of times. So, all things considered, my 'C1' was a bit of an achievement and made me the academic one in the family!

This was also the time, at the age of eleven, that I could start boxing competitively in the junior amateur tournaments. I looked forward to the fights but there was plenty of trepidation there as well. In particular, I remember always being afraid of the gypsy boxers. If I drew one of them in a tournament, I just thought this is game over, I'm dead here. They were renowned as all being very good fighters and just naturally hard kids. The mysticism about them spooked me too. There was a gypsy camp at the bottom of Tiger's Bay under the railway bridges near Yorkgate and we used to creep near and try to get chases off them. Just messing as kids do but I always feared they'd come at me with a sword or something. There were lots of them in west Belfast and they were starting to settle there more and more, but for us Prods they were still unknowns – something to be wary of!

Wary is probably a good word to describe how I felt in a lot of situations within boxing before the first bell would ring. And I think it's fair to say that being a Protestant in an environment largely dominated by Catholics was the main cause of it. In general there just aren't that many good Prods in the amateur game, and that's simply down to there being far more boxing clubs in Catholic areas compared with Protestant ones. In north Belfast alone you have the likes of Holy Family, Star, Belfast, Newington and the Dockers all within around a half-mile radius. Head west and there's even more; Oliver Plunkett, St Agnes, Immaculata, John Bosco, St Paul's to name just a few. For the Prods, after Cairnlodge and Albert Foundry on the Shankill and us at the Midland you'd probably need to go out to Monkstown for the next club. And it wasn't just the number of clubs that made a difference. It was the number of kids attending each one. The Catholic gyms would be packed to the rafters on any given night while the Protestant clubs often struggled to attract kids through the door. Why there is such a disparity I really don't know. Some will suggest it's down to the fact the ultimate goal for any amateur boxer in Ireland, North or South, is to pull on a green vest with a shamrock on it. The argument follows that parents in certain Protestant communities are never going to push their children down that route and would rather they dream of playing football for Linfield and Northern Ireland or pursue another discipline where the goal is to represent Team GB in the Olympics rather than Team Ireland. But I don't know. I was from as loyalist and Protestant an area as there is and I don't recall any of that ever mattering. I've never known of a boxer who was good enough not representing Ireland because of any sectarian or political reason. Rugby is an all-Ireland sport too and I'm sure all the kids playing that dream of representing Ulster then wearing the green jersey of Ireland. Whatever the reason, it could be a lonely existence being a Prod in amateur boxing in Belfast.

I've already said that the idea both sides of the divide readily united and became one big happy family in boxing is romanticising it all a little too much. It's probably true to say that, overall, it was always a more progressive environment compared with many sports, but you were still sure as fuck aware you were the different one in the group. There was no immunity to sectarianism, even if it only manifested itself in the form of muttered slurs as you passed. I was called an orange cunt a few times by kids and adults under their breaths. You're always conscious of it and you need to remember that up until this point I'd never really interacted with anyone who wasn't a Protestant. In primary school we'd be taken a few times each year to do sports or some outdoor activity with a school from the New Lodge. The idea was to integrate us all, but in reality it did more to highlight the segregation. If we went into a hall, all the Protestants went and stood on one side with the Catholics on the other. Then we'd be looking at each other, talking with your mates and laughing. Look at the state of them, we'd say. No chance I'm talking to any of them Fenians. We all went away hating each other even more. But at least in those situations there was always safety in numbers. I was with my own kind and comfortable. In boxing, apart from having Billy or Joe, I was always alone.

I had gained a reputation as one of the few decent Prods, so I went to spar in other clubs. I was often in Holy Family as Billy was good mates with Gerry Storey. I'd go there just to train as well, and Billy would drive us right up to the front of the club and in a couple of steps we'd be inside with the doors shut. The first time he couldn't take me for a spar it was left to Joe to bring me, and he suggested we just walk it. I thought he was fucking mad but away we went. The boxing club is in a community centre called the Reccy right in the heart of the New Lodge. We're walking through the New Lodge flats, past the murals, past the Up-The-RA and Fuck-The-Queen graffiti, past groups of people I'd never seen in my life. It's the evening time and winter so it's dark and I was terrified the whole way there and back. As a twelve-year-old from the Bay I'm thinking this is completely insane and we're liable to get jumped every time we turn a corner, but Joe didn't seem to have a care in the world.

I always felt it was me against everyone else when I walked into a tournament, that everyone was out to intimidate me. Looking back, I still don't doubt that but I suppose it's open to interpretation how much of a sectarian element there was to it. I remember my first time weighing in for the County Antrim's. It was taking place in the St Agnes Club on the Andersonstown Road one Sunday morning and naturally enough I was the clear outsider. It's boxing, so 99 per cent of the people involved are going to be working class and either genuinely tough or at least willing to fake it for appearances. Like happens at every boxing weigh-in, fighters are looking to prove they're not scared of anything and want to seize any opportunity to intimidate or gain some sort of psychological advantage. In St Agnes that day a group of wee lads asked me what boy I am. You get numbered, Boy 1, Boy 2, according to age group but it was my first time and I hadn't a clue. I said I didn't know and immediately the laughter and sneering starts. This dickhead doesn't know what number he is. Are you fucking simple or something? I was nervous walking in but now I'm shitting myself. Now, I'm the only Prod in that situation and a group of Catholic kids are ganging up against me. Whether I heard it or not there's little doubt at least one of them has made an orange bastard or stupid hun remark. I know that because at that time if the roles were reversed and I was with a group of my mates laughing at a solitary Catholic, someone amongst us would have muttered Fenian bastard or stupid taig. But the point of whether they went after me because of my background or simply because I was on my own, new to it all, smaller than the rest and an easy target, we'll never know. Maybe I could have been a Catholic from Armagh or Fermanagh making my debut and got the same treatment except I'd be a stupid culchie bastard instead of stupid orange bastard. Whatever the real truth, as an eleven-year-old kid you're not thinking too deeply about it. You're just shitting yourself.

I lost at some stage of the Antrim's the first couple of years. A kid called Steven Maxwell beat me once. He was a very good boxer but later got diagnosed with epilepsy and had to give it up. Another good fighter to beat me was John George. He went off the rails and his boxing suffered because of that but I still see him the odd time and, fair enough, he likes to remind me of his victory over me when we were thirteen. The first time I won the Antrim's I was fourteen and had to beat Paddy Barnes along the way. The wee man came flying at me as soon as the first bell sounded, windmilling all these crazy shots and basically pushing me through the ropes and almost out of the ring. He's since showed me the footage as his ma was filming on a camcorder and all you hear is her loving it and screaming, yahh get him Paddy!

Back then we were just rivals, always knowing there was a chance of drawing each other in the Antrim's or Ulster's. We met four times in competitive bouts, with me winning the first two and last one and Paddy bribing the judges to rob a victory in the third fight. But as soon as I outgrew the weight, and it became clear we wouldn't be facing each other anymore, we quickly became good pals. He'd started boxing under his uncle Jimmy Linden in Ardglass ABC.

Jimmy was a bit of a mad man, a real character. He never endeared himself to the officials and his boxers may have suffered because of that. It's well known that Paddy started his amateur career with a string of losses, but he stuck at it and ended up one of Ireland's most decorated Olympians. In the early days when I was fighting him, I just thought he was a wee eejit with his mad uncle smashing up the computer scoring systems at ringside! But by the time Paddy was training with Gerry Storey out of Holy Family we'd grown close and even starred together in a feature-length documentary about the Troubles.

Blackwhite was made by a Spanish documentary maker who came over and spent a couple of weeks with us when we were fifteen. We got £500 each for our time, which made us feel like millionaires. Gerry Adams, David Ervine, Mark Durkan and a few other politicians were interviewed for it but me and Paddy, the Prod and the Catholic boxers who'd become mates, were the undoubted stars. Looking back, the Spanish crew probably didn't know what to make of us. I remember Paddy acting the lad and forcing one of them to take a shot of Aftershock after his lunch like it was something crazy. This big Spanish guy just necks it with obviously no reaction because he's not a child and looks at us like, what are you clowns on about? They came to our schools and at mine someone lobbed a cream bun and smacked the sound guy on the head with it. Another time they wanted footage of me jogging through Tiger's Bay, but it took forever because every time I went past a worksite someone from up in the scaffolding would shout out 'dickhead!' or something along those lines. We had a great laugh filming it although some of the stuff they made us do was a bit wild. We had to act out these dream scenes at one point. In mine I'm in an alleyway with a gun in my hand and I have to start shooting these photos of people on the wall. I'm putting bullets into the likes of Maggie Thatcher and John Major and then Gerry Adams' photo appears. I shoot him too, but another photo of Gerry appears. I keep shooting but each time a younger version of Gerry is there until he's a kid and I hesitate and can't pull the trigger. Madness! In Paddy's dream scene he's on his knees blindfolded and a gun appears from off screen and executes him. Last you see of Paddy he's lying on the floor with a pool of blood forming around his head! In another scene they have us pretend sparring and they set the lights up so they can film our shadows on the wall. You can tell which shadow is which because I just start battering Paddy with body shots and he's covering up in the corner. It was all great craic and doing that documentary together probably cemented our friendship. Our families continue to get on well to this day. Christine is great mates with Paddy's wife Mari, Paddy was the best man at my wedding, and I'm the godfather of his firstborn, Eireann.

That year I beat Paddy in the Antrim's would have been my first appearance at the Irish Championships in the National Stadium in Dublin. The main man around my weight was always David Oliver Joyce, a fantastic amateur fighter who'd go on to have a good pro career too. My fear or sense of inferiority against fighters from the Traveller community meant I started fights against him already a point or two down in my mind. Davey beat me on countback to become Irish champion that first meeting, and he pretty much dominated the amateur game in Ireland for the next five or six years.

Right from the off, I was never a great loser. And I don't see that as a negative trait. Obviously as you get older and mature a bit, and especially later when you're in the public eye, you mask your true feelings and do and say the right things. But as a kid I took defeats bad. A bit of kicking and screaming, and it goes without saying it was worse when I knew I'd won. The earliest I remember getting robbed was in a club fight on the Grosvenor Road. I was bawling my eyes out in rage and frustration and my da is trying to explain that this is what happens in club shows – it's just what's known as a home decision and I had better get used to it. I'm not sure I ever did get used to it and I was on the receiving end of plenty. Another which stands out was a ridiculous one against John George in the Stella Maris Club down in the Docks. It's just not fair. You're a kid working your balls off in training and then giving it everything in the fight and at the end some ref lifts the hand of a fella you've just battered because he knows his da or helps train him or whatever. It's hard for a kid to take. It's hard to explain it to a kid. The nature of boxing and how it's judged or scored makes it pretty unique in terms of how sporting results can be predetermined. I was still playing a lot of competitive football at a decent level at this time and there'd be games where you'd come off feeling hard done by. A soft red card for your team, a blatant offside not given for their goal, a dodgy penalty and all the rest. But even if it didn't even itself out over the course of ninety minutes, or even a whole season, you still always felt you controlled your own destiny. That even if we sat there at half time – a goal down from a penalty that should never have been, everyone fully aware the ref was against us for whatever reason – we could still do something about it. If we score two without conceding in the second half, then we'd win. The ref can't blow the final whistle and then just arbitrarily point to our opponents and give them the three points. But in boxing he could. You wonder how many youngsters with talent have got fed up and walked away from the sport after being on the end of one robbery too many.

Sometimes I wasn't even a good winner, never mind a good loser. That all depended on the reward, the quality of the medal or wee trophy I got handed. Cooper used to laugh at me moaning if I didn't like the medal. I wanted fancy medals, big and shiny and looking like they were worth a few quid. I'd bring some of the cheaper efforts into the club and show everyone. Look at the state of that, I'd say in disgust. Call that a medal – that's shite!

I did well enough in those early years to soon get picked for Ireland. For me and those around me this was the natural progression of my boxing career, and no one viewed it in any other way. There was zero negativity about it, no sly digs or comments made about a Prod from the Bay fighting for Ireland. I was over the moon. My first international was in Ipswich and I lost my fight against an English lad but all I remember was being very happy. Happy to have been picked. Happy to have gone away on a boxing trip. Happy to get a vest and fight an international. I suppose it was a bit of validation for all the work too. Not just the work I put in personally but what Billy and Joe and everyone at the club were doing for me. The time they were taking away from their own families to dedicate to me. My own family had supported me from day one as well, so it was nice for them to see this was leading somewhere. We had no idea where of course at that point but very few kids who enter a boxing gym get picked to represent a country, so it gave us all a little boost.

The international call-ups probably hastened a decision I'd been dreading and putting off for as long as I could: boxing or football. Even at this stage when I was being picked to fight for Ireland, there were plenty of times I'd rather be up the Grove playing football. I was still turning out for Loughside Boys at a decent junior level, and I was a good wee player, good enough to join Crusaders under-16s and do a pre-season with them. But it's at that age you really have to choose between the two. You're at that level where if you've any true aspirations of achieving anything in your sport, you're better off focusing on one. Billy and Joe had long been voicing their displeasure that I was still going to the football; still using physical and mental energy up on it; and, worst of all, still getting injured doing it. I don't know if it's surprising to people or not, but I definitely got a lot more injuries growing up from playing football than I ever did in the boxing ring. On one occasion I went full-blooded into a tackle at the same time as both an opposition player and one of my own teammates. I came out of it worst, and it was my teammate who inflicted the damage. Somebody's da had to drive me home and I limped into the house. That kept me out for months and I ended up missing the County Antrim and Ulster novices, where the club would have been expecting me to win it. I can't blame Billy and Joe for wondering out loud why the fuck they're putting all this time into a kid who just goes and gets himself injured on the football pitch the next night. I think I already knew I was a better boxer than I was a footballer and, more importantly, I saw I had the potential to reach a level in boxing I never could in football. But a match in Mallusk helped end any doubts. We were playing a team from Ardoyne, and it all kicked off after I flew into a tackle. Some big fella called Joe charged up on my blind side, chinned me and I ended up needing stitches on the inside of my lip. I doubt anyone on the pitch could have landed a glove on me if we were moving around a boxing ring, but you need eyes in the back of your head in a football brawl. I shit myself. The County Antrim's were just around the corner, and I'd been flat out in the gym preparing for them. Billy had ordered me not to play in the match, and when he saw the state of me the next day I lied and said that I'd only been watching from the side when it kicked off and someone sucker-punched me. A few nights later I was in Loughside Leisure Centre with Billy, my da and my football coach, Davey Calder. Davey starts apologising to Billy, saying he'd never have let me play in the match had he known the Antrim's were so close. My heart just sank and I felt sick to the pit of my stomach. Billy didn't even say anything. He just looked at me then walked away. I saw out the season then hung up my boots for good.

***

I'd fought across the water in England, but my first real overseas trip with the Irish team was the World Cadets in Bucharest in June of 2003. I'd just turned sixteen and was away with David Oliver Joyce, John Joe Joyce, John Paul McDonagh, Keith Boyle and two more David Joyces – Big Davey and Southpaw Davey. Luckily enough I'd gotten more comfortable with the mystical ways of the Irish Travellers by now so was no longer worried about them pulling swords on me! I was fighting at 46kg, just over 100lbs. I beat a Pakistani fighter named Zeeshan Butt 32–15 in the first round and then faced a good Tunisian called Hamza Bin Mounaouer for a medal. The fella looked old enough to be my da and he beat me 17–14. He actually broke my nose midway through the fight, and it caused my eye to swell shut. An ambulance took me to the hospital to get my nose put back into place. I remember the doc getting his knee up on the bed to get enough purchase to realign the bone. It was insane – the worst pain I'd ever felt at that time in my life. Later that year, me and the same group of lads went to the European Schoolboy Championships in Rome where I fought at 50kg. I beat a very good Russian in Denis Sekretov 25–20 in the semi-final but got a flu ahead of the final. I shouldn't really have boxed but thought I'd give it a go against a Turkish fighter called Onur Sipal, who was nowhere near as accomplished as the Russian. I started well and won the opening round handily before my energy levels just evaporated and he hammered me throughout the second until the ref stepped in.

I loved being away with the Irish team. As much as who you fought and how you did, you remember who you met along the way and the craic we all had together. In Romania I got friendly with the Cuban fighter Yordenis Ugas, former WBA (World Boxing Association) welterweight champion, who beat Manny Pacquiao. He liked coming into our room to listen to the music we had with us. He loved 'Dilemma' by Nelly and Kelly Rowland, and kept asking me to play it. Even though he couldn't speak a word of English he was able to sing along with no clue what he was saying. The Cubans never had any money of their own to spend either, so I'd give him a few coins to go buy Pepsi. That was all he ever wanted so he'd do this wee whistle sound he used to make and say Pepsi, Pepsi. When the tournament was over, the Cubans would sell their gear to the other fighters just to go home with a few quid in their pockets.

Bucharest was also my first experience of a strip club. Sixteen years old, but looking around twelve, I went in with the rest of the boys and ordered the cheapest bottle of champagne on the menu. I thought we'd all get a wee sip but the smallest bottle you can imagine arrived and the girl filled her glass with all of it. A couple of minutes later she spied a guy in a suit come in and that was the last we saw of her. It wasn't long before our team manager burst through the doors and went ballistic. What are you all doing! Get out of here! We all sprinted out without paying, so he had to hang around and settle up. He was raging but the whole thing was hilarious. And one of the other coaches, Cathal O'Grady, knew we were in there, so he'd brought the camcorder they used to film the fights and recorded us all bombing out the door.

At the Schoolboy's in Rome, Amir Khan was one of the stars. He won it representing England, but we told him about this Cuban fella named Ugas who would beat him if they fought at the Youth Worlds later on that year. They did meet in the preliminaries and Khan destroyed him 21–6. There was a drum lying around the digs in Rome for some reason and I messed about with it, imitating what I'd seen the guys in the bands do marching past on the Twelfth. I don't know what Amir thought of me as a boxer, but he was impressed with my drumming skills even though I was shite.

After I got beat in Rome, I was lying in my bunk trying to get over the flu I had when an Azerbaijani light heavyweight barged into the room and grabbed me by the neck. He's about twice the size and weight of me so there's nothing I can do as he starts to put my Nike trainers on. Obviously, he can't get his big feet into them so he stands on the back of them and walks out wearing them. I just lay there in shock wondering what the fuck just happened. Tony Davitt later got them back for me somehow but those are the type of surreal things that went on during these trips. The next day I went with the team to visit the Vatican. Being from Tiger's Bay it wasn't the spiritual experience for me it was for all the other lads, and I misjudged the mood with an off-colour joke about some nuns ahead of us in the queue. You could normally say anything and get a laugh, but they were all furious with me!

My last big tournament before stepping up to senior level was the 2004 Commonwealth Youth Games in Australia. They took place in a student town called Bendigo outside Melbourne. I was still a 50kg fighter, but bantamweight was the lightest weight class going so I had to fight at 54kg. I won my first bout, beating a Kiwi called Angus Donaldson 15–8. In my second against the Scot Jason Hastie, I dropped him with a body shot that was incorrectly ruled a low blow. He was given an age to recover while I got a public warning. He went on to win 24–19 and then lost to England's Liam Walsh in the final. I was gutted but at the same time delighted to have been selected and have seen Australia while picking up a medal fighting a couple of divisions higher than I should have been. I was also proud to have represented Northern Ireland. Being the Commonwealth Games, this was one of the rare occasions at international level when the distinction was made between the north and the south of Ireland. And being born and raised in Belfast, I felt and still feel Northern Irish. You may not be able to get a passport stating Northern Irish but, if I had to tick a box on a form, I'd choose that ahead of British or Irish. Today, I hold both British and Irish passports and it doesn't bother me in the slightest how I'm referred to. Any boxer from Belfast who goes to fight in the US will invariably be called Irish. Maybe the UK will automatically label me as British as they're quick to claim any decent sportsperson they can find from Northern Ireland. I don't lose any sleep over what I get called but in my head I'm Northern Irish then British then Irish in that order – so when the opportunities arose to pull on a Northern Ireland vest, they were special moments for me.

***

I wore that Northern Ireland vest in my next fight back home. It was in Downpatrick against a local hero who was a bit older than me. The fight was scheduled for four two-minute rounds, and I battered him throughout the first three. The club ref there was a man called Seamus Kelly who also happened to be the brother of my opponent's coach. In between the third and fourth rounds Seamus came over and said he was going to call it now, that we weren't going to bother with a fourth round. Without saying it out loud, he meant that no one in the club that night wanted to see the local lad getting filled in for the final two minutes. He then called us both to the centre of the ring and declared the other lad the winner! I went ballistic. What the fuck do you mean he's the winner. This is a fucking joke. I went a bit Michael Conlan in Rio, and the crowd didn't take long to react. With N. IRELAND printed on the back of the vest I was wearing it was only going to go one way. A couple of 'orange bastards' and 'fuck off ya Brits' later we were on our way home empty handed.

I don't tell stories like that to shock or accuse or seek sympathy or anything like that. I wasn't traumatised by a minority in a crowd of people shouting sectarian abuse at me. I doubt many there that night were truly sectarian. They were people riled up watching

two guys fight who were raging that their guy got a hiding and
then further angered by the wee lad who'd filled him in effing and
blinding about not getting the decision they knew he deserved. I
was in the right and they were 100 per cent in the wrong, but most
of us in Belfast have thick enough skin to deal with getting called a
Brit or an orange so-and-so in the heat of a moment. Had I lost fair
and square after a great battle they'd be all smiles, patting me on the
back, shouting well done wee man as I left the ring – so while not
justifying them, I don't think you can really take it to heart.

Being honest, I'm reluctant to judge people in situations like
that because there is always an element of throwing stones in
glass houses. Relatively speaking, things in Northern Ireland had
calmed down considerably by the turn of the century, but there
was still plenty of trouble and I can't pretend I didn't willingly get
involved in some of it. Pretty much every young lad in Tiger's Bay
did, especially in the summer months when the rioting would start.
They call it recreational rioting, something for working-class kids
in interface areas of Belfast with not a lot of other options to do for a
bit of fun. I'd go with everyone else each evening and stand around
at either the Limestone Road or by the Orange Hall at Dunmore –
or even at the bottom of my own street – just waiting on a crowd
from the New Lodge to gather. It'd begin with a few stones being
thrown from either side and then it'd all kick off. Petrol bombs,
paint bombs, cars being driven into crowds, peelers arriving,
plastic bullets being fired, whatever. It was mad but like a big game
to us. As if we were playing cowboys and Indians. From no age
we'd be there, thinking you're a wee Jack-the-lad getting involved.
Maybe just throw a few stones your first time. It was childish stuff,
but we were children so what do you expect. It was a bit of craic
and nothing more to most of us. Rioting was good fun. It killed
a few hours in the evening and the buzz of adrenalin was class.
I remember making my own balaclava by cutting eye holes in a

woolly hat. Thought I was cool as fuck. In reality I was just another wee dickhead, but I didn't know any better. I didn't actually hate Catholics no matter what I shouted or what I threw towards the New Lodge. Same way I doubt the boys in Downpatrick calling me an orange bastard truly hated Protestants. The real scumbags are the adults at the riots who direct the whole thing. The men at the side getting the kids involved, coordinating everything, making it more sinister and taking advantage of situations for their own ends.

My mate Sam Sloan's older brother Glenn was one who suffered at their hands. When he was sixteen, Spacer, as he was known, joined the Ulster Youth Militants, which was the youth wing of the UDA. During a big riot one Remembrance Day they gave him a pipe bomb to light and throw. But it had a short fuse on it and exploded as he was throwing it, blowing the back of his head open and most of his arm off in the process. I didn't see it happen but was there for the immediate aftermath. I saw his feet and a crowd gathering round him on North Queen Street at the bottom of our street. Then I saw my brother stood completely still. He was ghostly white and in a state of total shock. He'd been close by and had witnessed the whole thing. At the funeral a few days later, we walked past the spot it happened and then turned down Duncairn Gardens. I remember people pointing and I looked towards the first row of houses on the New Lodge side. Someone was dangling a plastic arm out one of the first-floor windows. I still see Spacer's ma Mandy from time to time when I'm back in the Bay and we always stop and have a nice chat. She's a lovely woman and it breaks my heart thinking about how sad it must be for her to have lost a son so young.

On another occasion someone from the same area opened a window and fired a few shots towards the bonfire on the waste ground in front of our house on the Eleventh Night. Everyone panicked and started running in different directions, trampling over whoever fell in front of them. A guy called Mini Beggs was hit by one of the bullets. I'd just left with my da to take a look at Mount Vernon's bonfire and we came back to the chaos. It was crazy but maybe not as crazy as you'd think if you're not from a working-class housing estate in Belfast. It's a push to say you're used to seeing people shot, but you definitely get desensitised to the violence to a certain degree. You see some pretty wild things and it all becomes relative. I remember sitting in my mate Kenny Hotdog's house one day during the UDA and UVF feud. Kenny lived in Midland, just below the Bay, and one of his neighbours was a UVF guy called Carl Hoy. We heard a commotion and looked out the window to see a group of about thirty men trying to boot their way through Hoy's front door. Hoy was known to be both a mad and a brave bastard, and he suddenly charges out swinging a sword at anyone who tried to get near him. It sounds like something from a movie but that's the sort of crazy shit that went on.

***

I finished all my GCSEs at Glengormley High and did well enough to be allowed back in to do AS Levels. But all my mates had left school right after their GCSEs, so a year of ASs was more than enough for me and I left too. I went to Belfast Tech to do a Sports Studies diploma, and completing that was good enough to get me into the University of Ulster at Jordanstown to do a foundation degree. A year there and I would have been starting year one of the Sports Studies degree proper. The first night I went out to Jordanstown for a meeting I arrived at the room with nothing, and it turned out to be an actual class. Everyone else seemed to be a lot older and much more at home in the academic environment. The lecturer said to go quickly to the shop and buy a pen and notepad to get started, so away I went. I must have taken a wrong turn and ended up wandering lost into the library and asking the first person I came across if he knew where I could buy some stuff for class. He was a middle-class yuppy type and he just looked at me, replied that this is a library, then walked away. I turned around absolutely raging. This cunt thinks I'm a simple bastard. I know it's a fucking library mate, I'm asking if you know where the stationery shop is you prick. I found the shop myself, bought what I needed and returned to class still fuming. They gave us some sort of assignment to do that night for the next day. I went home, looked at it and couldn't do it, and that was that. I never went back to university.

My university life was short-lived but something else of note happened that first night at Jordanstown, which turned out to be far more important than any Sports Science degree. I'd been talking to a girl online for several months by then. I hate putting that down in print as it still sounds sad as fuck. We started on Bebo, which was the first social media platform we all used in those days. It was somewhere you could post photos or videos online and then you could add people as friends and send them messages. You had your top fifteen friends, which you moved about the rankings according to who was your best. Embarrassing stuff. I got followed by a girl one day and after seeing her profile pic I thought, happy days. First thing I wrote to her was ASL? Age, Sex, Location? She replied, fucking ASL you dickhead, so I had to pretend I was only joking. We started talking to each other every night on MSN. Turned out she was a genuine boxing fan. Her uncle would take her and her cousin Kerry to watch fights in the Andytown Leisure Centre and she watched the big fights on TV. She was a massive fan of Amir Khan, even going down to Dublin on the train to get a book signed by him once. She fancied him. Big Vladimir Klitschko too. Every night for months I rushed home to be able to speak with her. She was so funny and had me in stitches every night. But it took me a very long time to actually ask her out. I was no good with girls. I was too shy and needed to be drunk to pluck up the courage to approach one in person.

Before I got to that stage, on the same night I left university to never return, I saw her in the flesh for the first time. As I walked to the bus stop, I saw her and her mate Rachael. I knew it was her, but I shit myself and said nothing. It was a cold night, and I had my hood up so I kept it up and waited silently beside them. When the bus came, I let her get on first so I could check out her arse going up the steps. They sat down the back, and I took a seat at the front. The bus dropped me on the Shore Road, and I then sprinted home to log onto MSN and ask her if that was her on the bus! Weirdly, she has a similar story about me. I walked into Wetherspoon's one night with my da while unbeknownst to me she was there with a group of her pals. She told them there's that wee lad I speak to on MSN but by the time she went to look for me I'd apparently already left. I was none the wiser but just remember thinking thank fuck because I would have been scundered stood there with my da if she'd come over.

We were another couple of months chatting online until we discovered she was going to Kelly's Nightclub in Portrush one weekend on the same night a group of my mates were heading there. I went along and as soon as I got through the door, I saw her across the dance floor. She has a different version, but I swear to God she saw me then just marched across and stuck the lips on me. Big lumber. No talking or nothing. I was loving it and went to get us some drinks but by the time I got back from the bar she was gone. I couldn't find her anywhere. Turned out she'd been turfed out for being too steaming.

Even after that I still didn't have the balls to officially ask her out. I'd never had a proper girlfriend before so wasn't sure what to do. It was months again before I asked her if she wanted to go on a date. We were to meet outside McDonald's on Royal Avenue, and she was late. A local fighter I knew well, Ryan Lindberg, stopped to chat and asked me what I was doing. I said I was waiting on a bird, so he went on his way. About forty-five minutes later he walked past me still stood there alone, this time shaking his head and laughing his balls off. She finally turned up a while later blaming traffic. We went to Wetherspoon's, and she says I happily ate in front of her without getting her anything. Apparently, she politely refused a meal expecting me to quickly insist but I just said no worries and tucked into a big steak and chips while she watched on, starving. After Wetherspoon's we went to the Box Nightclub in the Odyssey, just the two of us. I couldn't match her drink for drink and ended up quickly blocked. At one point I banged into a table and spilt a load of drinks belonging to some group of girls. They all started screaming at me calling me a stupid cunt. I near got my ballix knocked in by a bunch of millies in front of her on our first date. Looking back, you wonder how and why she waited so long and then stuck with me once we finally did meet! And at the time, to be honest, I wasn't sure she had. A few nights later I asked her by text message, are we boyfriend and girlfriend now then? I got a yes in reply. Me and Christine Dorrian were an item.

Christine is from west Belfast, born in Lenadoon and raised in Poleglass. She went to St Dominic's Grammar School on the Falls Road where she got A Levels in English, Politics and IT before studying for her degree in Criminology at Jordanstown. She's from a Catholic and republican background, and although Poleglass is only a twenty-minute drive from Tiger's Bay, in reality it may as well be a million miles away. She'd never heard of the Bay when I first told her about it. I just said it's beside Yorkgate, which everyone knows because of the cinema and shopping centre there. Aside from the obvious of one being a Catholic and the other a Protestant area, the big difference between somewhere like

Poleglass and somewhere like Tiger's Bay is that only one is on an interface. Where there's an interface there's trouble. Where the two communities live a street apart that's where the tensions will be and where violence can erupt. West Belfast is a predominantly Catholic part of the city and, if you're born and raised in the middle of it, it can be kind of like a bubble of sorts. This is 2005 now, so Christine had no real experience of sectarian violence whereas I was used to the riots and people, like my brother, getting kickings for being the wrong religion on the wrong street. All that meant me and my family were more nervous about certain things when we first started going out than Christine and hers were. None of my own family cared one bit where she was from, but my ma would say to other people that Carl's seeing a wee girl from Glengormley to keep it vague and in our mind protect her a little bit when she'd come to our house.

The same way no one in my family cared Christine was Catholic, no one from her side batted an eyelid that I was a Protestant. The first night I met her ma we all sat in her house having a few drinks. There was a bowl of grapes sitting on the table and I was absentmindedly eating them all one by one. After a while her ma says, do you wanna leave them grapes alone – do Prods not get grapes in Tiger's Bay or something? Christine's older sister Lisa and her man Ciaran were there with us that night. Christine's da Dennis passed away from cancer when she was fourteen, so Ciaran saw himself as the man of the house. He's a great guy and we're good pals now but that night he just kept staring at me across the room as he got more and more drunk. After a while he motions for me to go over to him, so I get up off the sofa and walk to where he's sitting. Then he warns me in a drunken whisper, if you ever fucking mess her about, I'm going to stab you. I knew he was pissed so just sat back down without reacting, but his missus noticed something had gone on and started shouting at him, what the fuck did you just say you eejit. He shit himself. Nothing love, he said, I didn't say anything. I told Christine about it later and after she let her sister know, Lisa marched him into the bathroom for a bollocking. We could hear toilet rolls been flung about and everything!

Even though I knew Christine's family and friends genuinely didn't care, I was still very nervous myself in the early days about others finding out who I was and where I was from. Staying in her house one night I got woken by the sound of wee stones pinging off the window and someone trying the front door handle. It's maybe 2 a.m. and I panic. I shouted to Christine to phone the cops. Here we go I think, someone coming to do me in. I looked about for something to protect myself with and the best weapon I could find was a big bottle of hairspray. I stood at the top of the stairs waiting to blast the Provies in the eyes with it, but it turned out to be her ma coming home from a night out without her house keys. That shows you how on edge I was at the outset.

I blame those nerves for another incident that happened one of the first nights Christine and I shared a bed. I'd had a few drinks and when I woke in the middle of the night, I saw that I'd pissed myself and the sheet was soaked. Christine is lying on the side away from the wall but it's a small single bed, so I know it's only a matter of time before she moves and feels it. We were still in our early days, so I didn't know her too well – but I knew her well enough to sense that if she woke up next to a bed wetter, I'd be getting ditched before I left the house. I asked Christine to pass me the pint of water on the bedside table and then set it on my chest. I waited a while then calmly poured the water all over myself and faked a commotion like I'd just drifted back to sleep, and it had accidentally spilt. Somehow, I got away with it. And over the next week or so until she changed the sheet I'd sneak into the room and spray a load of deodorant over it to mask the smell of my stale piss. It wasn't until around a year later, when I felt confident enough she wouldn't dump me because of it, that I told her the truth!

I'd get black taxis up to her house all the time. The first time I didn't realise there were different rules in Catholic black taxis compared with Protestant ones. For us on the Shore Road we'd shout, let me off here mate or next stop is good, meaning next bus stop. So, we're on her way to hers and I shout in, let us off on the corner please mate. Christine looks at me like I'm an idiot. What the fuck are you doing, she says. You just rap the window up here when you want the taxi to stop. All the little giveaway signs. I was always conscious then of not giving the game away when I was travelling to her house alone. It was a £1.80 fare for me and for years I'd give the driver two quid and say, keep the change *mo chara*. That's Gaelic for my friend or mate, and if the driver knew I was a Prod from the Bay while saying it he probably pissed himself laughing as soon as he drove away. What a clown.

A few years later, after my pro career had already started, I did actually get a kicking from a gang in Beechmount where Christine's ma had moved to, but it wasn't sectarian. Not that that made me feel any better at the time! They were a gang of animals who hung around the area intimidating people, and apparently nobody could control them. We were in Christine's having a few drinks with her friend Kylie and her boyfriend Colin. The girls went for a Chinese and this gang followed them home, hoping to get into a house party or whatever. While we were eating, the bell went – so I went downstairs to tell them to fuck off and leave us in peace. There must have been about fifteen of them, mostly teenagers with one big fella leading the way. One spat at me, so I chucked some beer at them, closed the door and started back up the stairs. Next thing I know the door has been kicked through and this big brute is grabbing at me with an army of sixteen- to eighteen-year-olds piling in behind him. I was on the stair above the attackers, so I had a bit of an advantage to begin with. I grabbed the big man around the neck and hit him three or four digs, which appeared to have no effect whatsoever. A bit like when I fought Josh Warrington. He soon bundled me to the ground and they all battered me, kicks to the head and everything. Christine appeared and jumped on top of me to try and protect me, but these scumbags just kept going. They didn't care they were now booting a girl as well and she came out of it with bruises all over her arm and ribs. Kylie had run away squealing, and I think big Colin must have scarpered too because he was found unconscious up the stairs where someone had caught and chinned him. He ended up in an ambulance just to be safe. I picked my head up at one point thinking it was all over, and got another boot in the mouth from a big skinny fucker with massive ears. I was pretty beat up, so I let out a bit of a moan when they'd all gone back down the stairs. That's when we heard the big one shout, 'Are you whispering about me up there? I'll go up and knock your cunt in again.' It was all a bit mental. They used to stand outside Christine's ma's place after that just to intimidate me, but it eventually died down. And, like I say, it wasn't sectarian – so every cloud …

I was going to Poleglass to see Christine nearly every night. After training I'd walk a mile into town then get a taxi out west. She worked in the New Look shop on the Boucher Road, so sometimes I'd take the taxi up the Falls then get out and walk the mile and a half to Boucher to meet her. Then walk back to the Falls and another taxi to her house. A lot of walking and a lot of taxi fares. At that time I was skint, so we lived off her student loan. She was unbelievably generous. I still remember the embarrassment of checking my pockets leaving her house and only having £1.60. You feel shit needing to ask your girlfriend to borrow 20p to get home. My ma and da helped me out too and Billy would chip in for away trips so I could keep boxing at the highest level possible. They all helped me get my first car, a Ford Focus I bought off Christine's brother-in-law for £1,200. I reckon at least £800 came from Christine. I sometimes get slagged for never having had a real job but with boxing taking up most of my week it would have been tough to hold one down. I've only ever had one job interview in my life. It was to work in Big W at Yorkgate. The guy interviewing me called himself the team leader and I found that hilarious for some reason. Hi, I'm John. I'm the team leader. Are you, John. Good man. John never gave me the job anyway.

CHAPTER THREE

THE AMATEUR DAYS

My first senior tournament was the Irish National Championships in the Stadium in Dublin the week after my eighteenth birthday. They got Jamie Conlan and I to do the 51kg draw and we managed to pick ourselves against each other. We'd fought not long before in a cadet tournament and I'd come out on top of a competitive fight. This time I decided to box him rather than fight him and I made life a lot easier for myself, winning 16–6. I went on to beat Derek McArdle 19–8 in the semi-final and Derek Thorpe 14–4 in the final to become Irish Senior champion at the first attempt. I was delighted to win it so young but there was nothing special in any of the fights, and maybe because of that the memories aren't as strong as you'd imagine. Maybe the lack of fuss in winning it made me think this game is easy and presume there'd be plenty more to come as well.

The following month I was selected to travel with the Irish team to a Four Nations tournament in the Liverpool Olympia. There was quite a bit of attention on it with the BBC broadcasting some of the action live. Billy Walsh was the head coach and he asked me to carry the flag at the opening ceremony. That flag was obviously the Irish tricolour. I had to say no. A flat no. Times had changed but not that much. Everyone knew the stories of Wayne McCullough's house on the Shankill getting its windows put through when he carried the tricolour at the opening ceremony of the 1988 Olympics in Seoul. Maybe if it wasn't on the BBC I would have done it, but the thought of my ma and da sitting there while a brick came through the window because some dickhead saw me on TV with a flag he likes to burn on the bonfire each July meant I preferred not to risk it. I think it was a bit silly of Billy to put me in that situation. Maybe he saw it as a nod to 1988 as Wayne was chosen as the youngest member of the Irish team back then as well. Maybe he just didn't think about it at all in the context of the politics in Northern Ireland. It wasn't a big deal anyway. I quickly put it out of my mind, and it wasn't mentioned again. Everyone understood and respected my position. Darren O'Neill was the only one who would ask me about the politics and the Troubles and stuff, but he was a very clever guy and you could tell it was out of genuine interest in everything rather than some morbid fascination or an opportunity to gossip. You don't mind speaking to people like that on anything, although I'm not sure I was the man to enlighten him on much.

I lost to the English champion Stewart Langley in my first fight and that was my tournament over, but I had more a happy-to-be-there attitude. I still felt like a wee sprog, so to be accepted into a group by guys I'd always looked up to – the likes of Kenny Egan, Andy Lee, Conor Ahern and Darren – felt very special. I had a great relationship with big Kenny in particular. He took me under his wing a little and always looked out for me. I thought I was brilliant running around and going on the drink with these guys after a tournament. I remember in Liverpool on that trip Eric Donovan got knocked back from a nightclub because he was wearing trainers. He went around the corner, took his trainers and black socks off, put the trainers back on with the socks over the top, and strolled on into the club past the same bouncer. I was very impressed by the ingenuity. It reminded me of having to swap tops with my mate Woody to get past the bouncers in Kelly's once. Despite never having a problem in the past I got told I wasn't getting in because they could see the tattoos on my arms. Woody was a big lad, and I was a flyweight boxer wearing a slim-fit T-shirt, but we swapped and got in. Woody suffocating in my T-shirt with his chest hair bursting out, me tripping over Woody's long-sleeved shirt which came down past my knees. Another night in Kelly's the bouncers brought me and my mate Willy Marks into a room upstairs and strip-searched us down to our boxers. No idea what that was all about, and I try to suppress the memory, but I told my ma and she was all for going to the papers about it.

We got to go on a ten-day training camp to Cyprus around then. Apparently, there was some money left over in a budget which needed using up, so Billy took us away. I loved it, training every other day, shadow boxing underwater in the pool, staying in a class hotel. I roomed with the late Darren Sutherland during that one. An unbelievably talented fighter, but the tightest man I'd ever met at that point in my life. He used to pocket red-sauce sachets from the hotel restaurant to take home. In a taxi one night we were working out it'd probably be around €10 each to cover the fare home so he stopped the car and got out to walk a couple of miles back to the hotel rather than go out with us and have to pay it! On another night out – there were a few that trip – Eric Donovan sparked some fella out in the street for no reason. Next thing we knew a car full of lads pulls up and one emerges from it with a shotgun and points it directly at us. We all bombed off up some side street, me running in a zigzag like in the movies in case he's taking aim at my back. We ducked down behind some cars to hide and then our heavyweight, big Con Sheehan, full of drink, stands up and starts walking down the middle of the road towards the fella. Just an insane night.

That summer I fought in Italy, Estonia and Scotland. In Rome I won a Junior Six Nations Tournament and in Tallinn I got beat in the quarterfinals of the European Youth Championships. In Glasgow a big lanky Indian fighter called Arun Singh absolutely hammered me. I just couldn't get near him to pin him down, so he boxed the head off me. I loved all the trips and tournaments and travelling with the team. But I hated going to Dublin to train with the High-Performance Unit (HPU). I wasn't long started with Christine and now I had to travel down there every week from Monday to Thursday or from Tuesday to Friday. It was boring for me, just going down there to train and with fuck all else to do. The fighters stayed in a dorm above the Stadium and people just chilled out most of the time. The food was crap too. They told you it was all good healthy stuff that athletes need but it really wasn't. The other problem was dough. I wasn't getting funded at all then so only direct expenses were covered. Whenever I did receive a year of funding all I got was €1,000 per month. Not great really however you measure it, so I still had to rely on Christine and Billy and my folks to help me out. At different times there'd be other boxers receiving funding easily worth three or four times that, so it never sat right with me that as national senior champion, performing well internationally, I never got more than the bare minimum.

Towards the end of 2005 all eyes were on the upcoming Commonwealth Games in Melbourne, scheduled for March of the following year. I couldn't wait. The Youth Commonwealth Games in Bendigo had been one of the best experiences to date so to go to the full version and win a medal in a Northern Ireland vest was going to be special. In November, I twenty-pointed the Welsh fighter Chris Jenkins in the final to win a Multi-Nations in Ballybunion so I was feeling great entering the Ulster Senior's in the following week, despite a lingering hangover from the celebrations in Kerry. As the reigning Irish champion, I was a shoo-in for the Commonwealth squad and didn't need to prove anything in the Ulster's. I could have said I had a knock and sat them out to rubber stamp my ticket Down Under. But the thought of becoming Ulster champion in front of a packed Ulster Hall appealed to me so I never even considered withdrawing. I knew Ryan Lindberg was going to be my opponent and I saw nothing to fear there. Ryan just didn't look like a boxer. He was a quiet kid – into computers and stuff like that, I think. He seemed the type that had just been pushed into a boxing gym and was decent at it but had no real love for it. He'd go on to prove he was a brilliant amateur boxer – claiming victories over the likes of Luke Campbell, Scott Quigg and pretty much every Irish rival – but at the time I expected to deal with him handily and add the Ulster trophy to my Irish one. Instead, Ryan beat me. I boxed shit, but he was good and just very awkward with his style and long arms. He was a southpaw and I struggled with them in my early days. I think it was psychological more than anything. A southpaw in the amateurs tended to be a mover and a tricky counterpuncher. I probably tried too hard against them, thinking I needed to force the action. Although I could play the role of aggressor well when it suited me, I was a good boxer and a good counterpuncher myself – so more often than not I probably ended up fighting the wrong fight against them. Whatever the reason, Ryan beat me. I was distraught and raging in equal measure. I cried my eyes out the rest of that night, and missing out on those Commonwealth Games remains my biggest regret from my amateur days.

I was probably still feeling a bit sorry for myself a few weeks later when I lost my Irish title, with TJ Doheny beating me in the semi-finals. It was a low-scoring, cagey and awkward affair, but TJ was a very good fighter. A few months later I faced the best fighter I ever shared an amateur ring with, when Zou Shiming battered me at the Gee-Bee tournament in Finland. He just pinged the absolute head off me. Feeble shots but they tippy-tappied me to death. He was such a crafty fighter, able to hit you with clean one-twos on the break. I slag Paddy Barnes for losing 15–0 to him and say at least

I got a few points. Gallows humour though. I did actually keep it respectable for the first couple of rounds, staying within four or five points of him. But he pulled away with ease in the second half and it ended up 32–8 to China's greatest ever fighter.

Shiming would have beaten me that day regardless of my fitness levels, but fading in the second half of fights was common for me back then. I rarely had a good comeback win either. If I was behind in a fight, there was little chance of me turning it around. Killing myself to make weight was the main culprit for this. It's hilarious looking back at how I did the weight and how bad my eating habits were, even as a member of the Irish HPU. I used to look at a bag of crisps and a Mars Bar. What does that weigh? Okay, 30g and 60g. So, I'll have that instead of a 100g piece of steak. Silly bastard. Everything was so backward. Coaches would preach about eating healthy but there was zero follow-up. I'd lie or pretend in order to trick them. I pretty much lived in a sweatsuit, terrified of a set of scales. I'd starve myself for a day then suddenly neck three Mars Bars before training because I felt like I'd faint of hunger. The team had a girl acting as nutritionist, but it was nonsense really. If the English team had protein shakes for recovery, we had our choice of Nesquik flavour to be mixed with powdered skimmed milk and water. If other teams were being told to wise up and ignore cravings for junk or sweet food, we were told you could have a Turkish Delight or a handful of Jaffa Cakes! You couldn't make it up, but I was too immature to resist any urges, so I'd give myself a constant uphill battle to make whatever weight I was campaigning at. I enjoyed a few drinks like most young fellas do as well – often enjoying them a little too much at the weekend, even in the lead-up to a tournament. It took me a lot longer than it should have to wake up and realise I'd get nowhere the way I was carrying on.

I started 2007 still a bantamweight, but another defeat to Lindberg, this time in the Irish Senior semi-finals, was the death knell of my 54kg career. I don't actually think I lost that one, hurting him and giving him a standing count in the final round. But sometimes who you are or what club you're from can make more of a difference than how you fight in the judges' eyes. The decision to move to feather was accelerated by an injury to Davey Oliver, who was the number one at 57kg. He was forced to pull out of the EU Championships in Dublin, and I was chosen to take his place. Despite it being my first tournament at the new weight, I beat two decent opponents to make the final. It was shown live on RTÉ, and I was doing well until I gassed once again and lost out to the French fighter Khedafi Djelkhir in what was regarded as one of the fights of the tournament. Djelkhir went on to win a silver medal at the 2008 Beijing Olympics, with Vasyl Lomachenko beating him in the final – so he was a quality operator. That silver medal was massive for me. It proved to everyone, including myself, that I belonged at the elite level of amateur boxing.

With 2008 being an Olympic year, attention turned to qualification once those EU Championships ended. The first opportunity to book your place was by medalling at the World Championships being held in Chicago in October. As usual within Irish amateur boxing there was a bit of a power struggle at the top between various factions and individuals. The High-Performance Unit was still a relatively new set-up and there remained tensions in certain areas between it and the Irish Amateur Boxing Association (IABA). Where this affected me was when it came to Olympic qualification. Davey Oliver was the number one in Ireland at featherweight, but my performance at the EU Championships showed everyone I was a very close number two. Davey had the more established pedigree, the better résumé and the victory over me as Juniors, but I was flying now and outperforming him in sparring and in the training camps with all the coaches looking on. The only other weight class where the gap between one and two was as small was between the middleweights Darren Sutherland and Darren O'Neill. Because of this, Darren O'Neill and I had a status above all the other number twos. The coaches knew we were good enough to medal at the major tournaments and that we deserved the chance to prove that. That's why I kept getting invited to Olympic training camps and getting opportunities in internationals where I'd go away and invariably do well.

At the same time, Davey Oliver was on a bad run of form. He'd had to pull out of the EU's and, either side of that championship, he'd lost in Croatia, Poland, Ukraine and twice in Germany. I was at that same tournament in Germany and performed well in winning my fight so Billy, backed by Gerry Storey, made a strong case for me being selected ahead of Davey Oliver for the World's. Billy Walsh knew I deserved the chance too and it was him who suggested a box-off to decide which of the two of us went to Chicago. I was over the moon. The silver at the EU's had given me the confidence to match my ability so I was convinced I'd beat Davey Oliver in the box-off, collect a medal at the World Championships and secure my place at the Olympics before Christmas. Billy travelled down to the IABA Council meeting in Dublin where they were going to ratify the box-off decision and set a date. It was early September and the World Championships didn't begin until the very end of October, so there was plenty of time. But when it came to deciding where and when we'd fight, Dominic O'Rourke stood up and said it needed to be the following week. Dom was seven years into his first term as president of the IABA, so he was a very powerful and influential figure. He was also the head coach of St Michael's Boxing Club in Athy, Kildare. And St Michael's just happened to be Davey Oliver's home club. Dom's argument was that the rest of the team was already picked, and Davey didn't know whether he was coming or going with the uncertainty over his selection. That it wasn't fair to prolong it and the box-off must happen immediately.

Dom was also aware that I'd injured my eardrum during my victory in Germany the previous month and had been told not to spar for four weeks, thus making it impossible for me to be passed fit to box on the date he was suggesting. Billy never shied away from a debate, so he stood up at the meeting and argued the point. After a lot of heated back and forth, Dom walked out of the room saying he'd leave the rest alone to decide. Billy took offence to that. I suppose being the only Protestant on the Council he was more attuned to sleights when delivered no matter how subtle.

'Do you think you're better than me?' he said to Dom. 'If you're leaving the room then I'm leaving the room with you.'

When they returned a while later and asked what the decision was, they were told it had gone in Dom's favour. The box-off needed to take place the following week, which everyone in the room knew was impossible due to my ear injury.

'What was the vote?' Billy asked.

There wasn't one, he was told.

'So, it was unanimous then was it?' he said, looking pointedly at his colleagues from the Antrim Council in particular. He stormed out in disgust and that box-off never happened.

The whole thing deflated me. An out-of-sorts Davey went to Chicago and was beaten in the preliminary round. I didn't fight for the rest of the year. I think I was probably still feeling a little sorry for myself when I did return to the ring and Kevin Fennessy outpointed me in the 2008 Irish Senior's semi-final. I took that defeat very hard. I remember going straight to Christine's house when I got back to Belfast and breaking down in tears. With all due respect to Kevin, who wasn't a bad fighter at all, I knew I was head and shoulders above him and yet he'd just beaten me 13–7. The next day Davey beat him 22–4 in the final. I was embarrassed and frustrated, and very close to packing it all in. I hated spending my weeks down in Dublin and it suddenly seemed completely pointless if the end result was losing to Fennessy in a semi-final. I hated living on a pittance and having to keep scrounging off Christine and Billy and my parents. It was all too much effort for so little reward. I was as low as I'd ever been in boxing, and I honestly believe I would have hung the gloves up there and then if it wasn't for Christine. She was the one who talked me around. She told me not to think or worry about the money and made me believe this was the right path, that I had the talent and just needed the dedication to succeed in boxing. That loss to Fennessy was a bit of a turning point. It marked a before and after in my boxing career. It wasn't like everything immediately clicked into place for me, but certainly from that fight onwards I wised up a lot. I at least gave myself more of a chance of winning.

It was too little too late to make the Olympic team, however. I got my shot at Davey Oliver when box-offs were called across the board and every number one who hadn't yet qualified for Beijing had to fight their closest rival, with the winner going to the final European qualifying tournament in Athens. It was close, and his fitness more than anything made the difference down the stretch, but he beat me fair and square that day in Dublin.

At the Ulster Senior Championships in April, I fought Marco McCullough in the semi-final at the Dockers and beat him 11–7. A week later in Andytown Leisure Centre I twenty-pointed Eamon Finnegan to become champion. It was at that stage the best I'd ever boxed in my life. I felt like Prince Naseem in the ring that night. But I didn't really kick on from that performance at the Ulster's as I could or should have. I was still doing well in training and sparring but my results maybe didn't reflect that. I wouldn't say my head dropped, but certainly there was a nagging disappointment that I hadn't had a real opportunity to qualify for the Olympics and the Irish team set off for Beijing without a featherweight aboard the plane. I lost in tournaments in France and Turkey as well as another defeat to Davey in a box-off to see who went to the European

Championships in Liverpool. But if 2008 ended with a whimper, it made the bang with which 2009 began that much sweeter.

I was drawn to fight Tyrone McKenna in the quarterfinals of the Irish Championships. I actually mixed up my dates and started back up the road after the draw before I realised our fight was that day. We'd reached Newry before having to turn the car around and race back in time for the first bell. Tyrone's about six foot two and remains a bit of a freak today by making the 140lb super lightweight limit as a pro. But back then as a teenager he was already that height and somehow weighed in as a featherweight. It's hard to imagine two more different body shapes facing one another in the boxing ring, and there's a hilarious action photo which exaggerates the size disparity even more and makes me look like a dwarf. Regardless, I managed to jump high enough to reach his chin a couple of times and beat him 14–5. Next up was a rematch with Kevin Fennessy. The only motivation I needed was the memory of sitting crying in Christine's house a year earlier. This was the first fight where I physically felt the effects of a period of time spent living right, eating right, not boozing and not having to starve myself for two days to make weight. I battered Kevin that day. When I got ten points up his da and coach threw the towel in. He complained I was getting everything, but in reality he just didn't want to see his son take a hiding for the full nine minutes. That was a sweet victory but the true redemption I sought awaited me in the final.

If you reached the 57kg final at the Irish Senior Championships around that time it was a near certainty that David Oliver Joyce would be awaiting you in the opposite corner. Of the eleven times Davey entered the Senior's, he reached the final ten times, and won it six times. A phenomenal record. Including our first fight as kids back in 2001, he'd beaten me all three times we'd met. No one else has ever beaten me three times without reply so I think it's fair to say that Davey was my nemesis. I want to make clear the rivalry was only ever sporting. Davey is an absolutely lovely fella and we always got on great. He invited me to his wedding a few weeks before one of our fights and I was delighted to be there. We were pals and any rivalry was always respectful, but we all have egos – and maybe an athlete's ego is more inflated than most. When someone is getting the better of you, they become the focus. They're the one you need to beat before you can move on. The saga over the box-off that never was added spice to it. The feeling Billy and I had of us Prods from the North being the outsiders while Davey was Dom the president's boy raised the stakes higher in our minds. Even my old irrational fear of Travellers played a part in the build-up!

Unlike a lot of amateur boxers around that time, Davey and I had genuine pro styles. Basically, we didn't need to go looking for one another. We weren't hitting and moving and running around the ring. The Olympics had been four by two-minute rounds and that format suits that style. If your plan is to get on your bike, then it's easier to do that for eight minutes in total with another three spent in your corner having a drink of water. But we were back to three by three-minute rounds now. Nine minutes of fighting and only two of resting. That time frame is more suited to an aggressive fighter, one who saves energy for punching rather than running. But we were also two very skilled and very seasoned boxers. We were aggressive counterpunchers I suppose. There was a thought process behind everything we did. We were happy in close too – not because we were hard nuts just closing our eyes and swinging, but because we backed ourselves to catch and counter or use head and upper-body movement to hit our opponent more than he hit us. Styles make fights and ours guaranteed action at a high level. I think it's fair to say that it was one of the most anticipated fights of the night.

As soon as the first bell sounded, we met in the centre of the ring and got to work. I'm not sure if either of us touched the ropes at all in that opening three minutes. It was intense as both of us maintained our tight guards to catch everything incoming on arms or elbows or gloves while aiming to capitalise upon the smallest of gaps to land our own scoring shots. When we returned to our corners the live scoreboard read two for Joyce and two for Frampton. The bell went to start the second and we picked up where we'd left off in the first. Centre of the ring, tucked up tight, catch, catch, throw, catch. We were both putting everything into the punches now. Hooks to the head and body. An uppercut when it was on. I sensed him wince a couple of times from hooks I dug into his ribs, but the judges disagreed. I don't think a point was registered until the final minute of the round. Then in the last thirty seconds, Davey opened up with a flurry – maybe ten or twelve shots. One landed clean to earn him a point and I backed off a few steps before spinning into the centre of the ring to fire back. As Davey opened up again, I clipped him with a left hook and then shortened a right hand to ensure I landed first and caught him flush on the chin. He dropped hard and the ref started counting. He got up and saw out the final couple of seconds. The scores remained locked at four points each because a knockdown didn't get you anything extra, but I had all the momentum now.

Maybe people expected the usual Frampton fade down the stretch in a close, competitive fight but Billy and I knew better. We'd prepared better. I was ready to do another three minutes flat out. And I needed to be, as the pace did not slow. If anything, it actually increased. But I felt good. Without any fears about stamina, I remained calm and kept my shape better than Davey. He was winging in more shots, but they were getting wild, getting ragged. I was still picking mine and landing the cleaner. Halfway through the round I was three points clear. Davey had to chase it now and he did, getting more frantic with his attacks. I let him burn up all that energy and then put it on him with a minute to go. I landed another flush right hand, and it buzzed him bad. He stumbled across the ring and as I moved in to finish it the ref jumped between us and gave him a standing eight count. I didn't know the scores. In the heat of battle it can be hard to judge it accurately and I thought it was still probably pretty close. I was geared up to jump straight on him and unleash everything for the final thirty seconds. Had I done I reckon I would have forced a stoppage. But as his count reached eight, Billy and my da in the corner had seen the scoreboard. You're five points up son, Billy shouted. Get on your bike! At the final bell I dropped to my knees and let out a bit of a roar. That was as animated a celebration as I'd ever given in the amateurs. I'd done it. Redemption. Finally, a victory over my biggest rival. And Irish champion once again.

CHAPTER FOUR

THE JACKAL EMERGES

The first time I met Barry McGuigan was in the Holy Family Gym when I was fifteen or sixteen years old. It was an event in collaboration with an organisation called Fight for Peace, and Gerry Storey was running it. Global sporting-excellence organisation Laureus were involved and Amir Khan came over, so it was a relatively high-profile affair. I fought on it and afterwards I got a photo with Barry, and he spent a few minutes chatting to me about boxing. Barry was a legend of Irish boxing so for him to give me that time as a kid just coming through felt great. My first impression was just that he was a very nice man. The next time I saw Barry was at the 2007 EU Championships, when I won the silver. He congratulated me and we took another photo together. I didn't know it at the time but that was when he first expressed an interest in signing me as a professional. He approached Billy McKee and said I had all the makings of a very good pro. Billy said in no uncertain terms to leave me be for now, that I had aspirations of making the Olympic team the following year and that turning over was not yet a consideration. Barry was then ringside at the 2008 Ulster Senior's. He was there to support his son Shane, who was competing as a welterweight. Christine and her friend Leona had come along to watch me, and we all ended up at a table with a relation of Barry's. The old boy was enjoying himself and when I got up to get some drinks he leaned across and whispered to the girls that if he was twenty years younger, he'd be making love to the pair of them right now! He never propositioned me in the same way, but he did keep asking if I wanted to go and meet Barry. I said no. Like I say, Barry is a legend of Irish boxing and there were a lot of press and TV cameras around. He was there to watch his son fight so I'd have been embarrassed to approach and bother him.

A year later I was at a training camp in Jordanstown when I answered a call from a private number and heard Barry's voice. I was twenty-two years old and turning pro was definitely in my mind now. The focus was firmly on fighting at the World Championships in September in Milan, but at the same time I thought it was sensible to put a few feelers out and see what interest there was in me from the managers and promoters. Despite being Irish champion the funding still wasn't there for me, and I couldn't continue much longer with only getting my expenses covered. Barry told me he'd like to sign me and suggested we have a meeting at the Culloden Hotel. I was flattered and more than happy to go along. His sons Jake and Shane were there but when it came to talking it was just Barry, Billy and me. We had a cup of tea, and I ordered a cream bun. I remember him looking at it with a should-you-really-be-eating-stuff-like-that expression on his face. Nevertheless, he sold me the dream. He would be my manager and he had all the connections with the big promoters to get me the most lucrative deal and the opportunities on the biggest platforms. He said we'd start on Matchroom shows but mentioned Frank Warren too. He also spoke of doing his own shows in the Ulster Hall to grow the support at home. It was all music to my ears, but there were others sniffing around too. Local boxing figure Pat Magee had previously said to Billy that he'd start supporting me financially while I continued my amateur career. Officially there were no strings attached, but Pat

would rightly expect me to seriously consider signing with him
when I did decide to go pro. The Dublin-based promoter Tommy
Egan had also reached out. Egan had just done a deal with Artie
Pelullo of Banner Promotions in the US, which they were describing
as the New Deal for Irish boxing. The idea was that Irish fighters
could remain based in Ireland while benefitting from fighting on
US shows and networks. They seemed very keen to sign me. I'd
asked Gerry Storey's advice as I'd a good relationship with him and
he knew his way around the pro game a bit. He spoke to Warren
on my behalf, and I think a small offer may have been made but
nothing that signified they were too hot on me. Gerry also advised
me not to jump the gun, to bide my time on it all. He pointed out
that the World Championships in Milan were only a few months
away and, such was my form, I had every chance of going there
and picking up a medal. Billy Walsh was telling me the same. I
was reigning Irish champion, having dropped and nearly stopped
Davey Oliver in a brilliant final live on RTÉ. There'd been two major
tournaments in the months immediately after the Irish Senior's and
I'd performed excellently in those as well. At the prestigious Ahmet
Comert Tournament in Turkey, I won four fights in four days to
take the gold. I beat the Ukrainian number two in the quarter-final
along the way. It should have been against Lomachenko, but he was
injured. At least that's his story and he's sticking to it. I prefer to
think he watched me on RTÉ against Davey and shit himself, so he
faked an injury to avoid facing me in Istanbul. Joking aside, it would
have been nice to have fought Lomachenko. Just to be in the ring
with him and see first-hand how good he was and how I could have
done against him. To see how massively I would have lost by! After
Turkey I picked up another two good wins and a silver medal in the
Czech Republic, so I fancied myself to do very well in the Worlds.
Barry was saying this was the right moment to go professional and
I was tiring of the amateur grind and always being skint, but at the

same time the Worlds is something all fighters dream of competing in. I also knew a medal around my neck increased my commercial value as a pro fighter.

I remember standing with Christine in her sister's kitchen one night talking about the decision I was facing. The timing of the move was tricky, but we were all agreeing that Barry was the best option. Even my ma had heard of him so he was a name that would get me attention. But at the same time, it wasn't like I'd be signing up long-term to a Matchroom or a Queensberry where there's always a risk of just being another number in a stable of dozens, with most being far more established stars than I was. We talked about what Barry had been through as well in terms of his well-documented legal battles with his promoter, and reasoned he'd never do anything to screw over a fighter himself. I was playing the game and entertaining other suitors, but I think deep down I always knew I'd sign with Barry.

It wasn't long before Barry called back with a firm financial offer. Eight grand up front as a signing bonus, a grand a round starting off on four-round fights and the promise of securing me additional income from sponsorship deals. I was in Billy's office in the Midland when I took the call, and my gut reaction was one of disappointment. Gerry Storey was there too. I'm not sure I had actual figures in my head, but that seemed a pretty measly offer. Billy and Gerry agreed although Gerry's reaction was a little more diplomatic than Billy's rather pointed, tell him to fuck off. I called back and made my case for why I expected a higher sign-on.

'The grand a round is okay,' I said. 'But I'm looking for twenty grand sign-on.'

Barry said he'd need to think about that, but twenty minutes later the phone rang again.

'Twenty is agreed,' Barry said.

So that was that. I was turning pro.

One big regret I had was how I handled it all with Billy Walsh. Billy had always looked after me well. I don't know how he interacts with all his boxers, but he was always very good to me – and I really appreciated that. He made no secret of the fact he wanted me to continue my amateur career with the HPU for a few more years. The upcoming Worlds was a given as far as he was concerned, but he talked about the 2012 Olympics as well. He also told me things would change in terms of funding, but I'd need to wait for that. The amount each fighter received was reassessed annually and the financial year had not long started. So, I'd be broke for a good while yet if I did knock back Barry's offer. The truth is that Billy would never have convinced me once my mind was made up. But I'm still annoyed with myself for making my decision, and letting Barry know it, before I sat down and told Billy personally.

***

Before I got going as a pro, Barry said I needed a decent nickname. A few different ideas were bandied about, but when I suggested 'the Jackal', Barry absolutely loved it. My mate Marky Adamson was the one who coined that back when I was in school. First, I got called Carlos, after the Brazilian fullback Roberto Carlos who was in his pomp at the time. I also played fullback, was stocky and liked to stick the boot in so it wasn't a huge leap to add on two extra letters to my name. Somehow the pair of us then came across the Venezuelan terrorist Carlos the Jackal and the rest is history. At one point I heard that someone was trying to say the name came from a notorious UVF killer known as the Jackal. It's insane what people can dream up.

The first year of my professional career raced by. We signed a deal with Barry Hearn's Matchroom and they had plenty of shows to keep me busy. Six fights in six different venues, beginning with a four-rounder against Sandor Szinavel in the Olympia in Liverpool on the 12th of June 2009. I don't know if the place has had a refurb over the years, but it was a bit of a dive back then. I was the first fight on, very early evening. Around ten people had come over to watch me. I just remember being extremely nervous. Probably the most nervous I would ever be before a fight. It was the fear of the unknown, of course. I'd no idea what I was walking into. I'd never seen my opponent before. He was a southpaw, which is a strange choice for someone on debut. I used to have trouble with southpaws in my early amateur days. Am I going to struggle with them now as a pro? I'd never been hit in the head with an 8oz glove. How was that going to feel? Will I be able to take it? I'd never fought for twelve minutes before. What if this goes the distance and I run out of gas in the final round? My mind was going a million miles an hour. As we got close to the ringwalk I went to my bag for my gumshield, and it was nowhere to be found. Shit, I've left it in the hotel. No gumshield, no fight. Barry had to race to the hotel to get it for me, picking himself up a speeding ticket on the way back. When it was time to go, I remember looking down at my shorts and thinking, these look shit. Barry had sorted them out for me. I took a mental note to arrange my own gear going forward. Into the ring and it's a little like that night in Portstewart all those years ago, the little seven-year-old mutt straining at the leash. I looked across at my blonde Hungarian opponent and thought he could be a little boy himself. The bell went and he hit me. Not clean or anything, I think my glove deflected it onto the top of my head, but it felt very different to the amateur punches. These gloves are mental, I thought. I dropped him soon after and then sent him to the canvas twice more in the second round to force the stoppage. We were off and running.

Three months later and I was opening the card again, this time in the Eaton Sports Academy in Middlesbrough. They call it a Sports

Academy to make it sound grander than what it is, which is a local leisure centre. I had actually been due to fight there a month earlier, but the show got cancelled because the place was flooded. I fought a French guy called Yannis Lakrout and, other than being frustrated it went the full four rounds, I don't remember much about it. I guess like all young pros starting out I wanted to knock guys out. I felt that was how I made a statement and emphasised how much better than my opponent I was. But journeymen know how to survive. If they tuck their elbows in and don't take their gloves off their head, it's always going to be a challenge to stop them.

My first professional fight at home was up next on the undercard of a Paul McCloskey European title defence in Magherafelt. It was the same night as Frank Warren put a big Martin Rogan card on in the Odyssey in Belfast, but I still managed to take a couple of hundred out the M2 with me in support. Promoters take note of things like that, and this was the moment when Barry and Eddie Hearn realised I could do a big ticket for them. I stopped a guy called Ignac Kassai in the third round of a pretty nondescript fight, so it's two other memories that stick in my mind. The first is that it was fucking freezing. If Middlesbrough had a Sports Academy, Magherafelt had to go a step further and give themselves the Meadowbank Sports Arena. In reality it was an AstroTurf football pitch inside a tin hut, and it was absolutely baltic. The second was my ringwalk music. That was the last time I left that decision in the hands of someone else. Up until then I'd never given it much thought, and the venue DJ played whatever he wanted. I'm not sure I even noticed what was played in my first two fights. But as I made my way to the ring in Magherafelt I definitely noticed. What the fuck is this, I thought. Turned out to be a song called 'Kiss Me Thru the Phone' by Soulja Boy. People were literally laughing as I was walking, and I got a slagging for a while over it. From that night on I picked my own songs.

I had my final four-rounder in February of 2010, and it was decided to give me someone with a pulse. A 2–0 French kid named Yoan Boyeaux was chosen and it was clear that he and his team had crossed the Channel to win. The first three opponents had been pure journeymen, who understood and accepted they had no mission of winning. To non-boxing people this side of the game seems bizarre, but it's just a necessary part of the business when it comes to building prospects. So the difference between Boyeaux and those boys was striking. Not just in terms of performance in the ring, but in the build-up as well. At the weigh-in or seeing them in the hotel, their demeanour changed the whole feel of it – and I liked it. It felt like an actual fight. He was definitely supposed to be a small step-up in class, but this was only my fourth fight so it should still have been relatively easy work. I don't think anyone realised just how much of a step-up it was. I won it well, and although he drew one of the rounds, he ran more than he fought – but the rest of his career proved he was a very decent operator. Good enough to fight Naoya Inoue for his WBO (World Boxing Organization) World title a few years back and end up with a 43–7 record.

I had a quick three-week turnaround for my next outing, the first to be scheduled for six rounds. From sports academies to sports arenas, now I was in a good, honest Sports Centre in Huddersfield. And facing me was an absolute eejit in Istvan Szabo. Matchmakers will always be wary of an unbeaten fighter because you never know what someone's ceiling is until they're beat, but no one could have had any fears over this 1–0 Hungarian. When I arrived at the weigh-in he was nowhere to be seen and, after hanging around for a while, I was told he wouldn't be in until the evening. The British Boxing Board wouldn't allow me to weigh in without my opponent present, so I had to lie about the hotel, raging and starving, until he arrived. I don't know what time it was exactly but it was dark outside when he finally traipsed in, a skinny fella looking older than my da. He reminded me of Mr Bean. We're about to get on the scales and he suddenly dashes off for a piss. I'm thinking, oh he must be struggling here. Nope. I weigh bang on 122 pounds and then he steps up with his tracksuit bottoms still on and weighed around 110. They put him down as 116 to make it respectable but there's no chance he was anywhere near it. The fight the following night was one of those embarrassing ones you see every now and again early on cards. He had no proper boxing gear or anything. It looked like he'd found a pair of O'Neills GAA shorts to wear with no protector underneath. I think Sky TV were embarrassed by the whole thing. It was all over inside a minute when I barely touched him and he decided he'd had enough. It was so quick my da missed it as he'd run out for a slash while I was walking to the ring. And Istvan never fought again.

Fight number six took me back home again, this time to Belfast and the King's Hall on another McCloskey bill. I was matched with the English fighter Ian Bailey. He had a winning five and four record so I was guaranteed a more competitive night than auld Szabo had offered. I'm known for being short with a big head, but Bailey had me outmatched on both of those fronts. I nearly chinned him in the first round and got a bit excited. He survived it and I'd emptied a fair amount of my tank chasing the stoppage in the opening three minutes. That made for a very long five rounds until I'd earned a 60–55 points decision. I was absolutely knackered after it. I remember sitting there thinking, if that's what six rounds feels like how the fuck am I ever going to do twelve? As an amateur I'd mostly done four by two-minute rounds with some three by threes mixed in. But this was before AIBA (International Boxing Association) had launched the World Series of Boxing, so I'd never experienced the five three-minute rounds they fought in that competition. So, six rounds as a professional was essentially double what I'd ever done before. I would have sparred six tough rounds in the gym but it's not the same. I blew a gasket against Bailey, and he drew a round due to that fatigue. It was a bit of an eye-opener.

I was pretty happy with how the first twelve months of my pro career had played out. Six fights and a couple of respectable tests for the level I was at. The grand a round was fine as everyone knows you don't get rich in year one and that the activity is more important than the money. I felt it was all a decent foundation to kick on towards eight-rounders in year two. My only complaints were the lack of actual TV time I'd been promised at the outset and the size of show I was appearing on. Barry was true to his word on getting me on Matchroom cards, but I was never scheduled for the televised part of the bill. And in my head the events would be a bit more bright-lights-and-glamour type events than the reality of the shows on which I ended up fighting. With no disrespect meant to the lads involved, Nigel Wright in a Commonwealth title bout or Lenny Daws defending his British title or Gary Sykes fighting for a vacant British belt were not massive headline acts. And leisure centres in Huddersfield, Magherafelt and Middlesbrough were not the most glamorous of venues. Maybe I was getting ahead of myself, but even back then I felt I was destined for a bigger stage.

∗∗∗

One of the biggest decisions any young pro needs to make at the start of their journey is who is going to train them. I don't think it's an exaggeration to say that plenty of talented boxers with a lot of potential have started out with the wrong coach and been left playing catch-up for the rest of their career. Occasionally a fighter will continue with their amateur coach, but Billy had made clear he had no interest getting involved in the pro game so that wasn't an option. It's very rare that approach works out for the best anyway given the extent of the changes a successful amateur is required to make in order to develop an effective pro style. Back then the two main professional boxing trainers in Belfast were John Breen and Gerry Storey. Breen had the deeper résumé when it came to the pros, having guided the likes of Dave Boy McAuley, Paul Hodkinson, Crisanto Espana, Victor Cordoba and Fabrice Benichou to world-title glory in the 1980s and '90s. But Gerry was a legend of the amateur scene and had won professional British titles with guys like Michael Ayers, Tommy Waite and Tony Dodson. More importantly for me at the time, I knew and trusted Gerry and I was comfortable working with him in the gym. Barry wasn't sure about Gerry training me and tried to push me towards the Holy Trinity coach Harry Hawkins. It was strange as I thought Barry and Gerry were close but Barry worried that he was getting on a bit, and he had to prioritise my development over any friendships he might have had. I had nothing against Hawkins, but I didn't know him that well. Gerry was the coach for me.

Gerry had two people helping him out in the gym, his son Gerry Jr and Seamie McCann. Seamie is now the man basically running the Holy Family Club. When it comes to fitness, he's a freak of nature – the fittest man in the world. He did a lot of pads with me, and he'd help me out when I fancied a bit of sparring too. I could call him at any time of any day, and he'd come down.

'How many rounds do you want?' Seamie would say.

I'd ask if he could manage to do eight.

'Eight? I'll do fifteen with you if you want!'

And he could have as well. He entered the Belfast Marathon off his own bat once. He wasn't a competitive long-distance runner or a member of a club or anything, but he thought he'd give it a go. He ended up finishing seventh in sub two-and-a-half hours. That's just incredible to think of. By the latter stages of any marathon the runners involved all know one another from racing over the years. They must have wondered who the hell is this fella bombing past them at the 20-mile mark with people screaming, go on Seamie, from the side of the road!

Camp was standard enough with Gerry. I'd be up very early each morning to get a run in. A light middleweight from Bangor called Scott Jordan used to come with me. A lot of time we'd go up the Cavehill for these gruelling hill sprints and Seamie would jog alongside us chatting away. I'd be blowing out of my ass and then he'd say, do you want me to hit the button kid? Then he'd slap his own ass and speed off up the slope into the distance while I struggled on at what I thought was full pelt. Around midday or one o'clock we'd go to the gym for the second session and a load of pad or bag work. Gerry Sr was old school and would go over a combination for an hour if necessary until he was satisfied that I'd perfected it. Gerry Jr wasn't that type of taskmaster. If anything, I left the gym feeling I maybe hadn't pushed as hard as I should have after his sessions.

Towards the end of that first camp, Barry flew me over to England to do a few weeks with the trainer Kevin Maree. Kevin was originally from the south of Ireland but was now based just outside Manchester. He managed a gym connected to a hotel called Stirk House. He still manages and trains fighters today, but back then his only full-time boxer was another McGuigan-managed fighter, the Scottish super middleweight Kenny Anderson. Barry liked Kevin and it seemed he was his go-to trainer for the fighters he managed. I think the main idea of me going there was largely to get good sparring. Purely due to the much larger size of the talent pool on the mainland, it was far easier to arrange quality sparring there compared with back home. And as any pro at the beginning of their career will tell you, quality sparring at that stage is vital to your development. There is only so much you can learn in a fight against a journeyman so it's in competitive sparring sessions that you can really gauge your progression. I can have no complaints with the work I got those first couple of years. Barry was brilliant at bringing in the right people to help me along. He'd drive up from Kent where he lived and take me all over the place to visit other gyms and experience all sorts of styles and sizes and levels. I remember great sessions with the likes of Gary Buckland, John Simpson and Stevie Bell. Bell would have been fighting for English and Commonwealth titles around that time, so he was a good fighter and a lot bigger than me. Two days in succession he dropped me with the same body shot. One of those killer digs that has you rolling around the canvas Paddy Barnes style. I've never been dropped by a body shot since. The Mongolian Choi Tseveenpurev was another I had great spars with. Then just a load of experienced pros and journeymen of all shapes and sizes. It was exactly what I needed and I felt like I was learning a lot, even if I was at times coming out second best. When I did have success against a more established name, that would give me a lot of confidence. Confidence both in myself and in the process as my improvements were measurable and clear. A spar with Tyrone Nurse was one such occasion. Nurse was a big, lanky lightweight and he tried being a bit flash, so I jumped all over him and punched his head in that day.

I enjoyed going over to Kevin. He was a good man and a good trainer. I stayed in the Stirk House hotel and was well looked after. The chef cooked my food, and it was a pretty peaceful environment. If I had to be away from home, then I thought I could do a lot worse than there. And that first camp seemed to make sense. The majority of the work with Gerry, a couple of weeks quality sparring in Manchester, then meet up with the Storeys again to work my corner as lead and assistant trainer for the fight. Kevin would be in the corner as well and I think he enjoyed it as a young Irish trainer working under and learning from a legend like Gerry. I felt like I was getting the best of both worlds, and everyone seemed comfortable with the set-up. Gradually though, fight by fight, the proportion of each camp spent with Gerry decreased. Two weeks with Kevin became three during preparation for my second fight. Before long it was a month away, and soon after that more than half my camp was away from Belfast. Kevin has since said that Barry told him at the time that Gerry would soon be retiring from the professional side of boxing and so he wanted Kevin spending more time with me to smooth the transition when the day arrived. I wasn't aware of that back then, but it would make sense the way those first few camps went.

At some point during those first six fights, I also started to complete part of my fight preparation with Barry himself. He has a huge family home in Kent with a gym in the basement and he invited me to stay there and train with him for a few weeks. Training with Barry was very hard with a lot of focus on fitness. It was military-like as he whipped me into shape. There wasn't much emphasis on technique or correcting mistakes or tactics, it was all about power and throwing thousands of punches at 100mph. One day Barry had a meeting to go to and couldn't do a session, so he asked his son Shane to step in. Right from the off it was clear he was a far superior pad man than his old man. I enjoyed the session, so I was happy when it became a regular thing and Shane became another voice in my camp. Once again, kind of by stealth, the proportion of where my preparation took place shifted fight by fight with a clear trend towards more time with the McGuigans. They would also drive up to Manchester to watch me train with Kevin and look on at some of my spars. Shane was there one of the days I struggled against someone, and he shouted a bit of advice to me. I don't even know if Kevin knew exactly who Shane was at that stage but, as any trainer would be, he was a bit put out by someone coming into his gym and shouting to the fighter he was training. Kevin says he called Barry about it that night and said if his sons come to the gym then they need to keep their mouths shut during spars or sessions. He quite reasonably said that he was working on some specific things with me and didn't need additional voices muddying the waters. That was the last camp I ever did with Kevin.

***

By now Barry was keen to stage his own shows, so my next two fights moved away from Matchroom and the Sky Sports platform. They hadn't exactly been giving me primetime slots, so I was happy to get the opportunity to fight at home and headline a card in only my seventh pro fight. The opponent for this one was a little step up as well. Yuriy Voronin was an experienced Ukrainian who'd recently done okay against Scott Quigg, lasting until the sixth round against the 15–0 English prospect. Earlier in his career he'd fought for European and Intercontinental titles, and famously dropped Bernard Dunne in the final round of their battle in the National Stadium. I remembered watching that fight when Dunne was out on his feet and needed the ref to help him back to his stool, so I was nervous in the changing room. I needn't have been. I battered Voronin from the opening bell and stopped him towards the end of the third round when the ref stepped in to save him from himself. The atmosphere inside the Ulster Hall was brilliant as well. I was already able to sell it out pretty much single-handed, so Barry only needed three six-rounders and couple of fours on the undercard to give Setanta TV a bit more content. Among the crowd was the actor Daniel Day-Lewis, who drove up from Wexford on his motorbike to watch me. It was pretty cool having one of the greatest actors in the world do that and he was a lovely guy too.

Three months later we were back in the Ulster Hall for another Barry McGuigan-promoted show. Opponents struggled to get to Belfast due to a storm cancelling flights so this time there were only three fights on the undercard. A few lads who were suddenly without a fight ended up having boxing exhibitions against one another just to stretch the night out. I've no idea what Setanta, who had to try and make a televised spectacle of it, thought of that but no one else was concerned as I'd proven I could sell out the venue without help from undercard ticket sellers. It was another recent Scott Quigg opponent again too. The Scotsman Gavin Reid had lasted nine rounds with Quigg, so was seen as a legitimate foe for me and a competitive enough fight to be passed for the Celtic Super Bantamweight title. That meant it was scheduled for ten rounds and I did wonder how my stamina would be if it ended up going that far. It turned out Reid wasn't the man to ask those questions as I blasted him out inside two rounds. Given he'd nearly gone the distance with Quigg in his previous outing, it was a nice little statement to make.

From Belfast it was back to the bright lights of Huddersfield for fight number nine on another Matchroom card. It was supposed to be an eight-rounder but when the original opponent dropped out late it was moved to a six and the experienced Venezuelan Oscar Chacin stepped in. Chacin had just gone the distance with the European champion Kiko Martinez, so he was no mug. Not a threat as such, but wily and able to survive. As I'd prepared for eight rounds, I knew I could set a fast pace from the off and still be comfortable if it reached the final bell. Having watched him before I also knew his defence was good enough to block the first two or three shots thrown at him, but he'd struggle if a couple more followed to end the combination. I punished him to the body and heard him gasp and wince a few times, but he was a tough guy. With the final action of the third I feinted to the body and landed flush on his face, opening up a nasty cut over his eye. His corner didn't do anything to stem the flow of blood between rounds so it was only a matter of time before the ref called it off in the fourth. I was pleased with how I boxed that night and reckon even if it hadn't been for the cut, I would have gotten him out of there before the final bell. I was also excited because this was the first time I was scheduled late enough on a Matchroom bill that the Sky Sports cameras were actually turned on and rolling. Every young fighter is the same. You dream of that exposure from the biggest television platforms. My bout was only shown on the Ringside show, but it was still a big moment for me. You're buzzing to watch it back on TV and listen to Adam Smith and Johnny Nelson and these guys talking about you. Especially when they're being complimentary on your performances and feeding into the hype and expectation of how far your boxing career can go. The flipside is when they're ripping you to shreds live on TV, but I had a few fights to wait until I got that treatment.

Next up was a defence of my Celtic title against Robbie Turley in a fight which turned out to be one of the most important of my career. I was chief support in the Motorpoint Arena in Cardiff, with Gavin Rees versus Andy Murray for the EBU European Lightweight title topping the bill. That meant that finally I was truly in the Sky Sports spotlight, fighting live on television in a primetime slot. Finally, I had my opportunity to show a much wider boxing audience exactly what I was all about. Turley wasn't a bad fighter, and being Welsh fighting in front of a big home crowd I knew he'd be well up for it. But Barry and I were already stating in interviews that I felt ready for British or Commonwealth title fights, so I went in confident of a big performance. There is nothing wrong with entering the ring with that confidence and expectation, but looking back I can see I made a mistake in my interpretation of what a so-called big performance should look like. Rather than allowing my ability to organically deliver, I tried to force it. Rather than fighting my own fight and winning comfortably, I tried too hard to impress and produce something spectacular for the cameras. The result was I made life a lot more difficult for myself than it needed to be. Turley was active throughout and while he never hurt me, he did catch me

Not a bad-looking baby!

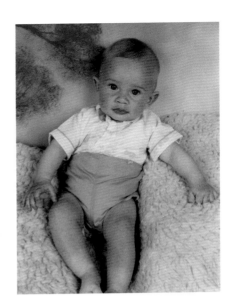

With my da and younger brother, both Craig, at my cousin's wedding, where I was on pageboy duty.

With my Granny Mary, who I absolutely adored.

ut-sized but not out-matched young K Frompton connects with his competitor
tephen Bowen of Carrickfergus. GC1238

K Frompton lays on the pressure in the boxing match
at Carrick Rangers Club in aid of Carrick Senior
Gateway Club. GC1239

'K Frompton' in action. The name 'Frompton' followed me around for years. On the left, you'll see me lining up a right-hand. If the big lad let that one land then he had no right being in a boxing ring!

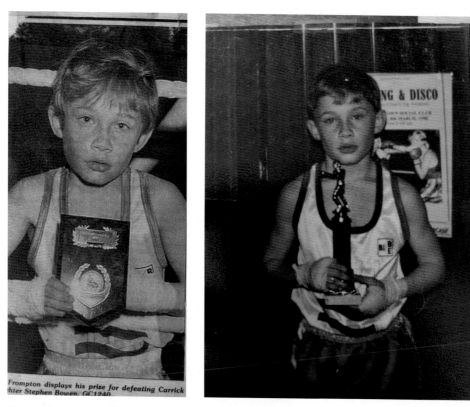

Frompton displays his prize for defeating Carrick
hter Stephen Bowen. GC1240

Despite having a big head, the headgear still didn't fit me, which tells you just how young I was when I started out boxing.

With Billy McKee, the founder and head coach of Midland Amateur Boxing Club. Billy was a huge inspiration to me throughout my career, right up until his sad passing in 2021.

At Midland ABC in 2000 with British and Commonwealth Champion Tommy Waite (centre).

With WBC Champion and Olympic silver-medallist Wayne 'Pocket Rocket' McCullough at the World Amateur Championships in Belfast in 2001. I think I took the whole week off school to watch as many fights as possible.

Wearing a sauna suit as a flyweight around the age of 19 or 20. I literally lived in a sauna suit as an amateur. It was only when I turned professional that I learned how to really look after my body and the importance of nutrition.

Me with no less than four Joyces in Bucharest in 2003. There are three Daves in the mix here: David Oliver Joyce, Big Davey Joyce, Southpaw Davey Joyce, John Joe Joyce, and John Paul McDonagh.

At the Commonwealth Youth Games in Bendigo, Australia in 2004 with (from left) Paddy Murphy, Mickey Hawkins and Dean McComb. I'm not sure why I'm looking so stern here as I came home with a bronze medal, having fought at 4kg above my usual weight.

'The Stocky Midget vs The Tall Lanky Beanpole'. Me and Tyrone McKenna at the National Boxing Championships in 2009. Joking aside, this picture highlights the height differential that was a constant for me throughout my career. © INPHO/Lorraine O'Sullivan

Standing outside Midland Boxing Club with Barry McGuigan, a mural of me on the wall behind. What's special to me about the mural is that it shows me in an Irish vest with a shamrock, yet nobody in Tiger's Bay has ever touched it.

At one of my Ulster Hall shows, with Gerry Storey in the background. I'm still incredibly fond of Gerry and I'll always appreciate everything he did for me.

Me and Paddy Barnes with legend 'Sugar' Ray Leonard at a meet and greet at Parkhead, Glasgow.

In the Europa Hotel with my ma, Flo, and granda Hughie, or Shughie as he was known, after a Commonwealth title fight. My grandas, Hughie and Jimmy, were always my biggest fans. Hughie died three weeks before I won my first world title and I dedicated that victory to him. It was an emotional moment.

Pure raw celebration after my gruelling first victory over Kiko Martinez to become European Champion in 2013. © WENN Rights Ltd/Alamy Stock Photo

My granda Hughie wiping the blood from my face as I sit with my new European belt. It's my favourite image from my entire career. © Mark Marlow

After successfully defending my world title against Chris Avalos in 2015. Avalos is probably the only opponent during my professional career that I didn't like. The ref did the right thing in ending the fight when he did to protect Avalos from serious damage, but I wish he had given me a couple of seconds more to clean him out. © PA Images/Alamy Stock Photo and frustrate me and drag me into a messier fight than I was used to. He cut me over the right eye in the fourth and the blood flowed quite freely. That was the first time in my life I'd been cut inside a boxing ring. I wouldn't say it flustered me, but I was certainly conscious of it. I dropped him in the seventh but ended the round landing one just after the bell, which cost me a point. I remained relatively calm. I knew I had to be winning on the scorecards. But I was also fully aware this wasn't going exactly as planned. Ten fights in, these were the first testing moments of my professional career. This was the first time I found myself genuinely looking around mid-fight for help or advice. And rather than Gerry Sr or Jr in the corner, it was to Shane sitting in the front row that I was looking for and listening to. That was meant as no slight on the Storeys or me putting Shane above them in terms of knowledge or ability or anything else. It was just my natural reaction in a moment of doubt to turn to the person I'd spent most of my camp with. The gradual shift from Belfast to Kent had continued and with each fight I did more of my preparation in England with the McGuigans. So, it was more Shane and I, rather than Gerry and I, who had put the plan together to beat Turley and it was more Shane and I who had discussed what might happen and how I may need to adapt. I've no doubt Gerry was giving me great advice and the right instructions between rounds, but I couldn't help myself from looking over his shoulder at Shane and focusing more on what he was shouting to me. In the heat of battle, you instinctively do whatever you have to do to survive and thrive. I finished the stronger, almost dropping Turley again at the death with a big left hook, and won a comfortable unanimous decision 98–91, 98–92 and 96–93 on the scorecards. From that point on, it was agreed that Shane would become an official part of the fight-night corner.

***

At the end of 2010, the week after I beat Gavin Reid, my daughter Carla was born. She'd stopped growing inside the womb, so they brought Christine in to induce the labour. Like most first-time dads, I'm a bit nervous and on edge hanging around the hospital waiting for this momentous moment in my life. I remember a couple of calls came through while I was pacing up and down beside Christine in the bed. One was from Mark Sidebottom, the BBC journalist. He wanted to do an interview with me, and when I told him where I was he asked if he could come up with a camera. I'm thinking, is this guy mad? Does he think he can get a shot in the delivery room or something? No, Mark. Let's leave it for another day mate. The next time the phone went it was Barry. Apparently, the boxing journo Leonard Gunning had put something on social media about me smoking a cigarette. I don't know if it was a joke or an attempt to stir some shit or what. Barry knew where I was but he called anyway, and here I am pleading my innocence down the phone to him, swearing I wasn't smoking, while Christine is about to pop. I shit myself when I saw the look on her face.

'Are you fucking serious?' she said when I hung up. 'I'm going into labour here and you're on the phone with your boxing manager. You want to get your fucking priorities straight!'

Carla was born, beautiful and perfect, on the 9th of December 2010, but not before she gave us a bit of a fright. We both noticed that as the labour was progressing, more and more medical staff were coming into the room. They'd all be looking at the monitor when Christine had a contraction, and you could see there was concern on their faces. It turned out the umbilical cord was wrapped around Carla's neck and with every contraction it was tightening, and her heartbeat was slowing down to almost nothing. I think at one point they were about to make the call to cut Christine open for an emergency C-section, but mercifully that wasn't necessary. The midwives were amazing, and they got Carla out safe and sound. We had a baby daughter. And really, all the clichés are true. I was just a kid myself. I mean, I was early twenties, but I was immature and naive and still had a lot of growing up to do. Christine was my first meaningful relationship and here we were with a child when I barely considered myself an adult. But it changes you. It's a mad feeling to suddenly be a father but you naturally embrace the responsibility. I made a lot of promises to myself and to Carla and to my family that night. Commitments to do everything in my power to look after her and provide for her and guarantee her the best life possible. Your child becomes your focus. They make the shit parts of life easier to handle because you know it's worth pushing on through for them. Like I say, it all sounds a bit clichéd – but if you're in tough moments in training or even in a fight, the realisation that you're doing it for your own baby rather than yourself can make the difference in how you respond to that adversity. Your dreams take on more resonance too. I was already dreaming of being a world champion but now I'm dreaming of doing it and holding Carla in my arms in the ring after. Now I'm dreaming it because I want to make my daughter proud that I'm her dad.

***

Kiko Martinez would go on to play a massive role in my boxing career. But back in 2010 he was still just the Spanish guy who'd blasted Bernard Dunne out in ninety seconds to claim the Dubliner's European title and then lost to Rendall Munroe a couple of times. That changed, however, towards the end of the year, when he reclaimed that European title from the French-Armenian, Arsen Martirosyan. He had a prize I wanted now, and given he had the Belfast-based Pat Magee involved in his management it was a fight all sides were interested in. It was first proposed for March 2011 in the Kings Hall, and I was all for it. I'd only had eight fights at that stage, and never faced anyone remotely close to the pedigree of Kiko, but I fancied it and so did Barry. It was only when a bout contract was sent to us that the fight collapsed. Pat Magee would own part of me going forward if I won, and that was a non-starter. Instead, we both faced Oscar Chacin within a couple of weeks of each other in early 2011 and, although you can't judge too much from such comparisons, I took confidence from the fact I did a better job on the Venezuelan than Kiko did. Coupled to the belief that Kiko's team insisting on having a piece of me was an open acknowledgement they expected me to beat their guy, I didn't hesitate when a second opportunity to make the fight, this time for September of 2011, presented itself. Even though I'd laboured at times against Turley, while Kiko looked good in knocking out Jason Booth in Madrid, Barry and I still believed I was ready.

It was only two weeks out when the fight fell through. I was sparring Martin J. Ward in Tony Sims' gym when I got the news. Something had happened to Kiko's father, and his leg had had to be amputated. Understandably, Kiko was in no fit state mentally to continue with a twelve-round European title fight in those circumstances. Barry never fully believed the story and publicly cast doubt on it in a video interview with the Irish journalist Gerry Callan. He said there was nothing in the Spanish press about leg amputations and he was cynical about these late pull-outs in boxing. Gerry made an off-colour joke about not having a leg to stand on and they had a wee laugh. I didn't know anything for sure but remember thinking that it's not the type of lie you're going to get away with. If you want out of a fight, there are a million excuses to make that would be easy to hide behind so why go with something as dramatic as your father losing a limb. My gut back then told me it was genuine, and now I know the type of man Kiko is it's clearly ridiculous that anyone doubted him.

At the time, I was hugely disappointed the fight was off. I'd trained harder than ever, partly because this was the biggest fight of my life and partly because I had been so poor against Turley in my previous outing. Everything had gone great in camp, and I was ready. The disappointment had barely subsided when the worry begins that not only am I not fighting Kiko for the European title, there is a danger I won't have a fight at all. Kiko agreed to vacate the title so it was mine to battle for if a suitable opponent could be found. Willie Casey was the obvious choice as he was my weight and was already training for a fight on a Tyson Fury undercard the week after. Having dropped him with a headshot in the amateurs I had no problem with that match-up. Willie turned down the offer anyway, so in the end an Australian fighter named Mark Quon was flown in and deemed adequate for a Commonwealth title defence.

I was just relieved they'd found someone willing to do twelve rounds and make weight at such short notice. It was a lot of messing around and late changes of opponents are never ideal – but I'd prepared for the best in Europe so, with all due respect to Quon, I wasn't fearful of the unknown in this case. I've no doubt Matchroom were relieved as well. The show was taking place in the Odyssey, the biggest indoor venue in Northern Ireland, and I was chief support to the Paul McCloskey versus Breidis Prescott main event. Being such a big arena, there was no limit on the number of tickets being allocated to fighters and I sold a shitload. McCloskey was popular enough as well but I'm sure there were more of my fans than his in there that night. There tended to be a bit of trouble between the two sets of supporters but nothing major. No doubt his would blame mine and vice versa. And drink would always play a part. In the ring I didn't have any trouble with Quon. I was grateful he'd stepped up last-minute, but he wasn't close to my level. It was also one of those rare occasions in which I was the taller man in the fight. And if I'm towering over you then you couldn't be more than five foot two max.

Having not seen any footage of Quon, I used the first to take a look at him and soon determined it should be a straightforward night. I did as I pleased with him for a couple of rounds and then in the fourth landed a right hand over his jab to send him to the canvas. He got up and fought on, but it was time to end it, so I put it on him. His corner had the towel in their hand, but before they had a chance to throw it the ref stepped in to end it himself.

I don't mind admitting now, with the benefit of hindsight, that the Kiko fight not happening as originally scheduled was a blessing in disguise. I'm not saying I would definitely have lost, but it's hard to deny it would have been taking on an extremely difficult challenge a few fights too early in my career. I do wonder now why we were all so prepared to take that risk. I didn't demand the fight because at that stage I didn't demand anything. Barry would tell me who I was fighting, and I did the rest. Thus far there had never been a suggested opponent to make me hesitate or think twice, so I was comfortable following orders. There was probably a bit of ego involved too. As a fighter you want to portray an image that you'll fight anyone, anytime, anywhere whether it's true or not. Your instinct is to automatically accept a fight and speak bullishly on it rather than ask that we all sit down and think this through. Money might have played a part as well. I think there was thirty grand for me to fight Kiko, a hell of a lot more than any purse I'd received to date. I backed myself to go on and be a world champion and make life-changing money, but at the same time I'd a baby at home now and thirty grand in the bank would make a massive difference to our lives. I guess the other factor at play was Barry's relationship with Matchroom. It's the promoter who pays the fighter who then pays the manager, so Barry would have been very conscious that without Matchroom life gets more difficult. Eddie Hearn had gone a little cold after the Turley fight. From the next big thing out of Northern Ireland, suddenly there were doubts over whether I really had it or not. Maybe Barry sensed Hearn's interest in me waning and felt this risk was necessary to keep him onside. The risk was likely music to Hearn's ears. He was probably sat in Essex looking at his stable and questioning whether Frampton is worth more investment if he's already losing rounds to a fighter of Turley's level. So, throwing me into the deep end with Kiko is a great idea to the promoter. He gets a brilliant fight for his show no matter what, and if I win then he has a European champion and a new Irish star. And even if I lose, he can view it like he's saved a few quid by not giving me the necessary development bouts to arrive at the same place. Win–win for the promoter, but a massive risk for the fighter.

I got out early in 2012, topping the bill in York Hall with a Commonwealth title defence against Kris Hughes. I picked 'The Boss' by James Brown as my entrance music and felt as cool as the man himself walking to the ring that night. After the fight was over, I was thinking I'd stick with this song for the rest of my career. Make it the song that everyone associates with me. Then for the next three or four months it felt like every time I turned the boxing on there was someone walking to the ring with James Brown singing 'Paid the cost to be the boss'! Billy Joe Saunders was one which sticks in my head as he was obviously high profile even back then. I swear no one was using it until I did, but now it was everywhere and that ruined it for me. I knew I was back to having to pick a new song next time out. In the end I never did land on 'my song' and each fight of my career saw me entering the ring to a different tune.

Hughes was 15–1 at the time and had lost narrowly in a fight for the Commonwealth title a little over a year before we met. The Scotsman was tall, tricky and a southpaw. I had my struggles with southpaws in the amateurs and this was to be the first proper test against one in the pros. It turned out I had little to worry about. Hughes wasn't good enough to beat me regardless of stance, but I realised that the advantages, psychological or otherwise, the southpaws had over me in the amateurs didn't translate to the pros. Lefties seem to always get automatically labelled as tricky, often by lazy journos or commentators in my opinion. It's probably true a lot more of them are in the amateurs, where that style can win you medals, but you need more than that in the pro game – and so the professional southpaws come in all shapes and sizes. Being a slick, tricky, awkward southpaw is sometimes enough to confuse an opponent for three rounds and tippy-tappy your way to a win as an amateur, but over twelve in the pro game – no chance. The best those guys could do is spoil for a few rounds until they get figured out, run out of steam or simply get marched down and roughed up by a stronger more aggressive rival.

I knew going in, and confirmed it in the opening exchanges, that Hughes didn't have the power to trouble me, so I set about him early in an aggressive start. When you know someone can't hurt you, your performance can appear more reckless than normal. But if you're doing it right, you're still in complete control. It's just that the risk analysis is different. You know you can put yourself in a more vulnerable position to land the shots you want than you would otherwise do against someone that can switch your lights off with a single punch. Against Hughes I was able to keep my hands low and throw a lot of lead rights. I won every minute of every round and hurt him repeatedly to the body. He was in survival mode from the off, continuously covering up and circling away from me. He didn't want to engage so I had to go looking for him. Halfway through he was well marked up and starting to gas. Then, early in the seventh, I landed an almighty right hand that nearly put him through the ropes. He somehow struggled to his feet, and fair play to Kris for having the heart and balls to do that, but there was no chance he could continue and the ref wisely waved it off.

I was pleased with my performance against Hughes. I dominated from start to finish and closed the show with a spectacular stoppage.

When I watched it back, nothing I saw made me think any different. But listening to the words of the commentators and pundits made me second guess myself. The general consensus from the Sky Sports team was that I was supposed to be a puncher and so should have got Hughes out of there a lot earlier. At the end of the fourth Jim Watt said I needed to make it more exciting for the fans and throw more punches. At the end of the fifth Adam Smith and Richie Woodhall echoed that sentiment, saying the crowd had gone quiet and I was lacking in combinations. To be honest, I took all of that to heart a lot more than I should have. Everyone is entitled to their own opinion, and those boys are paid to give theirs on live television, but I know now I shouldn't have allowed them to influence me like they did. Had I been a bit older and wiser I would have told them I'll box whatever way I want and whatever way wins me a fight. That while I can bang, I've never wanted to be known as a puncher as there is a lot more to my game than that. That actually I'm not the heavy-handed pressure fighter Nick Halling kept referencing but a much more versatile and cleverer fighter who, if anything, is more naturally a counterpunching boxer. Unfortunately, I was still young and immature and eager to please – and I remember thinking, shit, I better go out and throw more punches and bigger punches and try to get earlier stoppages.

The Hughes fight was my first experience of getting drug tested as a pro. As I moved up the levels and started fighting for major titles it became the norm, but when this guy came into the dressing room with a little plastic jar it was all new to me. He came in pre-fight as well, right in the middle of my warm-up and, even worse, right after I'd just been for a piss. I started drinking a bit of water to be able to go again, but I didn't want to be getting into the ring with a full belly either so I couldn't start necking litres of the stuff. It was preying on my mind now. I wasn't seasoned enough to forget about it and stick to my normal routine. I'm hitting the pads wondering, if I can't piss before first bell is the fight off? I wasn't sure what to do and then I felt a shite coming on. Happy days I thought as often when I sit down to take a shite a bit of piss comes out even though I didn't feel like I needed one. I'm walking to the toilet cubicle a bit more relaxed now and then the fella with the plastic jar drops his next bombshell: he needs to actually watch the sample being delivered. We started talking logistics and I couldn't hand on heart guarantee him that the piss wouldn't escape unexpectedly while I was squeezing the shite out. If that happened, I'm going to struggle to get him his sample. He told me not to worry, that the piss will definitely leak out first. He was adamant and I considered him the expert in this field, so we decided to give it a go. He was to watch me urinate then leave me in peace to complete my business. So I sat down, pushed his plastic jar between my legs and below little Carl, and looked up at this man I'd only just met watching me sit on a toilet seat. I then proceeded to learn the hard way that when you need to shit and piss, the shit always emerges first. As soon as I relaxed my bowels it started coming. 'I'm shitting, I'm shitting!' I shouted at him, and he screwed his face up in disgust at the smell. But he couldn't look away because he knew the piss wouldn't be far behind. What a way to earn a living. Scundered doesn't even begin to cover it for me, but I gave him his sample and they let me go batter Kris Hughes!

The six-and-a-bit rounds against Hughes were so comfortable that I had no problem going again with another Commonwealth title defence six weeks later when the chief support slot opened up for me on the undercard of Kell Brook versus Matthew Hatton. Prosper Ankrah, a 18–2 Ghanaian with a massively padded record, was in the opposite corner. I remember it kicking off a bit in our dressing room because the BBBofC (British Boxing Board of Control) official complained about the Vaseline being rubbed into my neck and shoulders. We told him it was to protect against rope burns but he made a song and dance about it being too much, so we had to remove it. All very unnecessary but the British Board is filled with these types of jobsworths, so you get on with it in the belief your opponent has someone just as officious in his room. That's why I was so surprised when I got in the ring and looked across at what was on Prosper's hands. He was supposed to be wearing the same Adidas gloves as me because that's who sponsored me at the time. Instead, he had on a pair of battered old Reyes, famous for being puncher's gloves. He was waving to the crowd, and it looked like he'd a pair of red oven mitts on! I whispered to Barry, what the fuck is going on here, but he did the right thing. He told me it doesn't matter a damn, we're here now and ready to fight. Afterwards though he was absolutely raging and went to find out how the hell a fighter got away with changing his gloves last second without telling us while we were having to towel off a little bit of excess Vaseline in the other room. Barry was also right that it didn't matter what this fella was wearing. He was pathetic. He ran around the ring in the first and collapsed in the second after what can generously be described as a glancing blow. When Shane got in the ring, I told him I'd barely touched him. Shush, Shane said. Say nothing.

In May, I was back for my third scheduled twelve-rounder in less than four months. And this one promised to be a lot more challenging than Prosper Ankrah. Raul Hirales was your stereotypical tough Mexican. He was unbeaten in his seventeen professional fights, and he'd been in with better opposition than I'd yet faced. He'd go on to lose a few more at a high level after me, but no one ever stopped him in a thirty-one-fight career. A few fights after we met, Hirales was the man who stopped Francisco Leal in the tragic bout from which Leal never woke up.

I was chief support again, this time to the massive Carl Froch versus Lucian Bute world-title fight in a sold-out Nottingham

Arena. The English cricket star Freddie Flintoff walked me to the ring carrying my Commonwealth belt. Big Freddie was training in the gym with Shane at the time, preparing for his own crack at the pro boxing game. My own preparation was based around going the full twelve rounds. Unlike against Hughes, Ankrah or Quon, I wasn't going into this one expecting a knockout. I knew I'd need to box a lot more and I knew I may spend some of the fight on the back foot. I had no problem doing that and treated it as an opportunity to show everyone my versatility. My approach meant the fight never caught fire as a spectacle, but those who understood what they were watching appreciated my performance as I controlled it from first bell to last. Perhaps the biggest plus from the night was proving to myself that I was definitely a twelve-round fighter. You can organise twelve-round spars in the gym all you want, but until you do it in a competitive fight under the lights you never know for sure. I paced myself perfectly, conserving energy while still winning every round, and felt fresh enough to be able to turn it on down the stretch. It was invaluable experience physically and mentally for someone who knew there'd be hard, twelve-round world-title fights a little further down the road.

We enjoyed ourselves at the hotel bar after this one. Eamonn Magee was there with his fighter Kieran Farrell who had fought on the undercard. Farrell's car got clamped and at one point in the night Magee and the Belfast journalist Nicky Fullerton arrived at the bar covered in grease with the clamp in their arms. God knows how they got it off the wheel. Christine's sister was with us and at one point her and Magee were having a back-and-forth at each other. She's a teacher and with a few drinks in her in social situations she sometimes forgets she's not addressing a classroom full of kids. I was keeping an eye on them and telling her to shush, praying please don't make me have to jump in and fight Eamonn Magee. There was a run on the bar when they called last orders, with Magee ordering fifteen pints of cider for himself. We sat there so long enjoying ourselves that people started coming down for breakfast.

The Kiko fight was made again at this point. A year and four fights wiser, it probably made more sense now. But six months out, the Spaniard picked up an unspecified injury and withdrew. So, in the end, the final fight of 2012 completed the set in terms of the boxes any good matchmaker will have a top prospect tick off on their way to the top. Hughes had been the tricky southpaw, Hirales was the tough Mexican and now Steve Molitor was the ex-world champ just past his best. The Canadian southpaw Molitor was actually a two-time world champion who had successfully defended his IBF (International Boxing Federation) Super Bantamweight belt on six occasions, so he was a genuine world-level operator. His record read 34–2 and he was thirty-two years old when I faced him, so although not in his prime he was certainly not a shot fighter either. In fact, *The Ring* magazine still had him ranked inside their Top Ten at 122lbs. This was my first time headlining in the Odyssey Arena and the place was bouncing when I got in the ring. The atmosphere carried on when the action started and, coupled with my fast and aggressive opening, I think Molitor was a little intimidated by the whole environment. I fed off the crowd and was brilliant that night. This was more of a front-foot performance, and I stayed up on my toes all the time. I kept the pressure on him every second of every round, cutting off the ring well, and giving him no respite. But it was a very controlled pressure. I didn't throw any shots for the sake of it and didn't chase him around the ring. He couldn't read from where and when my punches were coming and by the end my feints alone were almost causing him to fall from fear. He first went down at the very end of the third, a right hand buzzing him and causing him to kind of crouch or slump down with only the ropes preventing him from reaching the canvas. He was lucky the bell rang as I was swinging, and the ref gave him a standing eight count before allowing him back to his stool. I kept bossing him into the fourth, dropping him twice – although only the second was counted as legitimate – and fans were chanting, easy, easy, easy! He showed heart to survive the next, and to his credit started firing a few shots of his own in the sixth. But it was only a matter of time now and when I backed him onto the ropes for the umpteenth time and landed with a couple of head shots, he dropped to one knee and the ref knew he'd had enough.

I was delighted with how I went about Molitor and, of course, it was nice that the praise from pundits was universal as well. By taking the fight to him from the off and keeping that pace and pressure up until the stoppage, I delivered the type of performance that fans and TV execs alike want to see. A big crowd turned out to prove I was undoubtedly a huge draw and the atmosphere they generated came across fantastically on television too. Beating a guy of Molitor's calibre pushed me high up the rankings of all four governing bodies and brought attention from outside the UK and Europe for the first time. It felt like a bit of a coming-out party for me. I felt like I'd proved it wasn't just hype or wishful thinking when we talked about world titles in the future. Eddie was beaming after, talking about more big nights in Belfast and world-title shots in outdoor arenas. Barry was just as happy with how I'd delivered and the overall spectacle for the public. Basically, we all felt ready. The next fight would be a big one. The next fight would finally be Kiko.

CHAPTER FIVE

TOP OF THE WORLD

Finally. A year and a half on from our original date, Kiko Martinez and I were finally about to share a ring. A year and a half in which I'd only gotten better and banked invaluable rounds and experience. A year and a half in which my confidence that I'd beat the Spaniard had grown by the day. I loved the build-up during fight week to this one. It was intense and hostile, my first time being involved in a bout that had that true big-fight feel around it. Belfast was buzzing and tickets to be there at the Odyssey Arena on the night were selling fast. Even the Friday weigh-in at the Europa Hotel was standing room only. And Kiko fed off it too. I'd got under his skin at the previous day's presser when I delivered a line my da fed me about Kiko's hair being like his European title – he's losing both of them. It was pretty light-hearted banter to me, but it seemed to hit a real nerve with Kiko. His retort in Spanish was angry enough that the translator refused to translate it! So he was seriously hyped up the next day, getting in my face and shouting all sorts as soon as he stepped off the scale. He kept making throat slitting gestures and saying he was going to kill me. I couldn't understand much else but, with his Spanish flag draped over his shoulder and a wild look in his eye, I'm pretty sure none of it was complimentary. His whole demeanour that day guaranteed a bit of argy-bargy on the stage, but I kept relatively calm. He was a day early. The fight was on Saturday night.

As I was heading to leave the hotel via the back entrance, Gerry came up to me and asked if he could have a word. When you get off the scales having made championship weight, all you want to do is replenish and rehydrate so I said for him to come with us for a feed and a chat while I'm eating.

'No, Carl,' he said, 'I'd rather just do it right now, son.'

I could see by the look on his face this was something serious, but I still wasn't prepared for what he was about to say.

'I won't be in your corner tomorrow night, son. It doesn't feel right so I won't be there.'

My initial reaction was one of total shock. My trainer walking out on the eve of the biggest fight of my young career? It was hard to take in. But to be honest I then just said okay, gave him a hug and walked away. It was a really weird feeling. I felt deflated I suppose. But the initial disbelief subsided quickly because deep down I knew exactly why he was opting out. Things had only become more and more awkward with each passing bout. Although I was technically still Gerry's fighter, I did practically nothing with him in preparation for my fights now. That fact embarrassed both of us. I was paying Shane the full 10 per cent of my purse, which is the standard trainer's fee at that level, but then when I was home I'd get some cash out and drive to Gerry to give him something too. This strange conflict was becoming even more pronounced now that the fights were higher profile. There were conversations or disputes going on about who was the number two in the corner, Gerry Jr or Shane. Who'd get in the ring, who'd be seen on TV, who'd be listed as my official seconds and in what order. Some of it was egotistical nonsense and some of it was genuine concern about what's best for me. Gerry was never Barry's first choice to be my trainer, but he respected him. His son, however, was someone the McGuigans didn't want anywhere near my training in camp or my corner on the night. It was clear where we were heading as Gerry was getting on and Gerry Jr was being groomed to take over. And it was equally clear that my management team had other ideas. I just never in a million years thought the final decision on all of this would be taken minutes after weighing in for a European title fight. I remember my dad was raging with Gerry because of the poor timing. The McGuigans told me he wanted out because he thought I'd lose, and he didn't want to be associated with the failure. My dad was right to be angry, but I never believed the fear-of-losing theory. That's why rather than thinking, fuck you Gerry for doing this to me, I gave him a hug. I felt sorry for him. I knew that he knew we were all nearing the final stage of the process of removing the Storeys from Team Frampton. He'd been pushed and pushed, and now he was jumping before suffering the ignominy of facing the final shove. Whatever the rights and wrongs of it, the whole thing should never have dragged on that long. And maybe I need to accept some blame in that too. I think the fact that Gerry was such a big name in boxing and so respected within Irish boxing circles meant no one had the balls to sit down and have the difficult conversation. Instead, there was this gradual slow death of our relationship as Barry had me spend more and more time with Shane each camp. I felt bad about it all eating my lunch that day, thinking about how he'd been forced out. I also felt guilty that part of me was relieved. I was tired of the awkwardness and the situations I was constantly being put in, so at least this was a resolution. For better or worse, at least now I knew where I was. Shane McGuigan was my lead and sole trainer.

The fact I'd done the entire camp with Shane meant the impact on my mindset was minimal. It was far from ideal, but it wasn't necessarily the disaster or huge upheaval it may have appeared from the outside. I was used to having Gerry in the corner and it would be strange without him, but between the bells it was just

me and Kiko in the ring and the gameplan to combat the Spanish
champ had been developed with Shane. In essence, the tactics were
pretty straightforward. Stay up on my toes for the first half, wait for
him to slow down, then start to put it on him. All very simple in
theory, but in practice it's often a very different story.

I started well and won the first round off the back foot. My feet
have set me apart from the majority of opponents I've faced in
the ring, and I knew I'd need them against Kiko. It's a fair enough
comment that he only knows one way to fight but calling him
one-dimensional is not necessarily an insult when your single
dimension is as brutally effective as Kiko's was. Shane warned me
as I left my stool to start the second that the Spaniard would be
warmed up now, and so it proved. His style remained the same,
but the intensity and speed and ferocity increased. He bored into
range, hands high, a small boulder of a man. He's compact so he's
not a big target and there is more head movement than he's given
credit for. Even so, he's hittable and plenty do. But he doesn't mind
taking a few to land one. There's undoubtedly a cumulative impact
of continually punching him in the head, but as each single blow
lands he just marches on forward. When he's in any sort of range he
starts swinging, every punch thrown to hurt. Body, head, arms, he
doesn't really care. But there's variety and you need to be on guard.
He caught me several times and I definitely felt them. Rounds two,
three and four were fiercely contested. In the final thirty seconds
of the fourth he caught me with a looping left hook that sent me
back a step into the corner. The crowd had started the fight in party
mode but quickly realised this was not going to be a walk in the
park, and the mood had changed to one of focus and support. I
heard the audible gasp when he landed that one on me but when I
spun out of trouble and opened up, a left of my own causing Kiko to
stumble sideways, they erupted. The cheers at the end of the round
were what you'd expect for a fighter winning a world title never

mind edging the fourth round in a European title bout. I boxed extremely well in the fifth and he barely landed a glove on me while I capitalised on every chance to fire in accurate counters. He was swelling up badly now under his left eye and that gave me a target. In the sixth I got caught with a few but the old adage about getting wet in the rain holds true. When you share a ring with someone who is as relentless in his attacks as Kiko is, inevitably you're going to take a bit of punishment in places.

Halfway. I remember being sat in my corner ahead of the seventh round thinking that this fella doesn't seem like he's about to slow down like I'd been assured throughout camp he would. I could have started feeling a bit sorry for myself, but I showed a lot of mental strength to keep faith in our plan and wait for his tiredness to finally kick in. From the seventh onwards I began gradually holding my feet a little longer when punching with him. I wanted to stand up to him now – show him I wasn't planning on twelve rounds on the back foot, allowing him to be the aggressor throughout. It increased the risk of being hit myself, but this was how we had visualised winning the fight. I won the seventh with these tactics so pressed on into the eighth in a similar vein. How much was tactics and how much was tiredness and the feeling that I'd struggle to do another fifteen minutes on my toes I don't know. We traded flat footed in the early seconds of the eighth, and I came off worse. It was reckless and I knew it. I was looking for a balance between getting on my bike and standing toe-to-toe and that was far too close to the latter. It was too close to the type of fight Kiko wanted. The tactics and gameplan were sound, but I needed to be cleverer in implementing them.

Two of the official scorecards had me six rounds to two up, with the third scoring it five rounds to three in my favour. It's all subjective, but five–three was probably the more accurate reflection. And an extremely hard-fought five–three at that. I felt I might have lost the eighth and was determined not to give the ninth away as well. The last thing I wanted was to enter the championship rounds giving Kiko all the momentum. I held my feet even more. That combined with the fact my opponent was finally starting to feel the pace meant my punches landed differently on him. I could sense these were really hurting him now. I caught him coming in, and his knees dipped at one point. Then, for the first time in the fight, I didn't feel his strength against me in a clinch as he let me walk him backwards. It's good to get that confirmation that your opponent is as exhausted as you are. With less than thirty seconds left in the round I set myself and timed a short, sharp right to perfection as he came in with one of his overhand bombs. It landed flush on his chin and sent him onto his back. I was stood in the neutral corner, my arms resting on the top ropes, my body and mind absolutely shattered. In previous fights I would have been anxious to finish it. I would have been looking at the clock, thinking, come on ref, let me at him and I can get a spectacular knockout here for the highlight reel. But that night, to be honest, all I was thinking was, please don't get up, please don't get up. As the count was reaching four, Kiko was on his knees but his first attempt to stand up led to a wobble and he had to regroup. He did make it upright by around eight, but as the ref moved forward to make his judgement, Kiko stumbled backwards onto the ropes on shaky legs and there was no way he could continue. The ref waved it off and I, along with 9,000 in the Odyssey, went crazy. After just sixteen fights, I was the European Super Bantamweight champion.

A photo was taken that night which my da recently got framed for me. In it I'm sitting with my new European belt and my granda is wiping the blood from my face. It's my favourite image from my entire career.

This fight ended up being my last as a Matchroom fighter. The fallout started with a bit of disappointment when my purse arrived without an expected bonus attached. I was due £50,000 for the fight, but we had a deal whereby I got extra on top depending on how many tickets were sold. I can't remember the exact thresholds but once we hit a certain number, I was to get an extra five grand. Then another five grand for every 500 tickets sold beyond that. The Odyssey wasn't far off full that night, so I was expecting another twenty grand to come my way. Serious money for me at that point of my career. When no bonus at all materialised I asked Barry what the story was, and he said Hearn told him we were around 100 tickets short to earn the first five-grand bonus. I couldn't believe that. I said the place was jumping and there's no way we didn't get to the first bonus at the very least. Barry replied that a hell of a lot of comps were given out but even so I refused to accept it. My da suggested we just ask the venue to provide a breakdown of what was sold so I asked Barry to do that. He came back saying the venue wouldn't speak to him about it, claiming they'd signed a confidentiality agreement to not discuss the sales with anyone other than Matchroom. Basically, I was being told that Hearn had shafted us. I hated him from that point onwards. Told everyone he was a big, lanky cunt. Then, a month later, I got a text from him saying he can't work with Barry anymore so it's over. Our contract was up but I'd expected it to be renewed and was aware that Barry had been negotiating everything. I was driving at the time, and I shit myself. I'd been hating on Eddie but to be hit with the sudden reality that I no longer had a promoter or a television platform was frightening. Barry called me soon after and seemed a bit panicked himself. But he told me to relax, that Eddie was shafting us, and we'd be stronger alone. He said solicitors were involved and we were going to establish Cyclone Promotions. I'd be a partner in it and earn 30 per cent of the profits of each show. I was nervous but I liked the sound of that. Pretty quickly off the back of that it was announced at a press conference in London that I had signed a multi-fight deal with Frank Warren. In fact, what had happened was that Cyclone Promotions had signed a four-fight deal with the Warren-founded TV channel BoxNation to broadcast my fights. The first was scheduled for July on a Warren show in Wembley Arena featuring Billy Joe Saunders versus Spike O'Sullivan and Derek Chisora versus Malik Scott – hence, the presser alongside Frank. That deal saw me get a £35k sign-on and the same again guaranteed for a handy opponent at Wembley. I think it was the day that deal was made public that Hearn broke his silence on our split via a statement on Sky Sports News. It read:

We have enjoyed our time working with Carl Frampton as promoter of his boxing career. However, after the success of the last Frampton fight, we were informed by Barry McGuigan that he wanted to be joint promoter in future Frampton fights. Whilst we had no problem whatsoever in agreeing purses for Carl Frampton, we felt that such a relationship with Barry McGuigan represented a potential conflict of interest with Barry's role as Carl's manager and we could therefore not agree to be involved on this basis. Matchroom Sport and I wish Carl every success in his future boxing career.

Not long after he then gave another interview with iFL TV in which he was pushed again on what had caused the split. He said the only problem was that Barry wanted to be the promoter and that he knew that going into the Kiko fight. 'They had a motive from day one', he said, 'and this is where Barry wanted to get to. It's a family affair now.'

I was still sore over the fact I thought he'd stroked me out of a few grand for ticket sales, so I didn't pay any attention to him and didn't dwell on the fact I was no longer with Matchroom or Sky Sports. A few years later Eddie was asked in an interview about his biggest disappointments in boxing and he named our split high up his list. He said he thought he'd done a great job with me for the first sixteen bouts of my career, and it was a shame that my manager had suddenly wanted to be a promoter too and ruined the relationship. It did make me wonder what might have been when he said that, how things may have panned out differently. Matchroom were quickly emerging as the dominant promotional outfit in the UK and would soon go on to take over. I was a proven ticket seller, had acted as chief support in the UK for Froch versus Bute and had just won the European title in a fantastic fight. Maybe I could have been one of the Matchroom poster boys that benefitted from riding that wave Hearn was creating. We'll never know.

It caused a bit of a stir, Barry and I setting ourselves up as the promoters of my career. For the next couple of months, it was top of the list of questions each journalist had when I gave an interview. Everyone wanted to know what the arrangement was and how it was going to work. We didn't want to start putting figures and percentages in the public arena, but Barry and I were both happy to make clear it was a team effort now.

'I'm part of this promotional team and this is better for me as we know everything that's happening and going on,' I told the boxing reporter Steve Wellings at the end of May. 'There are no decisions made without me giving the go ahead. I'm involved in all discussions; nothing is done over my head because we are all on one team.' In a separate interview I stated that I was to play 'a key role in future career moves', and would be 'working on the promotional side of things alongside Barry'. A little later I spoke about having 'a bit more pressure obviously with me being part of the promotion'.

Barry was on the same page, telling the BBC that the new set-up 'gives us a chance to be more in control of Carl's career. Carl's part of the promotional team with us, Cyclone Promotions, he will be part of that.' Then, in his own interview with Wellings, he explained how 'after July 20th, the fights in Belfast will be our promotion. Team Frampton and McGuigan will be promoting over here.' There would come a time when the McGuigans would downplay both my own and Barry's roles in the promotion of my fights, but in real time, when the arrangement was fresh in our heads, these quotes speak for themselves.

I got back into camp and my opponent for 20 July was named as Fabian Orosco. He was the IBF Latino champ at the time, so he qualified for a defence of my IBF Intercontinental strap. Although he'd only lost a couple of his twenty-four fights, he wasn't expected to trouble me much. We never found out because, in pretty bizarre circumstances, he fought someone else in Argentina three weeks before our date and got himself knocked out. It took them a week to find a replacement in the shape of the two-time world-title challenger Everth Briceno. Briceno was a tough Nicaraguan who had mixed it at the highest level, albeit at lower weight classes. But he was now well past his best, so it was another one thought of as a relatively easy night after the Kiko war. Once again, we never found out. The Wednesday of fight week, the BBBofC said they wouldn't let me fight as I had a small perforation in my eardrum. It was a strange one because I'd recovered from the clip round the ear Kiko gave me back in February and my own Harley Street doctor had recently taken a look and said there was no problem. But the Board had made their decision and that was that. Barry thought there was something else going on. He told me that ticket sales were dire and the show was destined to flop, so Warren simply wanted my purse off the expenses.

Warren didn't seem to be involved in the remaining three fights of the deal, all of which were scheduled for Belfast. First up was the Frenchman Jeremy Parodi. He'd won the IBF International title and defended it a couple of times to secure a top-five world ranking. Coupled to an impressive 35–1–1 record he certainly looked the part on paper. The reality was he boasted one of the most padded records in the super bantamweight division. He was a lovely fella, and he was a hard man capable of taking a lot of punishment, but he was a clear step down in level from Kiko and it showed in the fight. He seemed overly tentative throughout, fearful of coming into any range that I could reach him. Because of that, most of his own shots fell short and I didn't even need to slip much. The noise from the crowd was immense too and it may have got to him. I controlled it from the off and did what I wanted that night. I put my foot down at the start of the fourth. With a little extra on my punches, I had him buzzed and stumbling backwards and he went back to his corner with a cut over his left eye and swelling underneath. It was more of the same in the fifth and sixth. He wasn't dancing so much now I'd taken the wind out of him, so quick feet allowed me to get in and out of range at will – landing damaging punches to head and body as I did so. But he was tough and game and never stopped trying. The commentators were starting to talk about him being one of those guys that can just absorb punishment all night long, but I knew I'd get him. The moment arrived at the end of the sixth when I timed a left hook to the body as we traded up close. It was one of those that takes a split second to register, a delayed reaction before you drop to your knee in pain. I knew he wasn't getting up.

Eight days later I was at The Old Inn in Crawfordsburn waiting for my beautiful bride to walk down the aisle. We were married on a Sunday, which is a bit unusual, but the Monday was a bank holiday so no one needed to hold back at the party. Carla was our flower girl and I started welling up when I saw her walking towards me, all dolled up in a miniature bride's dress like her mummy's. Then Christine arrived, thirty minutes late of course, and I had to catch a few tears as they rolled down my cheek. We chose a Humanist ceremony, and the celebrant was a woman named Myrtle Ewing. I think it's pretty much like a religious ceremony except you leave out the stuff about God. It was a beautiful service and a great day. We had about 120 people there so there was the traditional ding dong with mothers and mothers-in-law when distant relatives we'd never heard of appeared on the guestlist. We were like, who's paying for their dinner cos we don't fucking know who they are! Paddy Barnes was my best man, but his speech could have been better. He was so nervous he kept stuttering like a mad man. At the end he was supposed to sign off by saying 'thank you very much Mr Eastwood' as a dig at Barry who was in the audience, but he lapped it. I think the full McGuigan clan were there, and Shane and Jake were groomsmen. It actually got a bit heated between Shane and Cooper at one point. Cooper felt a bit aggrieved, and rightly so, that the only public narrative available was that Shane had made me the fighter I was. He was making the point that all the guys at the Midland, and Billy above all others, deserve a hell of a lot of credit too. That for fifteen years I was being educated and trained before I'd ever met a McGuigan. Shane was a bit dismissive, and Cooper was ready to flatten him. Fortunately for Shane a few others stepped in and calmed Cooper down. There was only going to be one winner there if punches started flying. By that stage everyone had had a fair few drinks. Me, more than most. May McFettridge was there doing her stuff and taking the piss out of everyone. I ended up on a table dancing while everyone was surrounding it clapping and laughing. Paddy, stirring shit as usual, said to Barry, 'you better keep an eye on your pot of gold there' and Barry came rushing over and told me to get off the table. I jumped down straight away, almost like a scolded kid. I probably would have laughed them off if my ma or da or hotel staff or whoever else had been the ones ordering me down.

***

Boxing can be a crazy sport at times. Two months after he was stopped by me, Kiko flew to Argentina for a comfortable comeback bout against a fighter with nine losses on his record. It was a two-round blowout win for him which somehow led to a shot at the IBF world champion, Jonathan Romero. The Colombian Romero was undefeated after twenty-three fights, so maybe his team saw Kiko as an easy voluntary defence before they looked for a big-money fight. If so, they were sadly mistaken. Kiko went to Atlantic City in August and battered Romero to become IBF champ via sixth-round stoppage. So, before I even had the chance to get into the ring again after victory over Kiko, here I was chasing another fight against him! To that end, I travelled to Elche on the Costa Blanca a few days before Christmas to watch Kiko make his first defence against the South African Jeffrey Mathebula. This was pure Kiko territory, a leisure centre right beside where he lives, so I got loads of stick from the crowd. The fact I was wearing a Santa hat and a Christmas jumper with lights on the front probably didn't help. I got dog's abuse the whole night, some good-natured banter and some a bit more vitriolic. One fella a few rows back never shut up, and from the look and sound of him he absolutely hated me. I was there with Barry and Christian Saunders, one of the business guys who pumped money into Cyclone. The point of the trip was just to draw a bit of attention to the fact we wanted to fight Kiko again. The rematch was being talked about but nothing had been agreed, so the hope was this could push things along. I wanted it immediately but Kiko was the champ, so he was able to call the shots to a large extent. He also had more options on the table, and I couldn't really blame him when he chose to take another voluntary defence against Hozumi Hasegawa in Japan rather than face me again. It would have been good money to go to Osaka and he'd have known Hasegawa was an easier night's work than me. I had to force Kiko's hand but without being mandatory challenger it was tough to do. And despite being the highest ranked challenger, the IBF seemed reluctant to name me official mandatory. The business and politics of boxing are murky at best and clearly someone on Team Kiko had enough sway with the IBF to delay the inevitable for a little while longer. When Kiko went on record saying I had nothing of value for him and he'd rather face Scott Quigg for the Manchester man's WBA Regular belt, we realised we may need to explore another route to a world-title shot.

That change of tack led to the two-weight world champion Hugo Fidel Cazares. The Mexican was the WBC's (World Boxing Council's) top-ranked contender, and as I was their number two it was an easy one to be approved as a final eliminator to become mandatory challenger for Leo Santa Cruz's WBC world title. Cazares had stepped up to Super Bantamweight after losing his Super Flyweight title, and was now on a five-fight winning streak. Although he was coming up the weights, he wasn't particularly small and was my match physically. But at thirty-six years old he was in the twilight of his career while I was entering my prime. And fighting him at home in the Odyssey, I couldn't see how I could lose. I said after the Parodi fight that the crowd gave me an extra 10 per cent and I truly believe that to be the case. I might even be underselling it. And that's not taking into account how it affects my opponent. Even the most seasoned of guys I fought would most likely never have experienced atmospheres like those which my fans could generate in Belfast. Very few fighters in the sport are fortunate to have such support.

By now I'd proven I could sell out the 9,000-seater Odyssey Arena by myself and so, just like he did at the Ulster Hall, Barry stripped the undercard down to the bare minimum required by television. Whereas Eddie put ten fights on the undercard when I fought Kiko, Barry had only put seven on the Parodi bill and reduced it to five for this one. It was a shame really because one of the benefits of having a popular fighter doing well and bringing big nights to a city is that a host of local prospects get on the undercard and start building their own names and records. I know from experience that it means a lot to a kid coming through to appear on a massive, televised show rather than always on a small-hall event in front of a couple of hundred people. All young boxers go through rough patches where they question whether all the hard graft and sacrifices are worth it, and it's the promise of the big nights under the bright lights that keeps many of them returning to the gym. A few boys probably packed it in when they saw they couldn't even get on a decent card in their own city never mind achieve something elsewhere. It's the promoter's right to do as they please in that regard and normally they find the right balance. The more fights on the undercard the more purses they have to pay out. But the smarter promoters always have an eye on the future and understand it's necessary to invest in the undercard so that two or three emerge and become headliners themselves a few years down the line. If you only put five other lads on you may make more money in the short term, but you're severely limiting your chances of developing the next big star. Cyclone clearly took the short-term view, and I remember thinking that the company must be making some serious dough with close to 9,000 tickets sold; a minimal undercard; and, judging from what I was getting paid, a relatively cheap main event too.

The fight against Cazares is best remembered for the slightly bizarre ending midway through the second round. It's a pity because in the four and a half minutes of action before that, Cazares showed enough to suggest he'd keep me honest. It was warming up into a nice little scrap. While predominantly a counterpuncher, Cazares could mix it up and wasn't afraid to go on the front foot when he wanted. It was fifteen years since he'd been stopped in a fight, and being Mexican he had that natural grit and toughness about him. I started positively and clearly landed the better, cleaner punches in the first round. But Cazares landed a couple of good shots of his own and seemed to grow into it as we approached the bell. He actually buzzed me pretty bad at one stage, but not many people noticed it. Shane had and, after double-checking I was okay during the sixty-second break, he told me I was boxing well but just waiting a little too long to begin my attacks. He sent me out for the second with the instruction to ping it in as soon as I see the shot is on. It felt like my opponent had been given similar advice from his corner as the round began with a flurry of action. Again, I was landing the heavier blows while Cazares did enough to remind everyone why he'd won two world titles. Then a minute in I landed a low one around his hip and he limped about milking a dead leg for thirty seconds. Referee Victor Loughlin wasn't in a sympathetic mood, however, and he waved us back into battle without much delay. I stalked Cazares around the ropes and backed him into my corner before exploding out of a crouching position to detonate a left hook on the side of his head. He didn't know what had hit him as his legs took on a mind of their own for a few steps and propelled him into the ropes and then onto both knees. By the count of four, he'd steadied himself on one knee with the help of an elbow resting on the second rope. By eight, he seemed to have recovered his senses and actually looked over to me in the neutral corner, smiled and gave a little nod of recognition at the quality of the shot I'd dropped him with. I could see he was pretty clear-headed at that point, so I was preparing myself to go back to work. Then, it was all over. Cazares and his team couldn't believe it and tried to argue their case to the ref. I doubt Victor understood a word of it and there was a school of thought that Cazares couldn't understand Victor's accent as he administered the count. That is far-fetched to say the least, and the ref clearly displayed the count using his fingers just in case. Watching it back, it does appear a little strange that Victor got to nine fingers and then jumped straight to a you're-out gesture, but I don't believe for one second that was the cause of the confusion. I think Cazares just fucked it up. He was too busy looking over at me trying to let me know he was fine, and he took his eye off the ball. I don't think it was one of those where a fighter deliberately lets the count beat him then jumps up and feigns surprise. I think he just got it horribly wrong. It took a little bit of a shine off what was a great left hook I threw. I remember when it landed, I caught sight out of the corner of my eye of the NI football legend David Healy leaping out of his chair like he was going up for a header!

My sights were now firmly set on Leo Santa Cruz. The talk was initially when and where rather than if the fight would happen. We wanted it in Belfast, of course, and venues like Ravenhill, the Ulster Rugby Team's ground, and the Balmoral Showgrounds were mentioned. At the same time, we were open to travelling to the US, East Coast or West. But that early clamour to make the fight quickly died down. I don't really know the ins and outs of what happened or didn't happen. I was official mandatory so it should have been a formality, but boxing is not like any other sport. Sporting merit often follows a distant third behind politics and money when it comes to the business of boxing. Almost without my realising it, the Santa Cruz chat had ended, and we were back onto Kiko. Less than two months after the Cazares fight, it was confirmed. It was Kiko again, but this time for the IBF World title.

I didn't feel any nerves ahead of this one. It was just pure excitement during the entire camp and build-up. A world title at home in Belfast. And not just in Belfast, but on the Titanic Slipways. Belfast is known around the world for having built the *Titanic*, so this was going to be an iconic setting. From where the ring was positioned you could even see Tiger's Bay in the distance. It was just a perfect place for me to win a world title. And I always believed I was going to win that one. There was a hell of a lot of pressure on me for the obvious reason that I'd already knocked Kiko out the previous year, but it didn't weigh heavy on me. People spoke as if the job was already done. There was so much expectation. It felt like people were buying tickets to simply see me handed the belt rather than having to battle a world-class fighter for it. But like I say, I had a confidence inside of me that allowed me to deal with that and actually embrace the pressure.

The weigh-in was another feisty one and I got into him. I can't even remember why I did it. It certainly wasn't something we'd planned or talked about. We kept him waiting then arrived at a packed Ulster Hall that was absolutely jumping. As soon as I saw him on stage, I thought he looked nervous. He would never have seen an atmosphere like that for a weigh-in. He may not even have felt that sort of emotion from a crowd in his actual fights. At the weigh-in for our first fight he'd been the aggressor but this time it was my turn. Maybe it was a subconscious payback for his theatrics the year before. But I think I just instinctively saw an opportunity to capitalise on his nerves and I took it. I wanted to bully him and exploit the contrasting emotions we both felt at that precise moment. His uncertainty and my unshakeable belief that this was my time. There is a great photo of me putting my head onto him and he looks like he doesn't know what to do. To put it bluntly, he shit himself. You don't win a fight with such mind games, but you can definitely gain an advantage ahead of the opening bell.

There was a surreal moment the following night as I approached the end of my ringwalk. Close to the corner in which I was to enter the ring, my ma of all people is stood with her arms spread out, clearly expecting a hug. Now, maybe for some people this would be pretty normal, but the Framptons aren't a hugging family. We just don't do it. Never have done. Now here's Flo, all five foot nothing of her, stood in my way, seconds before the biggest moment of my career so far. I'm thinking, agh what the fuck are you doing! We're on live television in ninety countries worldwide and in front of 16,000 here in the arena and you suddenly want a hug for the first time ever. What could I do? I can't just ignore my ma, so I give her a brief embrace and moved on. But I remember thinking as I climbed through the ropes, if I lose here because of that hug she's going to pay for it!

It was a special feeling walking to the ring that night. Special to think that they'd constructed a stadium just for me and for this fight. It was apparently the First Minister Peter Robinson who came up with the idea. There was nowhere indoors bigger than the Odyssey and I'd proven in lesser fights that I'd outgrown 9,000-seater venues. Different outdoor options were discussed but Robinson's suggestion guaranteed public funding and the backing of the NI Executive, Tourism NI, Tourism Ireland and the Belfast City Council – and so the Jackal's Den was conceived and built throughout fight week. There was a fear that we'd lose a lot of the atmosphere we'd come to expect at my fights in an outdoor arena. That without a roof for the noise to reverberate off, the chants and cheers would sail into the night sky without making it to me in the ring. I guess the fans must have cheered even louder than ever then because I still heard plenty. The other big unknown of fighting outdoors is the elements and, as well as everything else, that night has become famous for being the coldest ever world-title fight! Everyone who was at it remembers it as being absolutely baltic. Some of the fans who came underdressed may have struggled because of it, but it was great for the fighters. The Odyssey gets hot, and the Ulster Hall gets roasting, so feeling the cool sea breeze while I sat on my stool between rounds was a godsend. The conditions definitely helped me stay fresh throughout the fight.

Despite having already gone through the guts of nine rounds together, we used the first round of part two to weigh each other up once more. Kiko was more circumspect than everyone predicted, and I put that down to the stoppage in our first meeting. I had that psychological advantage over him. He was supposed to be the heavy-handed one, but I was the man with the knockout victory in the bank. He was slightly more gung-ho in the second round, and I

traded with him just to lay a marker down again. I had no intention
of fighting this way all night, but I wanted to prove I could, and he
won't be winning this fight with bullying tactics. I reverted back to
my boxing in the third and won it handsomely. There was a long
way to go, but I was in the groove and the confidence I had pre-
fight was only bolstered by the opening quarter.

At the very end of the fourth, as we clinched and stumbled
towards the ropes, our heads clashed and a small cut opened up
just above the corner of Kiko's left eye. He complained but nothing
was done. I wasn't a dirty fighter by any stretch of the imagination,
but I was streetwise enough to look after myself in the ring. I knew
exactly what I was doing in that clinch. At the start of the fifth, I
slipped and ended up on my knees and elbows, facing the canvas.
Kiko, probably still raging from the unpunished headbutt, took his
revenge with a punch to the back of my head. It wasn't full-blooded,
but it sent a message. Steve Gray was the referee that night, in my
opinion one of the best the British Board has. I walked to the
neutral corner, asking what the hell was that. The crowd are booing
because it was so blatant everyone saw it. Barry and the others are
on their feet at ringside screaming at the ref. Fighters have been
disqualified for less. Steve spoke to Kiko first – saying something
along the lines of, do that again and you're out. He then came to
me and whispered into my ear, 'I'm going to let him away with
that because I let you away with that blatant headbutt in the last.'
What can you say to that? Fairs fair. I apologised to Steve, and we
continued. Kiko landed a couple on me but in the closing seconds
of the round I delivered a short, right hand that chopped down
onto the side of his head and put him on his backside. It sealed a
10–8 round for me, and I was well on my way.

If it's not broken, then don't fix it. The second half of the fight
continued in the same vein. Kiko bobbed forward in varying
degrees of intent, while I boxed off the back foot, landing the cleaner

more damaging shots time and time again. The hearts of weaker-willed fighters than Kiko would definitely have been broken. But he never gives up. He'll always keep coming. Here and there he had fleeting moments of success, but I always answered emphatically. He wanted to bore in and fight his fight, dragging me into close-quarter combat in the trenches, but I was too accurate and too punishing. I clipped him so many times as he tried to enter the range he desperately wanted to fight in. There wasn't one round I returned to my stool thinking I'd just lost those three minutes.

Towards the end of the eleventh, with the finishing line in sight and feeling I still had plenty of gas in the tank, I held my feet and opened up. It stopped Kiko in his tracks. I kept throwing and now I was pushing him back. The crowd went mad, and when the bell rang I walked to my corner with one gloved fist raised in salute. It's not over till it's over in boxing, but I was feeling good. It's tradition to touch gloves with your opponent to begin a final round. Kiko and I hugged. It was a mark of the respect we already had for one another. I went for it that final round. I'd boxed out of my skin for eleven rounds and executed our gameplan to perfection. I'd pretty much won every round and dropped him for good measure. I believed I was the fresher fighter in the ring and with the crowd roaring me on I wanted to give them a grandstand finish. At one point midway through the last, I pinned him against the ropes with a twenty-second barrage and Steve Gray inched closer, suspecting he may need to step in. But Kiko wasn't going anywhere that night and he deserved to hear the final bell ninety seconds later. Two of the judges scored it 119–108 and another 118–111. I don't think you ever have an easy twelve rounds with a guy like Kiko, but in comparison to our first meeting this one was a clearer and wider and more comfortable victory. Kiko hadn't regressed, and he'd prove that by going on to achieve plenty in the remainder of his career – including picking up another world title by knocking out the undefeated Kid Galahad in 2021. But I had certainly improved and that's what gave me most satisfaction.

It was pandemonium in the ring at the end. It seemed like every man and his dog was piling in. My da managed to get in with Carla in his arms but she was out for the count. We'd got her these big headphones to protect her from the noise and she'd curled up in my ring jacket and fell asleep on my old man's lap as soon as the fight started. But I still wanted to hold her in the ring and get a photo so she'd have something to remember the night her daddy won the world title. It was chaotic in there and I didn't manage to get that shot. The MC, Craig Stephens, was actually the one shouting at my da to get Carla out of the ring for some reason. I reckon there were a few others who should have been turfed out before the new champ's daughter. Looking back now, I wish I'd told Stephens to fuck off. That if I wanted my daughter in the ring, then she should be in the ring.

It's hard to process your emotions in the moment during a night like that. The adrenalin of hearing the three words 'And The New …' was still coursing through my veins as I sat on the ring apron between Barry and Shane to be interviewed by BoxNation. I just wanted to thank everyone who'd help get me to this stage. My granda, my biggest fan, had died during camp so I had a special thank you for him. I dedicated the win to him and that got me very emotional. I felt a wee cry coming on, and as the adrenalin died down I felt a little lightheaded too. When the interview ended, all I wanted was to lie down.

I went to see Kiko first. Our changing rooms felt like a bit of an afterthought once they'd custom-built a boxing stadium. I was in a portacabin, which didn't really feel befitting of a world-title challenger, but when I saw where they'd put Kiko it made my quarters look like the Ritz. He was in a touring caravan, and it felt like a Brad Pitt scene from *Snatch*. A famous photo was taken there with our arms around each other's shoulders and Kiko pointing his finger to me. Both of our heads are swollen and as bumpy as a sock full of snooker balls. It's almost comical-looking but it is testament to the punishment we dished out to each other. Some said the dramatic swelling was the result of coming into a heated environment after so long punching each other in the freezing cold, but I don't know if there's any science to back that up. I always made an effort to go see my opponent after a fight – win, lose or draw. Most boxers do and you're pretty much always pals after the event, with any nonsense that's gone on to sell the fight quickly forgotten as part of the whole charade. After sharing the ring with someone you gain a respect for the man. You've both shared an experience that few people go through. But with Kiko the respect was deeper than usual. It's hard to put my finger on it. I guess I sensed we were similar in many ways. Working-class family men. I also had to admire the balls and determination of him. To get beat several times and come back to win a world title. Then to repeat that. To still be going, fighting at the highest level, to this day. I mean, the so-called experts were already saying he was past his best when I fought him ten years ago. It's crazy the drive he has. Obviously, there's a language barrier between us but with Google Translate and help from here and there we keep in touch and swap messages the odd time. I'll always be a massive Kiko Martinez fan.

Becoming world champion is life-changing in many ways. I'd like to think it didn't change my character or who I am in the slightest, but in terms of profile and attention you're suddenly on another level. We live within a bubble in which it seems like boxing is the be-all and end-all, but it is still a very niche sport and as you're making your way through the levels you tend to fly under the radar of most people. But when you win a world title, you break into the public consciousness. You're on the news and, back home at least, on the front pages. They replayed the fight on UTV a night

or two later and something crazy like 70 per cent of those who
turned their TV on were tuned in. People who have no interest in
boxing now recognise your name and face. I've been very lucky. It's
very rare I get any grief from people. You get the odd idiot spouting
off on social media but that's not even real life. On the street people
have always been brilliant with me. All they want is to say hello,
tell me well done, buy me a pint and maybe pose for a photo. Not a
bother. It's an honour to do stuff like that. I seem to be a particular
favourite with women of a certain age too. Auld dolls absolutely
love me for some reason! It's more Christine needs to watch herself
around them. She got into a spat with one years ago on Twitter who
wrote under a photo of Christine and I after one of my fights, look at
the millbag. Christine was far too quick for her and replied, you've
spelt millionaire wrong you pass-remarkable dickhead. A few years
later that woman's daughter came up to us in a bar in Belfast to
introduce herself and apologise for her mother's behaviour. As
ridiculous as it sounds it actually made it into the press, and her da
apparently slapped the paper down in front of her ma and said, it's
this type of behaviour makes me want a divorce. And they did get
divorced! So, I can't say fame has brought many challenges. And if
I'm being honest, I probably wanted the fame when I was younger.
I hate the word celebrity or the idea of being famous for fame's sake.
But fame to me means acknowledgment of my achievements as an
athlete. As a good sportsman from a small country that loves its
sport, of course I wanted recognised and acknowledged.

Ironically, one place I could go to become anonymous again
was camp. The gym was based in Battersea just across the River
Thames from Chelsea, and it was a part of the world where nobody
recognises a boxer. I came across plenty of other well-known
characters in my years there, though. I remember training one day
and, because it was warm outside, we had the shutters up. An older
lady pedalling along the road on her bicycle misjudged her stop

and came right off the bike. I ran across the road to help her up and it turned out to be the fashion designer Vivienne Westwood. She said, thank you very much young man, and then went on her way. Speaking of fashion designers, Victoria Beckham had an office in the same spot as the Cyclone's office. There was a little private shared courtyard inside and one day I saw David walking around it with his daughter. Victoria then joined them. That was the only time I ever saw Becks and I was dying to go get a photo with him. But then I thought, nah, leave him in peace, he's enjoying a private moment with his kid and wife so the last thing he wants is some eejit appearing looking to take a selfie with him. Without comparing myself to the great man, I was learning how that felt. So, I left him be. About thirty minutes later, Brian Walpole, who used to do some PR stuff for Cyclone, bursts in beaming from ear to ear saying he'd asked for a photo and Becks was more than happy to take it. I was raging! It wasn't just sporting royalty milling about either. The real thing arrived at the gym one day in the form of Prince Harry. It was a planned visit and I'd heard people discussing tipping off the paparazzi in order to get publicity for Cyclone and the gym. I was disgusted but thankfully they never went through with it. Harry was pretty sound. He did some pads with Shane and was then happy to chat away with us. I showed him some funny video that was doing the rounds back then and he was killing himself laughing. He said he normally just worked out in a commercial gym in Soho. That surprised us and we asked why he went in there with regular Joes and risked getting hassled. He replied that he always had a security detail with him and then went on to explain in that posh royal voice that the real reason he went was because 'the pussy was fantastic'.

The other period there was a bit of regular glitz and glamour about the place was when the cricketing superstar Freddie Flintoff teamed up with Shane to prepare for a real professional fight. My big mate Stevie Ward was one of the main sparring partners throughout an extended camp. The whole process was part of some documentary he was making. It was as big a circus as it sounds. Freddie was a lovely fella and an unbelievable sportsman in his own right, but boxing was not his sport and he shouldn't have been anywhere near a professional ring. Initially, the British Boxing Board of Control quite rightly refused to license him. When it is not someone with an amateur pedigree, Board representatives come out to the gym and watch you spar to see if it's safe to give you a pro boxing licence. They took one look at Fred and said no chance. The BBBofC take these things extremely seriously. They need to protect the integrity of boxing but, more important than that, they must ensure the safety of everyone who climbs through the ropes. It is not ever a joke in the ring. But a little while later I was told they'd come back out and changed their mind. Fred was licensed and passed fit and capable of fighting as a professional boxer. I was pretty appalled with the Board and everyone concerned. It was clearly a decision made for money and nothing else. And a very dangerous decision at that.

The legendary Mike Tyson rocked up one day when Flintoff was training. He'd been dragged in to help promote the whole charade and so was being very complimentary to Freddie, telling him he's looking good and all the rest. He then walked out of earshot and asked Barry what this was all about. Tyson presumed it was some sort of celebrity spar for charity. Like Fred was gonna do three minutes against someone from *EastEnders* on Sport Relief or something. When Barry said, no Mike, he's having a real professional bout, Mike couldn't believe it.

'That guy?' he said laughing his head off. 'That guy is fucking shit!'

Out of nowhere, Bob Geldof then wandered in. I'd see him about Chelsea before, wearing a bright-yellow corduroy suit and matching hat. Bob saw the lights and cameras so wanted to see what the commotion was. He stood watching Freddie hit the pads, but no one paid him any attention because Mike Tyson was in the building! Sugar Ray Leonard was another one who must have been paid to show his face. I remember being gutted I'd finished my session before he arrived. I would have loved him to have watched me train and then maybe given me a bit of advice. Instead, there was one of the pound-for-pound GOATs passing on his wisdom to Fred.

I actually went along as part of the team when Freddie had his fight. When it came to the pair having their hands wrapped, I was sent to watch the opponent Richard Dawson have his done. While I was there someone came in with the gloves, and I remember laughing at the reaction. This was a heavyweight contest so they should have been wearing 10oz gloves. Instead, they were handed a pair of 12oz Lonsdale sparring gloves. Basically, just massively padded pillow-like mitts. He couldn't even make a fist inside them. I've no idea how the Board allowed them to be used but, as I said earlier, influential people were making a lot of money in this farce so the Board played ball. Dawson was sat on a chair when he saw them and just said, 'ahhh man' in a really sad voice. He still managed to floor Freddie, but they gave it to the cricketer on points. Needless to say, it wasn't the finest display of pugilism and that was Flintoff's first and last fight. In fairness to him, though, he had come on leaps and bounds from the first day he walked through the gym door. Boxing wise, and also just general strength and fitness. He couldn't squat 50kg in the beginning and by the end he was doing sets with 100kg on the bar.

***

On 17 November 2014 my son Rossa arrived weighing in at 6lbs and 15oz. In comparison to Carla, who was a long and tricky labour, the wee man didn't hang around. Christine sent me to the shop to get her something and by the time I returned she was in the delivery ward and the show was on the road. It was nice to have a boy to complete the set. I also had a thing about the Frampton name living on into future generations, so it was good to know that was safe in his hands now. We had a Humanist naming ceremony for him, and the celebrant this time was a lady called Helen Madden. Helen was an actress as well and actually had a role as Bobby Sands' mother in the film *Hunger*. But my da and Christine's uncle Bernard were more fascinated by her because she was Miss Helen from the kid's show *The Romper Room*, which was a big deal when they were younger. That added a bit of razzamatazz to the occasion! At the bar, Bernard was saying to someone, did you see that Helen from *Romper Room* is here? I thought she was dead, he continued, completely oblivious to the fact that Helen was stood right behind him.

'Nope,' she said. 'I'm still very much alive!'

***

It was no secret that I wanted Scott Quigg next. I said it live on BoxNation while the blood and sweat from Kiko was still smeared all over me. But I'd said it a hundred times before that. It had been talked about for so long, and no matter how they tried to spin it they were the ones avoiding it. That became clearer than ever the day before I beat Kiko when Matchroom announced they were teaming up with Top Rank to co-promote Chris Avalos. Avalos was a pretty anonymous, run-of-the-mill American fighter with a couple of losses on his record and no standout wins. You may wonder why the hell the exclusively UK-based promoter Eddie Hearn would have any interest in him. The answer to that is he'd won an IBF final eliminator contest against a Japanese fighter with a 24–6 record to become mandatory challenger. He'd stepped aside to allow Kiko to face me, but now he was demanding his shot. Hearn knew he could use the situation to his advantage and hide Quigg from me for a while longer, so it was in his interest to get involved and ensure I was forced to fight my mandatory.

We were back into the warmth of the Odyssey for this one and the place was absolutely bouncing. It's difficult for me in the ring to judge and compare one atmosphere with another in my fights, but plenty of people who were there that night say it was the best. It was shown live on terrestrial ITV, and they brought the legendary American broadcaster Al Bernstein over to work it. When he was asked about the atmosphere and the support I have, he said he had seen a lot in thirty-five years of working in boxing but nothing to compare with what he had witnessed that week in Belfast. Michael Buffer was in town to MC the main event and when he roared his famous 'Let's Get Ready to Rumble', the roof near came off the arena.

Avalos is probably the only opponent during my professional career that I didn't like. Right from the off he rubbed me up the wrong way and there was genuine needle and animosity between us. He was a real arrogant prick. He thought he was better than me and made some comment about me being born with a silver spoon in my mouth. I remember replying with a laugh, asking him if he's ever been to Tiger's Bay! I didn't want to be anywhere near him at any stage. Even his family who had travelled over with him didn't seem like nice people. In the middle of a media scrum after the weigh-in, a piece of chewing gum came flying at me. We thought it was his mother who threw it, and after the fight Christine's ma Lils stormed up to her in the hotel and gave her a mouthful. Avalos' brother was sat there as Lils let fly and he didn't say a thing to protect his own mother. Then someone watched the footage of the incident back and apparently you can see it was actually the brother who took the gum out of his mouth and launched it across the room. It hit big Paul Douglas, one of the security guys, so the wanker wasn't even a decent shot. I just wanted to flatten him. It kicked off a bit on the stage at the weigh-in in the Europa Ballroom. We got in each other's faces and then he shoved me away. The crowd went ballistic and started chanting 'Easy! Easy! Easy!' Going into fight night I had it in my head that if I chin him, I'm not going to go and give him a hug as I always did to my opponents. I just wanted to hurt this dickhead.

I knew going in, but the first round confirmed beyond all doubt, that I was far superior to Avalos in every single department. And he knew it too. He was supposed to be all guns blazing but he was scared to really open up. He was just the stereotypical loudmouth unable to back it up when he was face to face with the man he'd been taunting. He nearly had a point deducted by the ref, Howard Foster, near the end of the first for a second punch on the break. But even in that it was pretty feeble. He risked losing points for two impudent little taps instead of really going for it and making it worthwhile. In comparison, I'd already landed four or five crisp right hands and had the feeling I could land them at will for as long as the night lasted.

He was a little more aggressive in the second but there was no class or guile to his work. He just sort of stumbled into range, squared up, and threw aimless wide punches from an orthodox or unorthodox stance which he appeared to find himself in at random. He was so bad that that was where the minimal danger lay. That you could get caught with something you're not expecting because no world-level fighter would ever throw it. But he was so slow that even that was an impossibility. I didn't respect him as a person, and he wasn't showing anything in the ring now to make me respect him as a fighter. With a minute to go in the second, I saw an opportunity to inflict a bit of pain when we tangled and his right arm straightened out across my midriff on the ref's blind side.

Locking it into place with my left glove, I applied force so that it bent the wrong way. I could have snapped it if I wanted, but I just wanted to punish him a bit for the chewing gum and everything else in the build-up. It's the only time in my career I've ever done anything like that. I wasn't one for dirty tactics or squeezing a neck a little longer than you should while the ref tried to split you up. But Avalos was an asshole, so he deserved it. He had a little moan to the ref and kind of shook out his arm, but we were clearly waved back into action. At that point he turned side on to keep whining, but I knew I hadn't done any real damage to him and he was milking it, so I didn't think twice about marching in and clipping him with a left hook. I guess it was my Floyd Mayweather versus Victor Ortiz moment.

For the first half of the third I stood inside right on his chest, just to show him I could and there was no position he could put me in that he could get the better of me. I battered him to the body and could tell he didn't like it. I caught him with an uppercut as well and sent him backwards. Then we stepped back and traded for the rest of the round. Had I been in any way concerned by what was coming back at me, that's not how I would have fought. But the crowd love it and I wanted to hurt him, so I felt comfortable with what I was doing. The beating continued into the fourth. Despite him having a five- or six-inch reach advantage over me, I was able to out-jab him – landing mine first through superior timing. I landed a cracking left hook right on the bell to end the round and he cut a sorry figure traipsing back to his corner.

When I got off my stool and looked across the ring to begin the fifth, I saw a beaten man reluctantly leaving his. I sensed there'd be no sixth round. A short, sharp, overhand right began the final onslaught. I unleashed with both hands as Avalos stumbled backwards from one side of the ring to another and onto a third. Referee Foster was already poised to step in when he lunged forward with his arms around my waist, and I stepped back and let him fall to the canvas. He was just lolling on unsteady legs in front of me now as I moved in for the kill. Lefts and rights were landing at will and I knew one clean one would flatten him. The ref did the right thing in ending it when he did to protect Avalos from serious damage, but I wish he had given me a couple of seconds more to clean him out. But I couldn't really complain. It was as easy a mandatory defence as any champion has ever had, and Shane had me up on his shoulder saluting the crowd. As usual, plenty piled into the ring to celebrate with me. But none made as spectacular an entrance between the ropes as Blain McGuigan. Actually, it wasn't between the ropes at all. He somehow managed to slither under the bottom rope and over the sponsorship toblerones to arrive in the ring flat on his stomach. I've never before or since seen anyone enter a boxing ring that way. Even when my kids could barely walk, they still instinctively clambered between first and second rope. It makes me think of those Tell-Me-Without-Telling-Me memes. Tell me you've never boxed without telling me you've never boxed!

One interesting character everyone saw sat front and centre beside Barry at ringside and then in the ring chatting with me after the fight was Anthony Constantinou. He was the CEO of the now infamous Forex brokerage firm CWM FX and was the McGuigans' main funder at that point. He put a tonne of money into the Kiko fight at the Titanic and was then welcomed as a kind of lead sponsor, meaning Cyclone Promotions officially became CWM Cyclone Promotions. CWM were pumping money into all sorts of sports sponsorship deals – with Chelsea FC, the Honda MotoGP team, the Wigan Warriors rugby league side and the London Boat Show all signing agreements with them. Barry and Sandra McGuigan's eyes lit up when he showed an interest in me and in backing us financially. He was pretty wild. He liked a party and thought he was Leonardo DiCaprio's character in *The Wolf of Wall Street*. He once tried to give me a watch he said had been worn by an astronaut on the moon, but I stupidly refused. Turns out that was Buzz Aldrin's timepiece, which mysteriously went missing en route to a museum and is valued at seven figures. There were stories of Constantinou smashing vodka bottles off walls during business meetings and he was later jailed for several sexual assaults on women who worked for him. So, although he was always very nice to me, it was clear from day one he was a wrong'un.

But he had the cash and seemed happy splashing it, so he became part of the team. It was weird seeing how Barry and Sandra acted in front of Anthony. I remember he brought us to his box at Stamford Bridge to watch Chelsea against Man City. I'm not a gambler but in an attempt to act flash around the high rollers I stuck £250 on a score draw and it came in around four to one. I was delighted but they probably wouldn't even have bothered sending their assistant to go pick up winnings of that size. There was a bigwig from Monster Energy drinks there and Anthony was saying I should be getting sponsored by him. I said my manager deals with all that stuff and then Barry came over and joined the conversation. But whereas he normally acted like the alpha male in the group, he was very meek around these guys. Anthony was well oiled up and after a while kind of dismissed Barry, calling him a clown and saying he'd handle it himself. I held my breath. Barry would be putting anyone else who spoke to him that way back in their place, but with Anthony he just kind of laughed it off. I saw Sandra do it too when Anthony was hurling all sorts of insults in her face. It was embarrassing to witness, but CWM were throwing money around like there was no tomorrow and the McGuigans were determined to get their share. Ahead of the Avalos fight, we were in his massive office in Heron Tower in London when Anthony asked me if I thought I'd beat Avalos by knockout. When I said yes, he offered me a £200,000 bonus if I got the job done. I laughed and told him he was mad, even though it would have practically doubled my purse. Shane was in earshot though and he soon joined in, saying in a jokey but deadly serious way, okay £100,000 each if we get the KO! So, in the ring Anthony took my gloves from my cornerman Steve Broughton as a memento and whispered to me that he was a man of his word and he'd pay me the £200,000. I still brushed it off but later gave him my shorts and robe, and during lunch the following day in James Street South in Belfast he asked for my bank details to make the transfer. At that point I just told him to sort it out with Sandra. I never found out what happened to that dough and a few days later the CWM offices were raided by City of London Police while Jake and Blain were there for a meeting. It turned out the company's income was largely from a Ponzi scheme that stole tens of millions of pounds from unsuspecting punters. Constantinou is currently on the run, having been sentenced in his absence to fourteen years in prison for fraud. And CWM Cyclone Promotions quietly returned to plain old Cyclone Promotions.

Scott Quigg was at ringside for the Avalos fight, and he joined Barry and I during the ITV interview immediately after. We both stated we wanted to face each other next. That the promoters just had to get together and negotiate where, when and how much. I had a dig about being the genuine world champion rather than the regular world champ or whatever the WBA were calling him that week, and I emphasised the fact I was the bigger draw. But there was also an acknowledgment it takes two to tango and that this was the biggest fight to be made in the UK. I really believed it would happen next, but boxing is rarely straightforward and a month or so later we were headed in a different direction when Jake McGuigan returned from the US with an offer burning a hole in his pocket.

Al Haymon was, and remains, one of the most influential powerbrokers in world boxing. Back in early 2015 his Premier Boxing Champions (PBC) was just about to launch, and he advised dozens of elite fighters. One of his favourites was Leo Santa Cruz, a man I had my eye on for a mega unification fight. Haymon is a secretive figure, and I could tell Jake was very proud of himself for having been blessed with a face-to-face. In fairness, the offer seemed a great one. Al would come on as my advisor but would only take a 10 per cent commission if I earned a purse above $2m. What more he or anyone else got out of the deal I never knew. In addition, my first fight under Al's guidance was to be on a PBC card in the US and I'd get paid $1m. Better still, I only had to fight a relatively unknown 25–1–2 career bantamweight named Alejandro Gonzalez to get those seven figures. What could possibly go wrong?

Plenty, as it turned out. My preparation was not as good as it should have been for Gonzalez. It all felt a little bit rushed with the match-up only being confirmed and announced a month in advance. It was taking place in El Paso, Texas, in the middle of July, yet we only arrived out there eight days in advance. That isn't nearly enough to acclimatise yourself to the six-hour time difference and the roasting heat of a Texas summer. I also have to admit I was over-confident going into it. I looked at the guy's record and assumed he was levels below me. I couldn't see any way Gonzalez could trouble me, so I entered fight week in the wrong frame of mind. I was too relaxed. I won't say I treated it like a holiday, but I didn't treat it like preparation for a tough, twelve-round world-title defence against a hungry Mexican challenger. Lying by the pool sunbathing and the like, it was incredibly naive. The first place I paid for that naivety was the weight cut. To say I struggled would be a major understatement. When I woke on the day of the weigh-in I was six-and-a-half pounds over the 122-pound limit. The most I'd ever left myself to lose on the morning was four pounds, so I panicked big time. Plenty of fighters might do cuts like that on the day but I don't, and I was already really dry. It was 100 degrees outside, but I went into the gym with a sauna suit and tracksuit over the top and told them to pump the heat up full blast. I skipped and shadow boxed and whatever I could do to sweat the weight off, but it was slow going. Cyclone even had a statement prepared for if I missed it. It was extreme. My strength and conditioning guy, Darryl Richards, walked into the gym from the 100-degree heat outside wearing shorts and a vest, said fuck me, and immediately turned around and walked back out when he felt the temperature. Looking back, I've no idea how I managed to make 122 that day – but I did. Just. But the weight battle still wasn't over. The IBF has a second weight check on the morning of the fight, and you must come in within ten pounds of the championship limit. It meant I couldn't go crazy refuelling but I'm not sure I was in any condition to do so anyway. At lunch my fingers and toes started cramping and curling. I had to physically pull my fingers straight to prevent them from turning into a fist. It was a little scary, something that had never happened before nor since. When I woke on fight day, I was half a pound heavier than I needed to be, so once again a mini weight-cut was necessary. I lost it in a hot bath at 8 a.m. and stepped on the scales bang on 132lbs.

I wore green-and-white shorts for this one. That was my compromise after being subjected to serious pressure from the McGuigans to play up the Irish thing for an American audience. Obviously I get it, and it would undoubtedly go down a storm in somewhere like Boston or New York. But there is a distinctly Latino feel about El Paso, Texas, so I could have walked out in a leprechaun outfit, playing the bodhrán while drinking a pint of Guinness and it still wouldn't have made a damn bit of difference. I also made sure a Northern Ireland badge was on the shorts so people from the Bay wouldn't think I was a complete sell-out! I gave those shorts to David Healy and in return he gave me the top he wore on the night he scored his thirty-sixth and final goal for our country against

Azerbaijan. It has pride of place in my house and remains one of my favourite bits of sporting memorabilia.

The set-up in El Paso was strange. I was scheduled in the ring around 3 p.m. local time to tie in with ITV's primetime slot in the UK. In the US it was being broadcast on CBS, which was amazing exposure for me on that side of the Atlantic. But then after my show, Julio Cesar Chavez Jr was topping another PBC event in the same Don Haskins Centre. They called mine the matinee show and while I knew in advance the timings, the struggle to make weight and then the on-the-day weight check meant I had so little time to get my body back into prime fighting condition. The other impact of being a starter for the Chavez card is that the ring was set up to cater for the Mexican super middleweight. He's a bit of a plodder so the canvas was super soft and spongy to aid his style and hinder anyone who likes getting up on their toes and using quick feet. My feet were, of course, one of my biggest assets. Despite everything, though, the dressing room was full of confidence. The venerable Nacho Beristain was doing my cuts that night. As a Mexican legend you listen when he speaks. He was telling me it was an easy night's work for me. Two- or three-round job, max. While I was getting my hands wrapped, Barry was in my opponent's room diligently observing what they were doing. He couldn't believe it when they started twisting the bandages until it was like a tough rope they were wrapping around his hand. Barry immediately questioned what they were playing at and apparently the commissioner just answered, 'you're in Texas now, son'. He came back to our dressing room and kept quiet about all of that. But I do remember his final words to me before the fight started. 'Keep your fucking hands up here.'

As first rounds of debuts on US soil go, this must be up there with the worst of them. Having never been dropped in a fight, or close to it, my entire amateur and pro career, Gonzalez put me on my arse twice in the opening three minutes. The first was little more than a short jab I walked onto. The second was a smart one–two from the Mexican, and in a crouching position my leg bent and my knee touched the canvas. Neither knockdown was damaging physically, but psychologically they were a nightmare. Physically it was just a weird sensation. Like my lights were switched off for a split second and then turned back on immediately. I wasn't hurt nor buzzed nor anything like that. But psychologically I was in a bit of a panic when I sat down on my stool. Twelve rounds provides you with a long time to make up ground, but you still don't want to start the second round already three points down. My overriding emotion was embarrassment. Here I was, the world champion, coming to town to show the American audience I was an elite fighter. Leo, the big fish I was chasing, was sat ringside and I imagined he was probably stifling a laugh at the idea I could trouble him. I was embarrassed.

I needed to settle down and settle down quick. The first round quickly rid me of any complacency. Now I had to forget about putting on a show or impressing anyone. Now I just had to settle down, box, win the fight and retain my world title. I won the second round but the third was competitive. Gonzalez lost a point for a third low blow, having been given a clear final warning after the second punch to my balls. Then, in the middle of the round, he caught me with an uppercut on the inside and unleashed a barrage of hooks. The exchange hurt me a hell of a lot more than either of the knockdowns and for a few seconds I panicked, thinking I was in real trouble here. It was another little reminder not to get too greedy, that boxing not fighting was going to beat this guy and there was no need for reckless aggression on my part. From the fourth onwards it was like the penny had finally dropped and I took complete control of the fight. I found the right balance in my work and felt more relaxed in the ring. I started to fight my fight, controlling the distance and tempo with my jab. I was still offensive, but I was more patient than the gung-ho opening rounds. I started setting traps and let him make mistakes I could capitalise on. I was now boxing as I should have from the opening bell.

By the eighth, I'd beaten a lot of the belief out of Gonzalez. He's a Mexican so there was zero chance of him giving up or anything close, but I could see in his body language he knew the fight was only going one way. I'd already landed some big blows but now I felt more comfortable showing more aggression. Now, rather than round one, was the correct time to do so. He responded with yet another low blow. I felt they were too numerous to be unintentional, so I took aim at his balls for once and the ref called us together and told us to wise up. He caught me with a few in the ninth and I had to respect his heart. I was countering him at will when he made the first move, but he kept coming. His chin was as solid as they come so I knew it was unlikely I'd knock him out, but the punishment he was shipping had caused a notable reduction in his power and speed. I spent most of the penultimate round on the back foot, forcing Gonzalez to make the first move so I could easily avoid and counter. His frustration expressed itself with yet another low blow and the ref had no choice other than docking another point from his tally. He continued giving it his all until the final bell, and for that he deserved enormous credit, but my class had shone through and I won it wide on the scorecards, 116–108 twice and 115–109 on the third card.

Despite the win I was in a foul mood that night when everyone was sitting about having a few drinks. I fell out with Christine because she put an Alejandro Gonzalez T-shirt on. People were winding me up about Andy O'Neill, the Irish cutman too. I don't know how it all came about exactly but he'd flown to Texas and managed to make himself part of Gonzalez's corner. I just thought that was a bit of a weird thing to do and, sat there with a few drinks in me, I started getting really riled up. I actually went for him at one point and luckily for everyone concerned I was pulled away before anything silly happened.

As a fighter, once you've calmed down you look to take the positives out of every situation. And despite the horrendous opening round, there were plenty from Gonzalez. My career was not going to be plain sailing from opening to final bell, and I knew that as I progressed the fights would become tougher and tougher. So, in a way it was good to have this test and overcome a sense of panic when I did. While still embarrassed by the first round, I was proud with how I recovered and boxed sensibly to win every other round. I was pleased with how I remained calm and quickly regained control. It showed a maturity in the ring that was sure to come in handy in future battles.

The other positive which emerged from being put on my arse twice was that it finally tempted Hearn and Quigg into accepting my challenge. Their balls suddenly grew when they watched me get dropped by some skinny unknown Mexican kid. It also helped that at the same time I was fighting in El Paso, Quigg was stopping Kiko in the second round in the MEN Arena, Manchester. What happened either side of the Atlantic that night gave Team Quigg a lot of confidence. Going into the fights there was a feeling I had a bit of a gimme while Scott was in for a very long and tough night. On the face of it, the opposite happened and that was enough for Hearn to finally play ball. But in reality, I had won ten or eleven of twelve rounds while Quigg had been battered round the ring for a round and then benefited from a reckless and over-confident Kiko walking straight onto one. To some people the narrative had changed somewhat, and it was now a 50–50 fight or Scott was the slight favourite. But I knew the reality so it was all music to my ears. Hearn and the McGuigans were finally able to do a deal, although by all accounts the negotiations were absolutely tortuous and Barry, my manager, had to be excluded from some meetings for fear he might snap and empty Eddie! Crazy. I wasn't involved, but the end result was the total income generated by the fight – every penny from television, the gate, sponsorship etc. – was to go into a central pot and be split 57.5–42.5 per cent in my favour. It should have been at least 60–40 per cent in my opinion, but I had the fight I'd wanted for four years so I was willing to take the hit.

It was a massive shock a few years later to learn of the tragic death of Alejandro Gonzalez. We'd taken Carla to an open farm to celebrate her birthday when I got the call. He'd been found in a car alongside his grandfather and a friend. All three were stripped to their underwear, had their hands and ankles tied together and they'd been executed. Apparently, they'd got mixed up with some cartel stuff in Mexico. Hard to believe really. I'd had a nice chat to him after our fight and he seemed a lovely fella. He was telling us about his young wife and child, and he was so happy to have earned enough to go home and buy a house in Mexico. He was a very likeable kid, so it was just so sad his life ended early and in such a violent way.

After El Paso some people wondered whether I was one of these guys who wins a world title and then takes his foot off the gas. Whether, even subconsciously, I had a feeling of job done, goal achieved, and I'd stop pushing and making the sacrifices I'd been making my whole career to date. I never felt that. It's a cliché but you simply set more goals. Higher goals. Defend your title. Win another title. Unify a division. Win a title in another weight class. Whatever it takes to keep driving you on. And within each fight then it felt like there was something new or different. Avalos was on ITV. Terrestrial television was an opportunity to sell myself to millions of new fans. It's a massive platform so I was determined to shine. And it turned out almost two million people watched me that night. Gonzalez was my first fight with Haymon; first million-dollar purse; first fight in the US and broadcast on CBS, which tens of millions have access to over there. So again, you're looking to impress. There was always something to motivate me. Complacency was never a problem. And had it been, the first round in El Paso would have dispelled it.

It was down to the Gonzalez knockdowns that I decided to go off the drink for a while. I wasn't someone who would regularly go crazy with the booze, but in certain social situations I'd certainly enjoy myself. Now, for a few months I decided to go completely teetotal. But with no fight date confirmed and no camp to start, it's hard to sit sipping juice when everyone around you is on the beer having great craic. So, one night in the autumn of 2015 I slipped off the wagon. It turned into a mad one and, after a few too many stumbles in the kitchen of our house in Banbridge, I got bundled into bed by Ciaran, my brother-in-law. He and his wife Lisa then went to sleep in the spare room while Christine conked out on the sofa. A couple of hours later, Lisa got up to use the bathroom and found me lying at the bottom of the stairs with a large pool of blood spreading out over the black-and-white tiles. I don't remember a thing, but I'd obviously fallen down the stairs and split my head open. There was a massive gash over my left eye and blood was still oozing out of it. It must have been pretty terrifying for Lisa, but she was brilliant. She didn't wake Christine because she'd freak out, but she got Ciaran up and they called an ambulance. The worrying thing was that I wasn't responding coherently, and no one had any idea how long I'd been lying there for. The paramedics were on the phone telling Lisa to put me in the recovery position, but when I started groaning they said just to leave me. Then I started trying to move myself and they told her to restrain me. When the paramedics arrived, they put me in a neck and back brace and loaded me into the ambulance. Ciaran got in too and the sight of the paramedics doing everything they could to try and keep me awake really spooked him. Lisa was left back in the house dealing with the police, who had arrived on the scene, and in her head I could have been dying on the journey. Then she cleaned up the blood and woke Christine and, of course, she starts going mental. Meanwhile I'm getting stitches, inside and out, in a wound that was open right to my skull. I'm still out for the count. Christine, Lisa and their ma arrive at Craigavon Hospital in a mad panic and get told I'm down in resuscitation. Oh Jesus, they think. He's dying. Turns out they only wheeled me in there to use the room as there was nowhere else to put me. With everyone there I finally wake up and the doctors are asking me the normal questions of where you are and what year is it, etc. I start rambling about being in Carrickfergus for something to eat with Christine and after some contemplation I decided it must be 1999. Everyone is thinking, Christ, he's brain-damaged. But less than an hour later I was on my way home. Doctors tend to be good at judging the difference between serious head trauma and just a bog-standard drunken eejit.

I can laugh about it all now, but it was genuinely scary for all concerned. My granda had died falling down the stairs, exactly one year to the day. It was while I was at Blain McGuigan's wedding. We think he went down to put the heating on and lost his footing on the way back up. My uncle Clarke found him in a pool of blood, just like Lisa found me. It could have been a lot worse for me. I was worried about telling Barry. He was always going on about leaving the drink alone until I hung up the gloves. The Quigg fight wasn't announced yet, but I knew it was almost there and I was probably a month away from starting camp. So, I hid it for as long as I could. Wore a lot of caps pulled down very low. I told Jake first and let him break it to Barry, that's how scared I was of his reaction. We all did a good job of keeping it quiet despite the fact the scar was very visible for months. The BBBofC then naturally demanded more neurological tests than usual before renewing my licence. I had a lot of busted blood vessels on my brain above the eye where the impact was and where the brain banged off the skull at the back. But the specialists gave me the all-clear and I was passed fit to fight and fit to start camp for Quigg.

Before preparation could begin, there was a three-day, three-city press tour to navigate. That's when the magnitude of this fight really hit home. I'd had plenty of massive nights already, packing arenas and winning world titles in Belfast, but this was the first huge domestic showdown and everything surrounding it just felt bigger. It also had Eddie Hearn driving it and if there is one thing he is good at, it is selling a product. It was a lot of pantomime but that's how you promote a fight. A full three months ahead of the opening bell, we were in London for a press-only news conference with Adam Smith acting as compere and arbitrator for the verbal exchanges. It started off diplomatically enough. Hearn describing it as the biggest fight in the super bantamweight division and Barry calling it a global event comparable to the famous Barrera–Morales rivalry. The trainers, Shane and Joe Gallagher, then weighed in – naturally, backing their own man. Joe described it as just another day at the office and predicted a convincing Quigg win. Scott chimed in to say he had all the tools necessary to beat me easy. Shane laughed their bullishness off and spoke about me being the more complete fighter and that I'd move on to bigger and better things. I concurred, saying I'd bamboozle then knock out the Bury man. It was Hearn who turned the heat up. After speaking about the tickets being split fifty–fifty, and Barry saying it would still feel like Belfast on the night, Eddie let fly.

'You're only here because we brought you here,' he said to me. 'We're going to provide you with a lot of money and Scott Quigg is going to relieve you of your belt.'

Quigg then went on to highlight that he'd just knocked out my best opponent in two rounds. I must confess they briefly got under my skin. The promoter I was facing more than the boxer. I told

Scott he'd been shitting himself as Kiko battered him round the ring and he then closed his eyes and landed a lucky one. We raised the fact that Hearn is on record saying Carl Frampton will knock Scott Quigg out and that he wanted nothing to do with the English fighter until I left Matchroom. It teed it up nicely for round two in Manchester the following day.

For some reason they chose the MEN Arena, and it looked ridiculous when around twenty people showed up to support Quigg. It hammered home the point we'd always made about who was the true A side. I questioned how Scott would feel on the night, being the home fighter but entering the ring to boos because the majority there would be my fans.

'He's not a ticket seller,' I concluded and Quigg, who sold a lot of his tickets out of his family's fish-and-chip shop, did well to fire back with 'the chippy is busy at the moment!' Little did he know though that I'd already sold my entire allocation and was directing my own fans to his chippy to buy tickets there.

I then had a pop at Quigg's status as world champion, saying for me this isn't really a true unification fight. The governing bodies that control the belts are often as bad as each other, but this was around the time when the WBA set themselves apart with some of their ridiculous decisions. One of them was the creation of so-called Super and Regular world champions. The Cuban bogeyman Guillermo Rigondeaux was the true WBA champion, but Hearn had managed to get them to order Quigg against someone called Yoandris Salinas for the vacant regular world title. Neither fighter had any wins on their résumé that suggested they were anywhere near world level, but Quigg's victory over Rendall Munroe had somehow made him the interim titlist. They fought to a draw but somewhere along the line the WBA had apparently upgraded Quigg from interim to regular champ, so he retained the belt. They then went a step further and upgraded him again to super champ, with

Rigondeaux becoming a champion in recess. It was all a bit mad, but good ammunition to target an opponent with. And of course, Team Quigg tried to give as good as they got. At one point Scott also said 'shut up Finbar' to Barry and that set him off. He blurted out that either Scott or Joe was a 'nonsense eejit' which doesn't make much sense but goes to show how riled he was. But whilst I didn't particularly like Scott at that moment in time, my stronger emotions were definitely directed towards Hearn and Gallagher. Towards the end of the Manchester presser, I described those two as the definition of arrogance and said that despite him being a big man, it wouldn't take me longer than thirty seconds to sort Eddie out.

The Europa Hotel the next day was absolutely packed for part three, probably the best press-conference atmosphere I've ever seen. Eddie, Joe and Scott all got absolute pelters from start to finish and it was impossible to hear the vast majority of what they said due to the constant heckling. It was generally good-natured and pretty funny stuff, but it was relentless. I referenced the trouble understanding them over the din when it was my time to speak, noting that had not been a problem the day before in Manchester. When Scott was talking, I held a piece of paper up with Real World Champion written on it and the crowd erupted. They would have erupted no matter what I did or said that day. Barry and Eddie got into another back-and-forth that quickly heated up.

'Don't be so smug mate. You're an asshole,' Barry told him to the delight of the crowd that was so raucous most people didn't even hear Eddie's comeback:

'No need to lose your rag. I just hope that all the people taking a percentage of Carl let him have some in the end'.

The traditional head-to-head then ended proceedings and gave me a break from looking into Quigg's beady little eyes and having to restrain myself from decking his smug promoter.

The next time I saw Scott was a couple of weeks out from the fight in the Sky Sports studio to record our episode of *The Gloves are Off*. That's the one where you sit facing your opponent in the dark with your chair turned backwards and Johnny Nelson is in the middle trying to stir the pot. You go back and forth for about forty-five minutes and then they edit it down to the best twenty or so for TV. It tends to be the usual bravado between two fighters about to face each other. I'm better than you. I know how I'm going to beat you. I'm the one who was pushing for this fight. I'm the A side. And so on and so forth. I went in very confident because I was better than him, I did know how to beat him, I had been crying out for the fight, and I was most certainly the A side! But more than all that, I knew I came across better on camera. I was more articulate than Scott and a lot more relaxed and polished when it came to talking. He got a lot of stick for his perceived lack of intelligence due to some of the things he said and how he'd stumble over his words on camera. It was also public knowledge that he'd left school at some crazy young age to focus on boxing. I didn't want to deliberately target that side of things but I was definitely planning to hammer him for his lack of boxing brain and ring intelligence, and the two kind of overlapped as things got heated. I remember leaving the studio that day thinking I'd really embarrassed him. That I'd made a complete fool out of him. But I was forgetting that I was on Sky Sports and that Scott was a Sky Sports fighter. Matchroom had the exclusive deal with Sky and no doubt had a hand in editorial decisions when it came to how a fighter or fight was presented to the public. Fair play to whoever it was who edited our show because they polished a turd in a way that managed to level things up. There was one part I couldn't wait to see when the show was first broadcast. After he'd needled me with his nonsense about being just as popular as me or having a higher ring IQ than I had, I said to him, 'your level of intelligence outside the ring reflects how you fight inside the ring – you're not a clever fighter'.

He replied, 'what do you mean?'

That was an open goal for me to fire back with, 'I think you've just answered your own question there,' to which Scott stared blankly back at me.

That was my best one-liner and they cut it out! I know it was a bit harsh on him but it would have helped sell the fight, and at the end of the day that's the only reason we're there doing the promotional stuff at all.

Next time we met was the fight-week press conference. It tends to be the day before you weigh in so fighters making championship weight are always more on edge than normal. You're already hungry and know what you've got ahead of you during the next twenty-four hours as you will your body down to a weight it shouldn't really be at. Emotions are very raw at this time, and it doesn't take much to set them off. People in the game know this is when you need to start tiptoeing around your fighter. At the head-to-head at the end of the presser, Hearn did the opposite. After a minute and a half of jabbering away in each other's faces, I gave Quigg a few patronising pats on the shoulder and he responded with a bit of a shove. I retaliated with one of my own and then this long arm comes over the top and pushes me back. It was Eddie.

'Get your fucking hands off me you big lanky cunt.'

I was deadly serious now and he could see it in my eyes this wasn't playing anymore. I saw fear in his.

'All right, all right, calm down,' he said in that cockney accent of his and then grew braver as the distance between us across the stage increased.

Blain was probably our biggest casualty from this final presser. He'd sat at the far end on the other side of Shane. The line-up was Adam Smith in the centre then moving out each side along the table it went fighter, promoter and trainer. Blain was nominally my promoter as he had got his licence from the BBBofC, but everyone knew it was really Barry and so it was the elder McGuigan rather than Blain who was placed as Eddie's counterpart. I think so as to keep up appearances and to not humiliate Blain, they squeezed him on the end of the table. Matchroom were obviously aware of the dynamic and probably prepped Quigg to take advantage. And he did just that after Blain asked him a question about doing the IBF's ten-pound, on-the-day weight check. After grinning at him for a while Quigg asked, 'what are you doing up here, asking questions like that?' and kept grinning. Hearn was a Cheshire cat too. Blain forlornly tried to argue he was the promoter, but they were already blanking him and chuckling to themselves. It was brutal. And there wasn't even anything Barry, Shane or I could do to defend him, so we just sort of dropped our heads and Adam Smith quickly moved on. Blain kept pretty quiet from there on in.

There were more handbags the next day as I made my way through the crowd and onto the scales on stage in the MEN. This time it was Barry and the retired heavyweight Clifton Mitchell at the forefront. Mitchell runs the security company that was handling things on the ground and as far as I know he took exception to us having our own guys and wanting them on stage with me. It got very heated and knowing Barry, he would have had no problem with a physical confrontation with Mitchell despite the size difference. He apparently teased the big man with the well-known gym rumour that Prince Naseem, as a featherweight, had dropped Mitchell in sparring. The ex-pro Paul Douglas was with us, and he stepped in to put an end to the nonsense. Paul later told us he'd knocked Mitchell out in the amateurs!

Six thousand people turned up just to watch us step on the scales. Far more than most professional boxers will ever fight in front of. I weighed in at 121½lbs and Quigg was 121¼lbs. It was a big effort from both of us, but I left the stage very happy. I thought he looked gaunt and drawn, and felt it had taken more out of him than it had me. I rehydrated, replenished and went to bed weighing 133lbs. I woke at 131½lbs and went downstairs in the Midland Hotel to comfortably make the 10lb weight check. Before me though, Quigg had been on the scales. He weighed just under 130lbs and jumped off delighted, claiming he was bang on and feeling very proud of himself. He then immediately started guzzling from the bottles he had with him, a tell-tale sign that it had not been an easy morning for him. I don't know how, but Team Quigg must have thought they had to make 130 rather than 132. Again, all music to my ears.

One hilarious sidenote to the whole build-up was the phoney war over dressing rooms. There was an ongoing and ill-tempered back-and-forth on that right up to fight night. This was Scott's back yard, somewhere he'd fought a few times before, and so he wanted the home changing room. The Arena was home to ice hockey and basketball teams, so the home dressing room was likely to be bigger and more luxurious than the rest. Having never fought there, I didn't know – and I couldn't give a fuck where I got changed. The key thing for me was that Scott did care and so I kept saying I was adamant as the A side and the only true champion I must have the home dressing room. It was hilarious really, but it got to the stage of brinkmanship where there were reports the fight would be called off if the issue wasn't resolved. They kept pushing so hard we guessed it must be a superstition thing more than ego driving it. That's when we'd started saying that superstition is a sign of mental or psychological weakness. At one of the pressers, I even started playing Stevie Wonder's 'Superstition' into the mic. I'm not even sure what happened with the rooms in the end, but I think I was told nobody was getting the main room. I really couldn't have cared less.

As predicted by all, the place was packed when we walked out. It may have been a fifty–fifty split on tickets at the outset, but we knew plenty of my fans had got their hands on a few from the Quigg section. Either that or they were just a lot louder than the locals. It was nice to see a few Northern Irish celebs there too. The managers of the Northern and Southern Irish football teams, Michael O'Neill and Martin O'Neill, both came to the dressing room to wish me luck. One of the greatest jockeys to ever ride a horse, A.P. McCoy, was there and the actor Jimmy Nesbitt certainly enjoyed himself at ringside in his retro NI top. Four of the current players – Gareth McAuley, Josh Magennis, Kyle Lafferty and Stuart Dallas – then walked me to the ring wearing my team kit and carrying my belts. It always feels nice to get that support from fellow athletes from different sports.

I was extremely confident that I could win this fight in several different ways – but there was one little variable I wouldn't be able to totally control, which was my only cause for concern. James Tennyson helped me prepare for this one and he was a great sparring partner. But in our final spar he opened up a cut over my eye. It was just typical. Barry, fearing the worst, was freaking out and that panicked me. It was actually David Haye who took control of the situation. We were in his gym and he was so calm about everything, which settled me down too. David made a few calls and made sure a doctor he knew and trusted would take care of me and help keep it all hush-hush. I went to hospital, and they used a surgical adhesive to glue it shut rather than stitches. We then kept it quiet as possible so as not to give Quigg and Gallagher anything to latch onto. I even wore makeup, right up to and including the weigh-in, to keep them from finding out. I skipped one media day, giving the excuse that I was feeling under the weather. Team Quigg smelled a rat, but they guessed wrong. They started saying I was struggling horribly to make the weight. That I couldn't be around food, so the spread laid out for the journos at the media day was enough for me to cancel! That was funny, but going into a world-title fight with a fresh wound over your eye is no laughing matter. It hadn't had the time to heal properly so it was liable to open up pretty easily. The last thing I wanted was to spend the entire fight blinking my own blood out of my eye and worrying about the ringside doc waving the fight off if it got too gruesome. The fact I made it through the thirty-six minutes without spilling a drop tells its own story.

The atmosphere was electric at the opening bell. Twenty thousand well-oiled fans were singing, 'There's only one –', with one side completing the line with 'Carl Frampton!' and the other with 'Scott Quigg!' The fact they were competing with each other meant a song which usually peters out within thirty seconds ended up continuing for about twenty verses! But as lively as it was outside the ring, between the ropes Scott and I weren't getting caught up in the emotion. The first round was the definition of a cagey opener, which I won by controlling the centre of the ring alone. The second was no better in terms of entertainment, with Scott stood pretty square behind his high guard and apparently reluctant to take any chances. I was relaxed, moved about the ring, landed a couple of shots and went two–nil up. The third round followed suit. It was hard to know what Scott was doing or what his gameplan could possibly be. I didn't expect him to be charging about the ring throwing haymakers and looking for an early KO, but I did expect some form of offence. Maybe the occasion had got to him. Again, he did nothing, and I took the round by simply controlling the centre and initiating what little action there was. Ditto the next, in which he actually threw a few punches but from so far outside of range that they had zero chance of troubling me. One weak looping right caught me, and I think that was literally the first blow I'd felt all night. A quarter of the bout gone, and I'd won every minute.

At this stage there was no denying the fight was shit. The crowd was doing their best, but we were giving them nothing to get excited about. Even as I was fighting, I was conscious how boring it must be and the way the noise levels had dropped it was clear that plenty were losing interest. But as far as we were concerned it was all going exactly to plan. I wasn't allowed to say this in the build-up when we were comparing ourselves to Barrera and Morales to hype the event and drive PPV sales, but I knew it was going to be a boring fight. I just didn't know it was going to be this easy. So, Shane's advice between rounds was absolutely spot on. You're winning so just keep doing what you're doing. Rounds five and six continued in the same vein as the first four. In the middle of the sixth, an uppercut on the inside landed flush on Quigg's jaw. It was the best punch of the night, and the way he immediately retreated and got his guard up high and glued to his face told me it had done some damage.

Into the second half and I felt I was cruising while Team Quigg knew they had to go for it. We got a few more engagements but it's all relative. An all-out war as promised, this was most definitely not. At the end of the eighth Joe Gallagher told Scott he was likely 6–2 down. He also told him Sky had me 6–1 up after the seventh. In fairness to Scott, he seemed genuinely shocked by this revelation – but he shouldn't have been, and his corner should never have let it get to this stage before telling him he was losing so badly. I guess it had the desired effect on him, however, as finally he came at me with something resembling intent. And at the same time, I was stuck in cruise control a little bit and didn't immediately adjust. The result was the final quarter of the fight being the most competitive, and at last the crowd had some action to cheer about. Starting the final round, we were convinced I only needed to be standing at the end to win by a country mile. I could have got on my bike and given the round away taking no risks. But I didn't like that he might be finishing with the momentum. I wanted to nip that in the bud and prove it was a very isolated period of success he'd had, and I had plenty left in the tank to turn it on if I wanted to. On my toes throughout, I made him miss and punished him time and again in the final three minutes.

It went to the scorecards and the first one read out declared Quigg the winner, 115–113. I thought I was hearing things. I knew I'd won the fight. Scott knew I'd won the fight. We embraced at the end, and it was nice to do that after so much animosity. With the noise and the commotion and all the other emotions that greet the end of a twelve-round world-title fight it's always tough to communicate with your opponent and catch everything they're saying into your ear. But I'm pretty sure the gist of Scott's message to me was, well done mate, you've got it. But now I'm stood there, and some American fella called Levi Martinez is telling me, nah, Scott Quigg won that, and he should take your belt home with him and leave you with nothing. It's hard to process what you're thinking as a fighter in those situations. It's another one of the countless examples of how fucked up the business of boxing is. And I say business because it is most definitely a business before it's a sport. These are career- and life-defining moments. Sometimes I watch football or golf and a player is standing over a last-minute penalty or a tournament-winning putt and the commentators are talking about the pressure and impact this will have either way on the player's career. As a fighter you're watching that thinking, wise up. There'll be another match in a few days. There'll be another tournament in a week. The true impact is minimal. The missed penalty or putt will be quickly forgotten about. The player in question will most likely bury the demon within weeks, and his career and life will continue in the exact same trajectory. In boxing, without even going into the macabre and very real prospect of life-threatening injuries, a loss can be all she wrote for a lot of fighters. But even worse than all of that is the fact that you don't even have complete control over your own destiny. If you miss the penalty or putt, no matter how gutting or what the circumstances, the outcome was all of your own making. You missed or made it. That night in Manchester, I did all the hard work, after years upon years of sacrifice and dedication, and now I had to stand there helpless and listen to how three people I don't know from Adam happened to think I did. Three people that, regardless of what they write on their scorecards, will fly home in their business-class seats the next morning and probably never think of me, my family or my life ever again. Three people that Christ knows who they're friendly with or where their allegiances lie or how susceptible they might be to outside influence. Standing in the ring waiting on the result, you suddenly get very paranoid. You see the big, smug promoter stood behind your opponent. The richest, most successful, most influential promoter in the UK. You see the Sky Sports cameras and team. The richest, most successful, most influential sports broadcaster in the UK. Your heart sinks as you consider that your opponent is a Sky Sports fighter and how if you beat him, they will no longer have an unbeaten world champion to market to their customers. It's a horrible, horrible feeling. But I'm one of the lucky ones. As a professional, I've never suffered the ultimate devastation of being robbed in the ring. The remaining two judges were slightly more competent than Levi and scored it 116–112 in my favour.

Even those two scores were far too close in my opinion. I tend to be extremely self-critical when scoring my own fights but, when I watched this one back, I struggled to give Scott more than two rounds. He won the tenth and the eleventh when he had nothing left to lose and had to go for it. And even then, I clearly won the last to put an exclamation point on the performance. That little burst from Quigg must be what gave rise to the post-fight narrative about him coming on strong as I faded. If I was fading so badly, how did I clearly win the twelfth? There was also the what-if chat. What if Quigg had started earlier? Like he deliberately decided to hand me the first six or so rounds on a plate for free and I had nothing to do with that. Or to be blunter in response, what if your granny had balls? Then she'd be your granda. I guess it was forlorn PR in case someone tried to make the rematch, but there was never going to be a public clamour to rerun that one. They also said Scott broke his jaw in the fourth round and that hindered him. Scott didn't break his jaw. I broke Scott's jaw. I did it by punching him really hard in the jaw, which, believe it or not, was part of my gameplan to win! I also think it was actually the sixth round I did it in but either way he deserves a lot of credit for going half a fight with that injury.

After sharing a ring with him, one thing I'd never question is Scott's heart and balls. Before leaving the MEN Arena that night I stopped by his dressing room to say goodbye. In my room there was champagne being drunk and Only-One-Carl-Frampton chants being sung. The contrast was jarring. You could see the damage that had been done to his jaw, but it was the defeat itself that was hurting him more. It was a sombre place and I felt like I was intruding a little. They clapped me out of the room when I'd given my thanks and well wishes, which was much appreciated. Then as I was walking out the door Wayne Rooney, who was there in support of Quigg, whispered something. I won't repeat it, but it was a friendly jab through gritted teeth as my victory had just lost him a bet he'd made public on Twitter with Rory McIlroy!

I met Quigg a few years later at Tommy Coyle's fight in Boston. Even then it appeared his initial instinct was to stare me out and start off on an aggressive footing like we were head-to-head at a press conference again. But as soon as I said, hello Scott, he loosened up and was sound. I definitely have no problem with Scott Quigg and never really did. It was good we had each other at that time and were able to enjoy a massive payday facing each other in a packed arena in a big domestic showdown. Fighters need those type of local rivalries to enter the public consciousness. We all dream of the glory nights in Vegas against the overseas superstars. But they tend to happen in the early hours of the morning, out of the sight and out of the mind of all but your diehard fans. We boosted each other's careers and I'll always be glad we had the opportunity.

***

The Quigg fight marked the end of my life as a super bantamweight. I'd just naturally grown too big to comfortably make 122lbs. It would have taken something very special and very lucrative to keep me in that division, and that fight just didn't exist. Both the IBF and the WBA were pushing mandatories onto me. The IBF's was Shingo Wake. With all the respect in the world to the Japanese fighter, that wasn't a match-up to get any pulses racing. The WBA's mandatory challenger was their champion in recess, Guillermo Rigondeaux. I presume part of the deal to get the WBA to upgrade Quigg to super champ ahead of our fight was to promise Rigondeaux an immediate shot at his belt, plus the IBF strap, after we were done. I often get asked why I never faced Rigondeaux, but the answer is pretty simple. At no time would it have been a sound career or business decision to fight him. He was a terrific fighter, a two-time Olympic gold medallist and a unified world champion. Technically and defensively, he was one of the best in the world. People maybe didn't like his style, but they had to acknowledge its effectiveness and the skill it took to fight that way. The competitor in me would have loved to have fought him to see who the best super bantamweight in the world was, but everyone around me correctly advised me to forget about it. As I say, boxing is a business before it's a sport and the risk-versus-reward calculation never added up for Rigo. His defensive style, how good he was, his lack of English, his lack of personality, poor management and promotion – whatever the reason, the Cuban wasn't a draw and forever remained on everyone's who-needs-him list. There was just no money in it. To put it in perspective, I got offered over five times more to fight Leo Santa Cruz. Even forgetting the fact that he was the one I had been chasing and, now WBA Featherweight champ, was in the correct weight class for me, on what planet would I have been better to accept five times less money for a more difficult fight?

There was no need for theatrics to make this one and it would have been hard to generate much hatred for Leo. Him, his brothers, his father, everyone we came in contact with, were good people. I remember during fight week we actually posed for a photo smiling together in the hotel lobby, Leo holding his young daughter while I had Rossa in my arms and Carla by my side. The contrast to my fight-week photos with Quigg is pretty striking! It was a fight the boxing world wanted to see, so it all happened pretty quickly. The fact we were both Al Haymon fighters would have sped up the process too. I vacated my super bantamweight belts and signed to fight Leo in New York in July. Giving away home advantage sealed my position as underdog with the bookies. This was the first time in my pro career I was not the favourite going in. It didn't bother me. In my head I fancied it. In my head I was the favourite.

We didn't want to make the same mistake as in El Paso, so we headed to the US a full month in advance and based ourselves in a place called New Rochelle in upstate New York. That gave me plenty of time to settle in and acclimatise. The town welcomed us with open arms. They even went so far as to announce a Carl Frampton Appreciation Day. And the date they chose? The glorious Twelfth of July! There was a ceremony and everything and during it I got chatting to some old boy, an ex-congressman or something from the area. He was telling me about his Irish ancestry, family from Mayo apparently, when he leant in and whispered, we were for the cause. I'm thinking, you're speaking to the wrong man here – see you later! We occasionally headed into New York City on the train. The first day we did, we got out at Grand Central and there was a busker playing 'The Boxer' by Simon and Garfunkel. I got goosebumps. I'm not superstitious, superstition being a mental weakness and all that, but I thought this must be a sign. I may not be the favourite with the bookies, but I know I'm gonna punch this fella's head in. I wish I'd used the song for my ringwalk, but I'd already decided on the 'Will Grigg's on Fire' tune. It was big at the time as he was banging in the goals for Wigan and had made the Northern Ireland squad for Euro 2016. Although I remember Michael O'Neill telling me he wished Grigg was as good as his fucking song! My da was in the changing room the whole time, and when I headed for the door I presumed he was part of the gang following me into the ring. He's one to shy away from any attention or limelight, but I knew he'd like to be part of it on this occasion. I was surprised then when everyone arrived and there was no sign of him. He only recently told me that Jake had tapped him on the shoulder leaving the dressing room and told him he couldn't be part of the ringwalk for some reason. My da, never wanting any fuss, just made his own way to his seat.

We fought in the Barclays Center in Brooklyn, an amazing venue. It sold well and once again there was an unreal atmosphere with both of us having thousands of supporters. And again, whether through sheer numbers or just individual effort, my fans made the most noise. I find that incredible and something I'm eternally grateful for. The size and passion of my fanbase is one of the things from my career I'm most proud of. I know Leo is from the West Coast and the US is a big place, but it is still the same country. His people didn't have to cross the Atlantic to be there like mine did. It was very cool to see a genuine global superstar like Rory McIlroy there as well. He'd unfortunately just missed the cut at the US PGA Championship, but instead of flying home he headed to Brooklyn to support me. I know a few boys who had actually put money on him to miss the cut as they reasoned he'd definitely prefer to watch me fight. The 'Ole Ole's kicked off as soon as the opening bell sounded, and I felt them with me. It is something I've thought about a lot, and in my mind there is no doubt that fans genuinely help an athlete. Look at team sports where across the board the home team performs better than the away. In a sport like football, the vast majority of teams are more offensive at home and set up a different way when on the road. There are other variables, but for me the vocal support being received is the biggest one. It gives athletes something. I've no idea if I could deliver the same performance if I entered the ring in a foreign country and only my ma and da were there clapping at ringside. There's an argument in boxing that at times a crowd roaring you on can work against you. An example being when you're struggling and should really run, hold or even take a knee. Instead, pushed on by the cheers and not wanting to let anyone down, you start swinging and get pulled into a war you've no business being in. Maybe for some, but I had proved throughout my career until then I can keep my wits about me regardless of the atmosphere. Quigg is possibly the best example of that. The atmosphere was unreal at the outset and even though I knew the fight was sucking the life out of the place, I stuck to a gameplan that delivered the easiest victory and the most boring spectacle.

There was more action in round one than in the entire Quigg fight. But then again, how could there not be when you're fighting Leo Santa Cruz. He was world renowned as an elite volume puncher, often throwing more than a hundred punches in a single round. It was a style that had already won him world titles in three different weight classes and kept him unbeaten since he turned pro, so we were confident he was going to take the exact same approach to facing me. My goal was to control the range of the fight so that he'd fall short with much of his work, to counter with hooks as he came

in, to vary the angles I showed him to deny him a rhythm and to hit
him hard in the early stages. The early hits would, I hoped, earn his
respect and ensure he didn't feel like he'd a free pass to just unload
a hundred punches every round all night long. It only took until
the second round for him to feel my power. He ducked under a
right hook, but I had a follow-up left hook already on the way that
detonated on his temple. He staggered and stumbled backwards
into the ropes. Had they not been there he may have ended up on
his back. The crowd went ballistic. I was saying to Leo, you can
throw a hundred punches if you like but I'll be throwing back in
between, and when I land you'll certainly know about it. And if I
land flush, that one blow will be worth more than your hundred.
The third continued in a similar vein, a right uppercut on the inside
being the shot of the round. My feet were frustrating him. I could
pick when he was launching his barrages and got myself back out
of range. I was causing him to fall in and punch leaning forward.
That completely negated his height and reach advantage, and kept
him in a range in which I could counter effectively. It was give and
take in the fourth. We both enjoyed success, but he landed nothing
substantial while I timed several left hooks that he definitely felt.
By the end of the fifth I'd apparently already thrown more punches
than I had needed to in the entire Quigg fight. Leo's style made you
throw, or he'd steamroller you with quantity as much as quality. I
fought the first half of the fifth on the front foot and the second
half on the back foot. I won both halves. Leo was guilty of lunging
forward as he advanced while letting his combinations go, and it
gave me the openings I needed to counter. If I wasn't five-nil up, it
was definitely four-one at worst to the Jackal. We put on a bit of a
show in the middle of the sixth, holding our feet and trading in the
centre of the ring. A bit of the macho stuff you get pulled into every
now and again. Ego is involved of course, but there is method to
the apparent madness too. I needed to keep reminding Leo that he

couldn't bully me like he did other opponents. If I was on the back foot it's because I chose to be, not because I was being pushed back or afraid to trade. He finished a little stronger at the end of the round and it may have been enough to nick it. But nothing was hurting me. We noticed he had the same hand-wrap guy as Gonzalez used. A real tough-looking Mexican with the dark weathered skin and all. His was the famous bandage-twisting technique that shocked Barry in Texas, so I had it in the back of my head throughout the fight that Leo could have the same advantage under his gloves. Whether he did or didn't, it wasn't enough to make any difference.

Into the second half. He started the seventh with that momentum but again I was landing the heavier shots. A toss-up between quality and quantity as to who won that one. Knowing the latter often convinces the judges I came out strong in the eighth and felt I did enough in another tough action-packed round. The crowd were still going nuts with standing ovations at the end of each round. Oohs and ahhs greeted every exchange. Sing-songs and chant duels raged in a friendly rivalry between different sets of fans. I'm a broken record talking about how amazing my fans are, and even in a fight as dull as the Quigg one they maintained an atmosphere. But when you're involved in a fight like this, when you can give them something as gripping as this to get their teeth into, it's another level. There was no let-up in the stands or in the ring. The ninth and tenth were well contested and we probably shared them. The eleventh was a bit of Rock 'Em Sock 'Em Robots, but a lot more educated than it may have appeared to the untrained eye. Both of us were very underrated infighters. We were adept at catching and throwing. It looked like we were just taking turns to hit each other. Some got through, some were blocked. I felt I did more hitting and more blocking. It was a mini war within the war. I went to my stool with gloved fist raised to the crowd who were all on their feet as the bell rang. The noise throughout the twelfth still gives me goosebumps just thinking about it. Leo must have known he needed a stoppage now, so he gave it his all. I read later he threw 114 punches that round, which is just an insane output. I could have got on my bike and saw it out at that stage, but it would have been doing a disservice to the previous eleven rounds of action. So, we went for it again. Right up until the final bell chimed, we stood toe-to-toe winging in the shots at one another.

We both celebrated, but I think deep down he knew he'd lost. It can be hard as a fighter in the thick of an action fight like that to accurately score it round by round, but you tend to have a feeling at the end whether you've won or lost. The scores were read out, one judge having it a draw while the other cards read 116–112 and 117–111. The six-point margin made me think, there's no way that's for Leo. When Jimmy Lennon Jr spoke those three little words, 'And The New ...', I erupted.

Jim Gray interviewed me in the ring immediately after. I told him that I wanted to be in fights that would be remembered for years to come, and that was certainly one of them. When Jim asked me what it means to be the first two-weight world champ from Northern Ireland, I joked that hopefully it means I don't need to buy a pint for the next twenty years. But it meant much more than that. This was my greatest achievement in a boxing ring. Leo was a massive name in world boxing. An undefeated, three-weight world champion, ranked in *The Ring* magazine pound-for-pound top ten. I was moving up in weight and travelling to this country. We were both Al Haymon fighters, but everyone knew Leo was his favourite. Leo even named his son Al! I was an underdog with the bookies, and the majority of US media had written me off after my Gonzalez and Quigg performances. To do what I did under all those circumstances was special. People asked whether it was the greatest performance by any Irish professional fighter ever. That's a big shout and it's not for me to say, but I don't think I'm being too arrogant to suggest it should be part of the conversation. It was certainly great enough to get individual recognition from the highest source in boxing when *The Ring* magazine made me their fighter of the year. That was just a totally unreal honour. Someone recently described it as like winning the Ballon d'Or in football. This is something that dates back to the 1920s and I was the first winner from Ireland and only the fifth from Europe. From the British Isles, only Ricky Hatton and Tyson Fury had received the award. That year, it was between me, Terence Crawford, Manny Pacquiao, Vasyl Lomachenko and Roman Gonzalez. I mean, just look at those names. Then you look at who has won it over the previous hundred-odd years. Joe Louis, Sugar Ray Robinson, Rocky Marciano, Muhammad Ali, Joe Frazier, Sugar Ray Leonard, Tommy Hearns, Marvin Hagler, Mike Tyson, Floyd Mayweather to name just a selection of the all-time greats on the list. That's there forever. For generations to come, boxing fans will read those names and talk about these legends and their deeds in awe. Then they'll ask, who the fuck was Carl Frampton! It took me a while to chase down a *Ring* belt because they weren't handing them out for a few years there, but it is one of my most prized possessions. I was lucky enough to be named the Boxing Writers Association of America fighter of the year too and travelled to the ceremony in New York to collect their Sugar Ray Robinson Award. I almost felt a bit embarrassed when I went up on stage to accept it. Looking out over the audience at all these legends from past and present, and many current or future Hall of Famers, I couldn't help wondering whether I was really worthy of the adulation. Like I say, it was all just incredibly special.

The celebrations in New York the day after I beat Santa Cruz are legendary. We spread the word to head to a bar called Annie Moore's where I'd done a press thing a few days earlier. Everyone was warning me to take it easy, that I'd just done twelve rounds and as we were starting at lunchtime it would be a long day. Yeah, definitely, I agreed. Then, as soon as I walked through the door someone hoisted me up onto their shoulders and gave me a pint. I downed in one go, the place erupted and that was that. I went full Frank the Tank. While I was still vaguely sober enough to do so, it was great being able to interact with fans who'd made the trip. It still humbles me to think of people spending their hard-earned dough to travel the world and watch me fight. Keith Dallas, a former boxer who now helps out in the Midland, sold his car to be able to go to New York. Another fella I met recently told me how he'd taken his deposit back on a flat he was going to move into in Hamburg so he'd have enough for flights to the US. It makes me emotional thinking that I received that level of support throughout my career. And it's why I'll always make an effort to express my gratitude when given the chance. In Annie Moore's, I stuck five grand behind the bar and let everyone go for it. I thought it'd last most of the day. Inside an hour a barmaid came up and said that's the five grand gone! So, I put another five grand down, this time with some rules in place to stop randoms walking in and ordering ten quadruple whiskeys at a time. It wasn't long before I was in an absolute state, so those close to me decided to get me out of the madness. We headed to the rooftop bar of the hotel where our mates Mags and Colin were staying. They actually got engaged that trip. I was so poleaxed, however, that I was soon put in their bed for a sleep while everyone else continued the party. People took it in turns to sit in the room and keep an eye on me, with one fella sitting himself on a chair to do the first shift. An hour or so later a mate came down to take over and found my guardian curled up on the bed beside me. A bit weird he thought, but woke him, ushered him out, and positioned himself on the chair to begin his watch. After a few seconds, he felt his arse getting wet and jumped up in disgust. So that's why your man had changed position! He then sat on the bed beside me instead. A few seconds later, he leapt up again. Jesus Christ, he said. How many times did that fella piss himself in here? The unnamed pant-wetter has never lived it down, and needless to say Mags and Colin didn't get the romantic engagement night in their bed they'd been dreaming of.

***

Although I wasn't too sure myself at the time, there was apparently a rematch clause and so I was contractually obliged to get straight back in with Leo again. Whether you agree with them or not it's relatively standard that a champion's team will use rematch clauses to protect their man, so it neither surprised nor bothered me. I don't remember any negotiation over date or venue either, but although anywhere near the West Coast of the US was going to be Leo's territory, I was willing to deal with that for the chance to fight in Las Vegas. Leo tried in vain to convince everyone that Vegas, just three hours from his home, was neutral and that he had been the away fighter in New York! Headlining in Vegas is a dream for any fighter, so to go do it at the MGM Grand as a world champion was going to be something I'd remember for the rest of my life. I got goosebumps when I arrived on the strip and saw my face on a massive billboard beside the likes of Britney Spears and David Copperfield. That's pretty surreal stuff.

We followed the template from the first fight and flew out to the US about a month ahead of the fight. The changes in time zone and climate are even more pronounced when you travel to the West Coast, so it was vital I got settled in Las Vegas early and adapted to my new surroundings. I'd been sparring twelve rounds in London before we left, madness in itself by the way, but my first session in Vegas saw me have to stop after five rounds. It's amazing the toll the travel takes on the body, but it was only a couple of days before I was back firing on all cylinders. We rented a house from the American welterweight Robert Guerrero in which to base ourselves. Located in Blue Diamond about half an hour west of the city, it was the perfect spot away from the hustle and bustle of the strip. The first fortnight went well. It was me, Barry, Shane, Jake, my sparring partner Jon Fernández, Josh Taylor, who was on the undercard, Darryl Richards, and a documentary maker called Tom Magnus, who was doing something for the BBC and capturing more footage for a feature-length documentary we'd been working on covering my entire career. I didn't like it that my mate Conrad Cummings, who was a big part of the gym and had just been unlucky to lose a decision I thought he won, was kind of shunned and not included in any plans. I later invited him out and covered the costs myself, which seemed to annoy the McGuigans for some reason.

Barry was a firm believer that a boxer should be kept away from family when preparing for a fight. Partly down to the living-like-a-warrior-type thing, but he was also paranoid about a fighter picking up a bug or something from your wife or kids. Even when I was fighting in Belfast and my house was a couple of minutes down the road, he'd make me stay in a hotel and hated it if I said I wanted to nip home to see Christine, Carla and Rossa for an hour. But I saw where Barry was coming from, so I went along with it. I'd go to England for my camps and be away from home for months on end. For me, that was the toughest part of being a boxer. Most say it's the weight cut – and don't get me wrong, that was never fun – but it killed me kissing my wife and kids goodbye, knowing I wouldn't be seeing them for a long time. I wouldn't say I ever got used to it as in it became easy. But it became ingrained in me, and my body and mind became accustomed to this being the natural state of preparing for a fight. No kids, no wife, no mother, no female influence at all really. It was gym or back in the gaff with other fighters. My world for a couple of months became a lads-only dynamic so those first couple of weeks in Vegas was business as usual. Then the girls arrived.

Two weeks out, Sandra, Barry's daughter Nika and Shane's wife
Sophie entered the house. As if we're on *Big Brother* and it had all got
a bit stale, so the producers send in a wild card or two to spice things
up. It wasn't like there was loads of space when there were eight of
us staying there, but now we had twelve to accommodate because
Shane's gym assistant Josh Pritchard arrived out too. Jon, who as
my lead sparring partner is possibly the most important guy there
and certainly the one after me doing the most work, had his own
bed before the newcomers arrived. Now though he found himself
sleeping in a hallway on an inflatable mattress. It was insulting to
Jon, and it embarrassed me. It also meant he wasn't getting ideal
preparation to get himself up each morning and help get me into
the best shape to defend my world title. The other big impact was
the complete change of dynamic and atmosphere in the house. I
love my wife. She's my best friend and the person I always choose to
spend my time with above all others. But it had been hammered into
me from day one that when you're getting ready to go to war, you
need a completely different environment and mindset. You have
to focus fully on the fight and nothing else. You surround yourself
with other men, other fighters, other people that are shedding their
own blood, sweat and tears each day alongside you as part of the
preparation. Also, as the fighter is the person in the group putting
his life on the line to provide for everyone else, it's all about you. It's
all about the fighter. Whatever the fighter needs to be comfortable
and be in the best shape mentally and physically, that's what the
fighter gets. That house in Blue Diamond for the final ten days was
anything but that. For starters, I couldn't help resenting the fact
that I'd been forbidden from seeing my wife or kids but the same
rule didn't seem to apply to my manager or trainer. If the big worry
was catching an illness from an outsider, are they saying Christine
is more likely to be carrying a bug than Sandra, Nika or Sophie?
It couldn't possibly be that so it must be the need to keep me in

this warrior frame of mind, focused on taking myself to the limit and trying to punch another man unconscious. Well, I can promise you the atmosphere in the house became the furthest thing in the world from an eve-of-war army barracks. From a male-only zone, there were now three females. More than that, the females were the mothers, wives, daughters and sisters of the men helping me to get ready. People change a lot in those circumstances. The easiest way to explain it is that it became a very girly house. Lots of sitting around and chit chat about nothing. Simple things like the music being played or the programmes on the TV all become very different. We had a chef come in each day to prepare our meals. A nice fella, he came across as a camp Mickey Rourke. At the start he'd come in, cook the food, make simple conversation then leave. When the girls were there, he was suddenly hanging around for hours and the campness levels went through the roof for the time he was there. It wasn't a big enough house that there were different spaces to chill out and everyone could do their own things. So communal areas became dominated by the girls, and I found myself retreating to my room about 8 p.m. every night, bored and angry. I was on to Christine every night complaining. Telling her this doesn't feel like a training camp anymore. How could it when Nika and Sophie are there purely on holiday? It wasn't right and the whole scene put me in a really shit frame of mind in the run-up to fight week.

Once the fight-week obligations began, I got a room in the MGM Grand Hotel. Actually, it was much more than a room; it was a huge suite with its own massive living area. I thought it was unreal until the next day they swapped me to a Skylofts' room. It's in the MGM but like its own separate, boutique entity. There I had a room with two floors to myself, a steam room in the bathroom, big platters of fresh fruit delivered each day, butler service and all the rest. It was unreal. A special private elevator takes guests up to the Skylofts, and the guy bringing me up whispered into my ear that as a Skyloft guest they can get me anything, at any time, and be very discreet about it. In my head I'm thinking, does he mean hookers, drugs and firearms here?

'Nah, mate,' I said. 'Just a couple of fresh towels each day will be sound.'

The fight was in the MGM, but the place is so big that you still needed a car to collect you and drive you around the building to reach the entrance we were to use. On fight night, Barry, Sandra, Shane and the rest all jumped in the waiting cars and headed off. That left Christine, Jake and me waiting for the next one. We hung about for a while, but nothing arrived. Jake made a few calls but had no luck. Finally, he suggested we just walk it. I'm there with all my gear on my back, my wife on my arm, and about to get into the ring for the biggest fight of my life – but being me, I just said, aye okay let's go. It was mental. We had to run across about eight lanes of traffic at one point. Then we got to a door, but of course it wasn't the right door for us. The security woman just starts shaking her head saying we're not supposed to be there. They're always extremely anal about security in the US, but you can understand why and the people on doors are just following orders and doing their job. Even so, it's a bit crazy when I'm pointing to the lanyard around her neck saying, see that fella there, that's me, I need to get in here to fight or this has been a big waste of time for everyone! Finally, she was convinced.

Despite that little adventure, I got into the ring in the MGM Grand on 28 January 2017 fully expecting to beat Leo Santa Cruz again. There was a lot of talk that Leo was going to box more this time. It was said publicly – before, during and after the first fight – that his father, who trains him, wanted him to box against me. In between rounds in New York, you can hear him imploring his son to get on his toes and use his physical advantages. But for whatever reason, he didn't do it in the Barclays Center and Shane was adamant he wasn't going to do it in Vegas. Speaking to the Irish News during fight week Shane said,

'He's talking crap and trying to lead us up the garden path by saying, I'm going to box more and use my reach and distance. He can't do that. How can a guy programmed to do things suddenly change? He is going to have to do what he does best, only a bit more and hope for the best.'

That was all I'd heard throughout camp as well. Basically, I'd prepared for a rerun of fight one and nothing else. David Haye was around us that camp and he talks about how not only did we focus a lot on the first fight but we only focused on the rounds I did well in, as if we'd simply repeat those in Vegas twelve times. It only took a round to realise we'd made a massive mistake. This was a completely different Leo Santa Cruz I was facing. He was on his toes, controlling the range, peppering me with jabs and countering to great effect when I attacked. Then when we planted our feet and traded, he came out of those exchanges on top as well. He won that first round convincingly and it set the tone to a large extent. I was probably a couple of rounds down before I had any real joy, and that came when I stopped marching forward. But I couldn't find and maintain a rhythm to build on the small pockets of success I enjoyed. Carl Froch on commentary said I looked shocked by the tactics Leo was employing and he was right. I shouldn't have been, but I was. This was a more patient fighter in front of me. A more calculating fighter. In our first meeting he threw over one thousand punches and lost quite clearly. He'd end up throwing less than nine hundred in Vegas, but he was the man in control. The sixth and seventh were close rounds, but his flurries at the end might have swayed the judges. I was convinced I won the eighth and that he was starting to tire, and I looked for confirmation of that when I sat down. Dr Anderson who was doing the cuts nodded and said, great round Carl. But then Shane told me I'd lost the round. Fuck me, I thought. If I lost that one, then I definitely lost the others I had marked down as close affairs. I don't know if Shane genuinely thought the eighth was Leo's round, or whether it was an attempt at reverse psychology to fire me up, but it backfired either way. I went out and forced the action again like I had early on, and that just played right into Leo's hands. I got ragged and I fell short with my punches, leaving me open to easy counters. I stood and traded in places and came out second best. By the time I stood up for the final round, I felt like the fight had slipped away from me in the preceding three rounds. I went for it in the last, and I probably did enough to earn the round, but deep down I knew I'd come up short. The judges agreed, scoring it 114–114, 113–115 and 113–115 to the new champion. I could only applaud and readily admitted in my interview that I'd no excuses, that the best man on the night had won the fight.

This was a new experience for us as a team: me losing a fight. Some people dealt with it better than others. While I went with the doping guy to give a urine sample, Shane threw a bit of a hissy fit in the changing rooms. Christine was there talking with Ruth Gorman from UTV, and they saw the whole thing. Carl was shit, Shane said. Fuck this, we're never coming back to Vegas, they all wanted us to get beat. So on and so forth, blaming everyone he could think of. Sophie and Nika are putting arms around him consoling him and telling him it's not his fault, that he's a great coach! Geraldine Davies, a woman with decades of experience in boxing from working with the likes of Frank Maloney and Lennox Lewis, was working for Cyclone at the time. She witnessed it and actually came up and apologised to us about it. The next night I went out with Christine and a few friends on the lash to drown my sorrows. As usual, I couldn't handle my drink so was plastered by the time we were back in the room. Shane and Sophie had come up by that stage and Christine, never a shrinking violet, tells Shane he was out of order the way he acted in the changing room and the way he was talking about me. Shane starts slabbering back telling her she's talking shit, so Christine said to Sophie, you were there, isn't that what he said. Caught in the middle, Sophie just bursts out crying and they left. The next day an interview Shane gave the *Belfast Telegraph* was published. He just lashed me. 'Carl's feet were not very fast.' 'In the changing room he seemed a little bit drowsy.' 'He became a bit too predictable, walking into hard shots and got caught far too square.' 'If he had used more head movement then it would have been different.' 'He was trying to force it too much.' I could go on. It's disappointing to see your trainer speak like that publicly the day after a defeat. It wasn't a stellar performance, but I'd lost a majority decision in Vegas against an elite fighter. Had I picked up one single round more, it would have been a majority draw. And regardless of the manner of the defeat, blame should be shared. Ultimately, I agree it always comes down to the fighter who has to actually climb through the ropes, but no one had any problem sharing the credit when I won so why the different approach now that I'd lost. It was also clear he was on the defensive because he'd been picked up on Sky Sports by Johnny Nelson for giving me shit advice between rounds:

'I'm a bit disappointed with Carl's corner and I say this as a big fan of Shane McGuigan. I didn't think the corner was very helpful. We heard every round what Carl was doing wrong but we weren't actually told what he needed to actually do. I found that very frustrating.'

That was a big blow to Shane's ego, so he was making sure the narrative was changed to how shit I was. I would never have done it and thrown him under the bus back then, but a big part of me wanted to give my own interview and say how insane it was that we didn't prepare a Plan B. How naive we were to treat a three-weight champion like he was one-dimensional and wouldn't make any adjustments after suffering the first defeat of his career. How the final two weeks stuck in a house with Shane's mother, sister and wife had been horrendous preparation for a bout of this magnitude. Of course, I didn't. And for the first time ever, it went quiet between me and all of the McGuigans for a few weeks. Then it was me who reached out to Shane. We'd heard from fighters in the gym that he'd apparently been badmouthing Christine, calling her a cunt and everything. I should have been onto him in a flash asking him who the fuck he thought he was speaking about my wife like that. It hurts me now thinking back, because instead of doing that I'm sending messages saying things like, tensions were high; it's okay, don't worry. That I'd never criticise him as a coach and that I'd improve and perform better and beat Leo in the decider. Anyone else would have just knocked his cunt in.

I was never given the opportunity for revenge against Leo. It turned out that when Barry asked for a rematch clause in the contract of the second fight, Al told him he expected me to win and that it wouldn't be necessary. Instead, he offered his hand in a gentleman's agreement, going as far as to say Leo would travel to Belfast for it in the summer. A handshake. No standard rematch clause in a contract, just a handshake. It was a level of naivety that is scarcely believable. But that's where I was. Leo had his title back and had zero intention of even fighting me again, never mind doing it in front of 25,000 at Windsor Park. I was licking my wounds at home, feeling a distinctly cold shoulder from my promoter slash manager and trainer, wondering what was next. It was going to be an interesting year.

CHAPTER SIX

MEET THE McGUIGANS

Just before I flew home to face Andres Gutierrez in the Odyssey Arena on 29 July 2017, Christine opened the door of our family home with Rossa in her arms to be faced with an officer from Her Majesty's Revenue & Customs. The taxman handed my wife a bill for £397,000 to cover VAT unpaid by Cyclone Promotions. He went on to say that I am the only director of the company they can track down and so I am on the hook for it. If I don't pay up, they can come for our assets. A window cleaner happened to be doing his job at that precise moment and he looked on with his mouth open. The door closed and Christine was left standing in a state of shock while our two young kids asked, what's the matter mummy? She tried to call me but I was in the middle of a spar so she called Jake, asking what the fuck is going on. When I got out of the ring, Jake's face was as white as a ghost. To fully understand how we all ended up in that situation, however, we need to rewind about eight years.

When I signed with Barry McGuigan back in 2009, I thought I was agreeing to allow Barry to manage my boxing career. Nothing more and nothing less. It turns out that what I actually agreed to was the entire McGuigan family controlling every aspect of my professional life. As it was happening in real time, it all appeared to fall into place organically or by happy coincidence and make perfect sense. But looking back now, I believe a plan emerged and I was earmarked for the most vital role within that plan – the cash cow.

Within a year of choosing Barry as my manager, I was spending as much time living with him and his family in their Kent mansion as I was at home with my own family. It's a massive house and at times it was difficult to keep track of the comings and goings, but wife Sandra and children Blain, Nika, Jake and Shane were invariably there when I was. Shane's future wife, Sophie, seemed to live there too. It goes without saying that the environment and atmosphere was very different to what I was used to from my own upbringing. The early days were weird and they were tough, to say the least. In comparison to my own family, the McGuigans all seemed to be into each other's lives and be constantly talking and giving opinions. There were plenty of times I'd be relaxing somewhere, on my phone or whatever, and one or several of them would appear and start talking the ear off me. I was always on the lookout for ways to escape to my own room without looking like an ignorant bastard. They were know-it-alls, but they were also nice to me, and I gradually got used to my new surroundings. Sandra would feed me and even do my laundry at times, while I started becoming more relaxed in the company of the kids. And they were all just kids to me, like I was still a kid myself. Shane and Jake are younger than me and Nika was a few months older. I think Blain was around twenty-five when I entered the McGuigan house, but he seemed like the biggest kid of all. He called himself a musician and his band mates were always hanging around too. They'd practise in a studio attached to the house and then chill out in this caravan they had out in the garden. They came in one night while Christine was visiting with Carla. We had these baby biscuits in a bag in the kitchen and they kept eating them. I had to say, 'come on lads, they're biscuits for the baby'. They were all very apologetic but when we came down for breakfast the next morning, they were all gone! That was Blain to me. Nice enough fella but hard to take too seriously. Jake was probably the one I was closest to. He was the one who would have a drink and be the most normal. Shane was okay, but a little strange and not as easy to immediately relate to. He was big into his personal training as that was his background at the time. Nutrition as well and diets were a big thing in the family in general. They were all very judgmental and quick to comment on other people being overweight. I think it was the caveman diet they were all into back then. Christine found it tougher than me to adapt to being around them all, despite the efforts of the girls to welcome her in. Nika took her shopping one day, and Christine told me later how she'd spoke at length about the problems her dad had had with managers or promoters during his career and how he'd never ever let something like that happen to me. Christine liked Nika and Sophie, but she was never going to see eye-to-eye with the family as a whole. That caused a lot of tension between us because as I was with them so much it meant Christine had to be as well if we were to spend any time together.

From the off, Barry was on me constantly. All day every day, whether I was in Kent, up in Manchester with Kevin Maree or back home with Christine. It was interesting getting to know him. He's famous for having a dictionary or thesaurus around so when the camera is on him, he throws in some big word and comes across as well-spoken and intelligent. Off camera he's a different character. There were so many occasions over the years when he'd act or say something so bizarre, I reached the conclusion that he must like to shock those around him every now and again. There are mild examples like when he watched Christine order a steak and chips in the Europa and told her if she cleaned up her diet, she could be very lean. Christine just told him she's very happy the way she is, thank you very much. Then there are awkward examples like when he took the piss out of Christine's disabled cousin. Ryan, who has sadly since passed away, had spina bifida and was wheelchair bound. He'd go to a lot of my fights with his da, Bernard, so Barry was aware of him and knew he was somehow related to Christine. One morning after a fight he came up to us and said, 'Did you see that fella in the wheelchair last night rolling up shouting my name and asking for a photo?' Then he did a horrifically offensive impression of someone with a severe disability speaking. Christine just looked at him and said, 'Barry, that's my cousin.'

If I'm being honest though, lots of different people warned me off Barry at the very beginning, urging me to be cautious in trusting him with my career. But boxing is a dirty business in general and there are a lot of different egos at play, so I squared it in my own mind that these were individual and personal grievances rather than widespread beliefs. His public image seemed so good outside of Northern Irish boxing circles as well, so I wondered if it was all just a bit of jealousy back home. Billy McKee never wanted me anywhere near the McGuigans and he never tried to hide that opinion. My da wasn't happy I'd signed with them either, but he doesn't say much. He lets me make my own decisions and my own mistakes. Then, for my sake, he made an effort with them. They were my team whether he liked it or not, so he felt he had to support me and support my career. He could just never get over how stingy they could be. There are so many examples, but the one my da always recalls is Barry getting a round of drinks in at Carla's naming ceremony. It came to around £19.80 or something similar so Barry handed over a twenty-pound note. My da was helping him with the drinks and couldn't believe it when Barry then stood at a packed bar waiting patiently for his 20p change!

People were always quick to tell me little anecdotal stories about Barry, trying to open my eyes to what he is. Several involved fans looking for autographs away from the cameras. Christine's ma says

she was walking down Castle Street with their Denise years ago
and saw Barry outside Eastwood's Gym. When she asked for an
autograph for wee Denise, Barry brushed them off and said he was
in a hurry. I remember being in Dublin Zoo one day and some
punter asked for a photo. After he took it we chatted for a bit, and he
told me about meeting Barry somewhere on a school trip and when
a few of the kids asked for an autograph Barry told them he didn't
have the time. He said that him and his mates had hated him ever
since. It was a common theme but back then I decided to ignore
that noise and judge it for myself. And as far as I was concerned,
Barry was doing all right by me. He wasn't fulfilling every promise
– learning a trade in case boxing didn't work out never materialised
and neither did the car mentioned at the outset, for example – but I
was fighting regular, being paid okay and I believed my career was
on the right path.

It's hard to pinpoint the exact moment when each individual
McGuigan became an earning member of Team Frampton. I've
explained how I was gradually manoeuvred away from Gerry
Storey to Shane via Kevin Maree, and that sort of assumption of
a position by stealth happened across the board. Whenever Barry
started doing his own little shows in the Ulster Hall for me to top
the bill, Sandra suddenly morphed from the chatty woman who
sometimes washed my training gear in Kent into the business mind
behind the shows. None of the kids was involved then, other than
Shane helping with the training. Barry was the promoter; Sandra
did a lot of the work; and they had a guy called Fergus Turner, who I
think provided some funding. There was invariably always a money
man somewhere behind the scenes who could fund everything.
He'd hang around until they fell out with each other or someone
with deeper pockets came along. After Fergus it was a lovely guy
called Christian Saunders who was known as Nelson. He gifted
them the dough to get the gym in Battersea going and did a lot

more for them over the years. He was a good man and unbelievably generous with his money. He flew Barry and Shane first-class to Vegas to watch Mayweather versus Canelo Álvarez, and Jake and I the same for another Mayweather fight once. In return, Nelson liked to come in and do sessions with Shane. I couldn't believe it then when Shane had a bit of a moan to me that Nelson was taking liberties and was talking about needing to start charging him. It's hard to wrap your head around that type of mentality. To be so focused on the money and so determined to squeeze as much out of everything for yourself. I remember Shane said to me I could stay in his spare room while in camp. I was grateful and was going to, then he started talking about rent. I'm on seven figures now and he's getting 10 per cent. Across Gonzalez, Quigg and the two Santa Cruz fights he probably earned half a million off me, so I thought he'd let me crash for free in a spare room he wasn't using – but obviously not. I politely said thanks but I reckon I'll just stay in a hotel, mate. That worked out more expensive for me, but it was the principle.

So, within barely a year of turning pro and signing a management contract with Barry, another two of his family, in the form of his wife and youngest son, were already on board. Jake was probably next – although again, the lines were constantly blurred. Then, after the Matchroom fallout, Blain was pulled in and dressed up in a suit to act as a promoter when we started doing our own shows under the Cyclone banner. Jake had a real job with some sports agency in London, so I guess there was a semblance of logic behind him doing something for the business. But I was always embarrassed when I had to act like Blain was legitimately my promoter. By this stage I was a European champion talking about moving to world level, and rather than a Bob Arum or an Oscar De La Hoya or an Eddie Hearn representing me, I had the fella who stole my kid's biscuits and would arrive to work on a skateboard. It was humiliating but I swallowed it because I knew it was just for show, and I trusted Barry that he was doing the real work in terms of promoting my career.

It was a genuine trust I felt towards Barry and his family. They spoke of me like the fourth son now. Barry always did a great job bigging me up in the media and while I was constantly reading all this lovely stuff he was saying about me, it was impossible to imagine he didn't have my best interests at heart. The trust was absolute and led me quite quickly to a situation where I just did exactly as I was told. My career was going well, so why wouldn't I listen to what my promoter, manager, advisor and trainer were telling me? When I won the European title in early 2013, I realised I was in a position to start earning the sort of money that required me getting financial advice on how to handle it all. I hired an accountant in Belfast, and they emailed Sandra in April of that year with a simple breakdown of how they saw it working. Basically, I'd set up a company and all the money I earned would go into it. I'd then pay out any expenses, which would include trainer or manager fees and the like. Sandra's response was to tell me they didn't know what they were talking about. That they didn't understand how boxing worked. Her and Barry then organised a meeting for me with their accountant, Jeff Lermer. The pair of them went with me to the meeting. And at the end of it, Jeff Lermer was my accountant too. I was so naive or whatever you want to call it that I didn't think twice about the fact their accountant was now also my accountant. Ditto when it came to someone advising on commercial or legal or any other matters you could think of. If a contract was put in front of me and a McGuigan told me it was good for me and fine to sign, I signed it. We were a team. If I do well, we all do well, so why would they do anything other than the best by me?

I was made to feel that from day one, but it rang especially true in my ears once we left Matchroom and went on our own, with me promised a 30 per cent share of the profits Cyclone made on shows. It was an us-against-the-world-type mentality then. And we were the good guys. Everyone else was a cunt. Hearn was robbing me. Warren was trying to get out of paying me. I spoke to Richard Schaefer once at a media day ahead of Santa Cruz II and Sandra was over in a flash straight after. She was livid, asking me what the hell I was talking to him about. We hadn't been talking about anything really. We were just shooting the breeze because we found ourselves next to one another. She went on a rant that the likes of Schaefer and other high-profile boxing figures are snakes who are always going to badmouth the McGuigans because they're worried about them entering the US market. It was delusional stuff on so many levels, but I fell for it time and again. I believed everyone else in boxing was a scumbag and out to get us. I believed I needed Barry and his family to protect me and keep getting me the best deals.

There were only two things I ever queried back in those days, in and around beating Kiko the second time. The first was why I didn't have more sponsors of my own. I used to look at my opponents' shorts, or my peers within British and Irish boxing, and see them plastered with logos. Even the boys fighting at low levels, often away from the TV cameras, would tell me they could pull in a few grand a month from businesses to cover their training expenses or food or whatever. The bigger names, the guys fighting at the level I was at and beyond, then had recognisable brands behind them. I knew they were getting big bucks and, as well as the money, it raised their profiles and opened more doors for them. I'd look at these boxers on TV and wonder why a company would prefer them over me. Without blowing my own trumpet too hard, I'd compare myself and believe I was more talented, more articulate, often more likeable and a genuine world champion to boot. I remember asking Barry what the story was, and he just told me I didn't want to look like a racing driver, covered from head to toe in different logos. That threw me. Why do I not want that? Everyone else seems to want it. It's a short career that can be over with one punch, so why the fuck would I not want to maximise my earnings if all I have to do is print a company's name on my shorts. It made no sense, but I was stuck in a space where I just accepted things I was told. I just let it go. Then my fight shorts would arrive and there might be a random logo on it. In El Paso it was something with a cactus I'd never heard of. Against Quigg it was a company called Mosaic. I knew about them, but never saw any cash from being their human billboard. It was only a lot later that the penny dropped. These were essentially my sponsors. These were companies wanting to be associated with Carl Frampton and paying for that privilege. A guy called Ryan McGee who was involved with his da in Mosaic at the time told me they paid around £50,000 to get their logo on my fight shorts. God knows what the others paid over the years. I never knew because, in my opinion, Barry or Sandra or Jake or whoever went out and sourced the sponsorship were leveraging my name but then keeping the dough. They were telling sponsors my shorts would be clear of anything else, so it was a blank canvas for their brand. The other fighters were affected too. Conrad was refused permission to put on his gear the logos of local companies in Coalisland who wanted to give him a few quid. It would weaken Cyclone's sales pitch when they were selling their advertising space if someone else was already there. Then the money would come in and disappear again without me even knowing of its existence. It was a real eye-opener when I got away from them and had some transparency from the people handling that side of things for me. Despite the fact I was by then past my best and no longer a reigning world champion or *The Ring* magazine Fighter of the Year when my value peaked, companies were still all over me with offers. In the space of a couple of years I got over £300k into my bank account from companies like 32 Red, JD Sports, 11 Degrees, Everlast and R Kings. I can only imagine what I could have earned when I was on top of the world.

The second query I would half-heartedly raise from time to time was why I wasn't receiving anything from our profit-sharing agreement. That was the big promise to keep me sweet when everyone was in a bit of a panic after Matchroom walked away. Barry, my manager, had become pretty much unapproachable to discuss money or any business matters, so I would go to Jake and Blain. By this stage, Jake was really the one managing me. Their separate answers were almost identical, as if they were reciting lines they'd been fed. 'The shows don't make any money,' they said. 'We're lucky if we break even and obviously, we need a wage for our work too.' Like a mug, I just accepted it. I didn't do any of the things I should have done, didn't ask any of the questions I should have asked. Show me the accounts? What are all the expenses? Why do you keep doing it if we're just losing money each time? Who is paying your salaries every month if the show doesn't bring income into the business? I didn't have the balls at the time to push the issue. I didn't even sit there quietly and do a bit of the math myself. That came later, when the shit hit the fan and they had to open the books a little. And the truth was staggering.

For Kiko II, Ticketmaster confirmed they had £1,215,000 worth of tickets for sale. The place was packed. It was also confirmed that CMW sponsored the event to the tune of £330,000. BoxNation confirmed they paid £100,000 for the UK rights. Previously, because there was plenty of controversy as to why Cyclone was receiving so much public money, the Irish news reported that the Department of Enterprise gave £150,000; the Department of Culture, Arts and Leisure £100,000; and Belfast City Council £50,000 towards the show. Then, as Barry was never slow to tell everyone, over ninety countries worldwide paid for the rights to broadcast it. That's nearly £2,000,000 in the pot. From that two million, I was given a purse of around £145,000 – about 7 per cent of the budget. Show me another main event fighter who sells out arenas and only gets 7 per cent of the budget. All of them would tell me over and over again that I was the best-paid super bantamweight in the world. The inference being that I was greedy looking to earn more. But boxing doesn't work like that. Fighters' purses aren't plucked from thin air. Even if I was the best-paid 122-pounder, that was because I generated the most income by a country mile. If purses were calculated as a percentage of that income, no doubt I was one of the worst paid. Kiko was unfortunately also getting robbed left, right and centre, with four or five different parties leeching off him, so the pot to keep all those mouths fed was £425,000. That still leaves around £1.4m. Again, nothing was ever disclosed to me or explained to me in terms of the expenses involved when putting on a boxing event, but I'm damn sure it doesn't cost £1.4m! Especially given the standard of my undercards, which were notoriously weak. In my first fight away from the McGuigans, there were three twelve-rounders, including two world-title bouts, on my undercard. That night in the Titanic the only other twelve-rounder was Eamonn O'Kane against a 23–3 Lithuanian. It's hard to comprehend how much profit there must have been that night, but I was told it was zero. And 30 per cent of zero is still zero unfortunately.

That's jumping forward a little to when my eyes were finally opened, but back in real time I think the first moment I started to have any doubts over what was going on money-wise was when I received my purse after the Alejandro Gonzalez fight in El Paso. That was the debut fight under Al Haymon, and I was to receive a cool $1m. It was my first truly big purse, around four times the size of anything I'd been paid previously. The fact it was seven figures as well made it an extra special moment in my career. It was a strange feeling of deflation then when it hit my account and was around £360k. But my problem was I didn't really know what to expect. I knew I wasn't getting the full million, but deductions from my purses were never clear and never uniform. When you're only getting a few grand it doesn't really matter so much. Now we were into big numbers it obviously did, but other than understanding Shane got a flat 10 per cent trainer's fee I was never certain who else took what. One of the big problems was that my money never came to me until everyone else had been paid off. I presumed that was normal. Now I know better. As embarrassing as it is to admit this, I didn't even question it when I got that £360k. I just sort of mentioned it to Jake in passing, how it was less than I was expecting. He reacted with a bit of mild surprise and said it does sound low. That was the end of the conversation, and I never raised it with anyone else. That's how it was back then. The fight before, against Avalos, I'd been waiting months and months to be paid when I finally spoke to Jake and asked him what the story was. He blamed the CWM affair and even said his parents were re-mortgaging their own house to get me my money. I believed every word of it. I was then the one feeling bad and sympathising with him, telling him there's no rush and I don't want them to be struggling. Madness, but that's the dynamic that had been firmly established between me and Team McGuigan. I was just the dumb fighter. Do your work in the gym, Carl, then get in the ring and fight. Don't worry about anything else, we're all taking care of that for you.

Nevertheless, the seeds of doubt were definitely planted now. Events surrounding the Quigg fight then ensured they sprouted and grew. The purse split had been the biggest bone of contention in the run-up. I'd wanted 60–40 but, in the end, settled for 57.5–42.5. That was still a sizeable amount in my favour, but when I used it as ammunition in the verbal sparring we got into there was always a twinkle in Scott's eyes. At one stage he said to me he knew for a fact he was getting more money than me. I want to think, you're an idiot, Scott – the split is there for all to see. But he had a kind of calm, knowing smile that made me think he wasn't lying. Quigg always had his intelligence attacked but he later remarked that out of the two of us, he wasn't the one being fleeced by his own management team for years. Then there was Hearn's comment at the presser in Belfast: 'I just hope that all the people taking a percentage of Carl let him have some in the end.' Again, it was said with confidence. It didn't have the feel of a wild accusation in the heat of the moment. What's more, no one on my side reacted. Barry was sat a couple of feet from Eddie, and he just lowered his head as if he hadn't heard it. He wasn't slow telling Hearn and Gallagher they were talking nonsense, so why the silence now?

Christine was picking up on more and more things as well. She was with Sophie and Nika in the Midland Hotel and went to pay for her sandwich and soup. They told her, don't be silly, put your money away and just charge it to the Cyclone account. Over the course of that week, she realised all sorts of people would merrily charge food and drinks to this account. Christine mentioned it to me, and I was none the wiser. But in my head I start thinking, is her soup and sandwich coming out of my purse here! It turns out it was, and that was far from the most ridiculous expense I incurred, but it would be a long time before I knew that for sure. It was a long time before I received anything never mind knew what had been deducted. Despite fighting Scott Quigg in February of 2016, I didn't receive a penny until late December. More than ten months I was asking to be paid. Again, Barry wasn't engaged with me as a manager anymore, so it was Jake I chased repeatedly for this one. His new favourite line was that they're waiting so they can give me the money in the most tax-efficient way possible. He knew he brought me well out of my comfort zone talking about tax and things like that. So, I just swallowed it and kept waiting. It was bollocks, of course. A fighter gets paid and is responsible for his own tax affairs. But I'm all at sea now, with no idea who I can turn to for help or impartial advice. Shane got married that year to Sophie and I was invited to what looked like a castle in the hills of Mallorca where it was hosted.

It is by a very large distance the most spectacular wedding I have ever seen. I mean, the type of thing you'd see in movies. Or rather, if two movie stars married each other. Forget Christine's tomato soup, I'm now thinking, is my Quigg purse covering this as well?

That was my mindset now. I almost want to call it paranoia but, on the basis all my fears would eventually prove to be completely founded, I don't think that's the right word. I was looking at everything differently, trying to figure out how this business was being funded. We were a month in a hotel in New York before the first Santa Cruz fight. Myself, Barry, Shane, Josh Taylor, Conrad Cummings and Darryl the S&C guy. The rest of the McGuigan squad followed out later. Am I paying for all this? Every flight, every hotel room, every meal? Josh and Conrad are good mates, but they're just two other boxers fighting on the undercard. Surely, that can't be my expense? One night near the start, we all went out for dinner together and I stuck my hand in my pocket and paid for everything. Next time we're out, Barry says, don't worry about it, I'll get this. He then sticks it on the Cyclone bank card! My heart sank. Jesus Christ, I'm paying for this entire trip too then.

In the hotel lobby in New York during fight week, Christine found herself at a table with Sandra and Luis de Cubas. Unbeknownst to Sandra, I had just introduced Luis to Christine – so he was fully aware she was my wife. De Cubas wears different hats but he was there discussing promotional matters and, in particular, tickets for the fight that Saturday. At one point, while talking to Sandra but looking directly at Christine, he said, 'so that's coming out of Carl's purse?' In response, Sandra just nodded. When he left, Christine was straight onto Sandra asking what tickets they were talking about and who is getting them. Sandra brushed her off, saying, don't worry, Carl is getting the same purse as promised. But that was de Cubas' way of trying to alert us. He was just another in the long list of people who tried to warn me over the years.

Tickets were constantly a hassle with the McGuigans. Boxers always get comps to give to family, friends and sponsors – not that I had many of the latter to worry about! In the early days of your career you'd maybe get five or six, but if you're a world champion headlining the card you'd receive a lot more. Later when I was fighting on Top Rank or Frank Warren bills, twenty-five to thirty comps were no problem at all. And it would be agreed well ahead of time where the seats would be. Ten ringside, ten of the next best and five cheaper ones or whatever. Any special request above and beyond the contracted entitlement would invariably be met as well. With Cyclone, I reckon I got around fifteen if I was lucky. And there was never any clarity on it. It was more a we'll-see-what-we-can-do type thing. I used to go, cap in hand, asking if it might be possible to get a couple of tickets for my brother and sister, for example. Or Christine's sister and husband who travelled all over the world to watch me. More than once the response I got was, hopefully we can get them some ringsides but tell them to buy some cheap seats just in case. Unreal. I would have to buy tickets for people for my own fight just to avoid the embarrassment of not being able to source them a couple of seats. If I couldn't get them for my own brother and sister, then there was no point thinking I'd be given extra comps for uncles or anyone like that. What I didn't know at the time was that they were hoarding those tickets they'd taken off the ticketing platform and trying to sell some of them. These should have been comps for me and other fighters, but they were flogging them instead. I was absolutely scundered when it was revealed that they'd charged Rory McIlroy £1,280 to attend the Santa Cruz fight. It was an honour to have him there, and everyone from venue to TV to sponsors would have been delighted too. He's the type of superstar you'd pay to attend your event. But no, Cyclone had made him log onto his banking app and transfer them £1,280 before giving him and his mates a seat. There were others too; Colin Murray, the DJ and TV personality; Gary Lightbody from the band Snow Patrol. All told to cough up if they want to watch me fight. Each a major source of embarrassment for me when I found out. And God only knows how many others there were over the years.

The flipside was, the McGuigans and their partners, and their partners' families, and even sometimes the partners of those families, never seemed to struggle for a ringside seat. The vast majority of these people meant absolutely nothing to me, but there they'd be at ringside while I was fighting. More than that, they'd be all over the place in the fight hotel and even into my dressing room after the show. When I beat Kiko to win the world title, all I wanted was a little bit of time with Christine to chill for a second and try to soak everything in. She actually told her ma and a few others who were hoping to see and congratulate me just to leave it for a bit. Me and her headed back alone to the changing room and when we opened the door Shane's girlfriend was holding my new belt alongside her sister and mother as they posed for photos. Within minutes the place was rammed with McGuigans and their friends. It was insane. I've just fulfilled a lifelong dream and wanted to be alone or with the people closest to me. Instead, I'm asking for my world title belt back from my trainer's girlfriend's ma. Christine was disgusted. It happened all the time from there on in. None of them had been in Huddersfield or Magherafelt, but now it was glamorous there were dozens of them. Even before the fight there'd be people there that had no right to be. Josh Pritchard, Shane's wee assistant in the gym, strolled in with his girlfriend ahead of the Quigg fight. I didn't even want him there, never mind his bird playing on her phone. I couldn't believe it. This is close to the bell for the biggest fight of my life up until that point. I was raging but didn't know how to react, so I went and just stood facing the corner of the wall until Shane came over and asked what was wrong. I said, 'Get her the fuck out of here right now.' I don't know if she came back after the fight. There was so many crammed in it was impossible to tell. I tried to get into the toilet to take a piss for the drug test, but I couldn't because various girlfriends were doing their makeup. Again, totally insane. All these things really annoyed me, and I wish I'd spoken up more at the time. Christine always told me to make clear up front who was or was not allowed in my dressing room before and after fights. If anyone really wants to see me and congratulate or commiserate, they're all welcome at the hotel bar later. But the bottom line is I didn't have the balls to do that. I was always too scared to rock the boat.

More evidence of the McGuigan family's selfishness was on full display the morning after I beat Santa Cruz that night in Brooklyn. I'd made plans to stay on in New York for a week. Me, Christine, our kids, my parents and her ma were all going to enjoy a holiday in the Big Apple. The McGuigans were doing the same, so I'd asked them to book me the necessary rooms in the same hotel they were going to. Of course, no problem, I was told. That morning we all woke early and packed up to move out of the fight hotel and into our new digs for the week. There was no sign of the McGuigan clan at breakfast or as we were checking out, and me and Christine actually remarked to each other that that's a bit weird. They never got up early like that to do anything, so it felt funny. It all made sense once we tried to check into our new hotel. 'Sorry Mr Frampton, I don't see your booking here. Oh wait, here you are but you're a day early. You check in with us tomorrow.' No that's not right I say. But no worries, can we have three rooms now please? 'I'm very sorry, Mr Frampton, but we're completely booked up tonight.' Right at that moment the hotel-lobby elevator doors open and out pile most of the McGuigans. It dawned on me what had happened. They'd ballsed up the booking, so they all got up early and scrambled over en masse to make sure they got themselves safely checked in to the remaining rooms. Barry and Sandra were in one. Shane and Sophie in another. With Nika and her boyfriend in the third. They feigned surprise. Then they pushed the blame onto Geraldine Davies, who was working in the office back in England. Geraldine has decades of experience and is a very safe pair of hands so that seemed unlikely. Then they called it a miscommunication. I was angry, but Christine was absolutely livid. Right there in the lobby she's shouting at me to book some flights to Belfast, that this is fucking out of order and we're going home. Sandra was very uncomfortable because she'd never seen Christine that raging before. I'm trying to calm things down, saying we've a holiday planned so let's just get tonight sorted and then enjoy ourselves. Half an hour later, there's me, world champion having just headlined the Barclays Center and beaten a pound-for-pound great, dragging my suitcases around a boiling hot Lower East Side, trying to find rooms for me and my extended family. It was the final straw for Christine as far as her relationship with the McGuigans was concerned. We were back in the same hotel as them the next day, but barely a word passed between us for the rest of the week. My reaction should have been the same as Christine's, but as usual I was just trying to keep the peace.

The delays over receiving my wages were never-ending. In the Barclays changing rooms after the fight, I was given a cheque for the $500,000 we were officially declaring as the fight purse, minus the US withholding tax. For a split second, I was actually getting paid. Then Barry took it off me and soon after told me he'd ripped it up and that they'd later pay me in full. So I flew home empty-handed – now awaiting my wages for two fights, Quigg and Leo. Nevertheless, despite the fact I was chasing for two purses worth millions each, the McGuigans started hounding me for hundreds of thousands of pounds they'd suddenly decided I owed them! A guy called Rupert Phillips had come in to work with the McGuigans as some sort of financial consultant and he was pressuring Jeff Lermer to reissue historical invoices with the VAT element attached.

Basically, Cyclone were claiming I owed them over £200k in VAT dating back over three years. And the reason they had suddenly dreamt up this scheme was because they had just become liable to pay over £300,000 in VAT from the Quigg joint venture and needed invoices to net off against that. It was all over my head so Jeff broke it down in an email to me that August, not long after the McGuigans had dismissed him as their accountant. He used an example of me getting paid $1m. The McGuigans were now saying that was actually $833k plus 20 per cent VAT they'd paid me. Jeff was having none of it, though. He responded to Rupert making a number of points very clear. Firstly, it was known that my company was not VAT registered. Jeff had highlighted that fact to Barry a couple of years earlier in an email in which he wrote that I should be paid the net amount, with no VAT. Secondly, the reason my company was not VAT registered was because the payments to me were made on a profit-sharing basis, which would not attract VAT. Thirdly, he said no final invoices at all could be issued because I had not seen final auditable accounts of each fight to understand what I was due. What I'd received up until then was only a payment on account until proper reconciliation of the shows was produced. Finally, he also made the point to Rupert that even if VAT had been applicable, to use the above example I should have received $1m plus the 20 per cent VAT on top to make a total of $1.2m. I didn't know Jeff at all. I'd met him twice, and at least one McGuigan was there alongside me on both occasions. I also didn't really have a clue what was going on regarding the VAT issue, but I felt I needed someone closer to home to help me with it. But before I appointed Sean McCrory in Belfast to be my accountant in October, Jeff did his best to alert me to what was happening. An email that September read, 'I showed the previous payments to you as a profit share, therefore no VAT on the basis that was exactly what was happening. Was your position vis-à-vis Cyclone properly documented?' The question at the end was the red flag, but he went even further in a telephone call in which he said to be careful and gave me the impression that this lot were trying to screw me over.

Sean came in and did a great job for me. He took a look at the limited info and documentation I had and quickly concluded that it wasn't adding up. We organised a meeting in London that Rupert, Jake, Blain and Barry attended from the other side. Sean's what you'd expect from an accountant, straight as a die. He had a list of questions he wanted answered and documentation he wanted provided, and that was all he was interested in. For whatever reason, the majority of the answers and documentation was not forthcoming. Barry didn't say much but he was doing his hard-man act he puts on when someone or a situation is frustrating him. He kind of loudly exhales through his nostrils and stares at the person. I started to feel uncomfortable and bad for Sean as he's a regular nice man, but he didn't seem bothered in the slightest. He kept his cool and continued calmly asking the questions he'd flown over to pose on my behalf. The guts of it was, where the hell is my money? Connected to that, what the hell are these deductions? When I finally did receive a purse, there'd be no explanation as to why it was always a lot less than I was anticipating. Lump-sum camp expenses would be listed as a single figure. A massive single figure. An approaching-one-hundred-grand-type figure. I could have sparred Floyd Mayweather for two weeks and it wouldn't have added up to this much! There was missing money from non-boxing income too. A company called Benchmark arranged appearances for me. They paid Cyclone and, after their inevitable deductions – for what, your guess is as good as mine – Cyclone were to forward it on. The outstanding money there was increasing rapidly so that was another £60,000 to £70,000 Sean was chasing down. Sean kept plugging away, and the McGuigans kept ducking and diving. We didn't know it then, but it would take legal proceedings to finally get the answers we deserved.

On top of still not having received a penny or a cent for the Quigg or first Santa Cruz fight, we ploughed on ahead into the Santa Cruz rematch. This time I didn't even know what the purse was. As far as I'd been told, it had been $1m for Gonzalez and $1.5m for the first fight with Santa Cruz. Now I'm in everyone's pound-for-pound top ten I'm expecting at least $2m and preferably closer to $2.5m for the rematch. But everyone was very vague when I asked what the purse was. 'Around $1.75m' was the closest I got to any clarity. They used to have their story straight well in advance, but it seemed like they weren't even bothering to do that anymore. Jake slipped up as well during that camp when he pulled me to one side to tell me Josh Pritchard was going to fly out to join us in Vegas. 'We'll pay for his flights,' Jake said. I'm thinking, who is 'we' exactly, but okay. Then he follows up with, 'and okay to pay him a grand a week for being here?' What? Your kid in the gym coming out for a holiday. Maybe he'll squirt water into my mouth between sparring rounds. Are you serious? By the look on his face, he realised he'd dropped the ball. Normally he would never have discussed it with me. The normal way of things would have been Josh turning up and me not cottoning on he was enjoying himself on my dollar.

Things went downhill fast after Leo beat me. Suddenly, I was no longer the fourth son. Or if I was, Josh Taylor was now the fifth, and currently more favoured, son. It was as if they sensed I was on the way out and Josh was the man to now keep their business model running. Money dribbled in, largely thanks to Sean's persistence. A few weeks before heading to Vegas, I got my Quigg purse. I later found out Cyclone had received all the money in early July. So just the five months to forward on my share, then. Just after the Vegas fight, I got my first Santa Cruz purse. My understanding was I was fighting for $1.5m, but I later found out it was actually $1.665m all in. Cyclone had received a wire transfer of $1.242m in August of 2016, a month after the fight. They finally forwarded on my purse in February of 2017. A full seven months after I'd fought. Of that $1.242m, I received just £592,000. In Vegas, the promoter there gave me a cheque for the officially declared purse of $1m, minus withholding tax and other sanctioning fees. This time I batted the McGuigans away when they tried to repeat the old ripping up the cheque routine. I told my da to take it and not give it to Sandra. At least I had something I thought. At some point in my hungover departure from Sin City I lost the cheque, but Richard Schaefer was good enough to quickly sort me out with a wire transfer for the same amount. Schaefer was also good enough to disclose what the real pot was for that one as, needless to say, it wasn't the $1.75m I'd been told. His promotional outfit had wired a total of $1.948m for that fight, including $850,000 in January of 2017 to a Cyclone company and Cyclone bank account that I didn't even know existed. Barry, Shane and Blain representing Cyclone the promoter had taken their cuts out of the $1.75m they disclosed to me, presumably in the hope I'd never find out that the actual pot was closer to $2.2m.

The relationship between the McGuigans and myself was dead in the water now. As a fighter, they thought I was finished, and the exceptionally talented Taylor was coming through to replace me. They arranged a comeback for me against a Mexican called Andres Gutierrez in Belfast and told me I was basically on a ticket deal. A ticket deal is how novice pros start off getting paid at the beginning of their career if they don't have a proper promotional contract. The small-time local promoter will put on a show and give them tickets to sell. They then get a percentage of that cash after the cost of their opponent and a few other bits and pieces have been deducted. As the reigning *Ring* magazine Fighter of the Year, I thought I deserved a little more respect than being told you'll get X if you sell this many tickets, but the purse will drop considerably if you don't hit those targets. I didn't even care, though. Fuck them. I just wanted away from them now. The only thing I wanted was to win so I could leave on my own terms rather than being accused of only changing as if it was an excuse for the loss to Leo.

Camp was horrible. It was a terrible environment to be in. I was mentally all over the place and sparred awfully because of it. I hurt my neck as well, to the extent where I could barely keep my hands up. My balls have never been questioned since I first walked into the Midland, but it was clear I shouldn't be sparring with my neck the way it was. Shane forced me to complete the spar in which an average kid proceeded to punch the head of me. He was being the hard man outside the ropes, the brave trainer. A man who never turned pro because he once got some headaches after Frank Buglioni battered him in a spar. He had a mild concussion and that was it, he never fought again. Yet, he had no problem watching me get pinged repeatedly that day when I couldn't keep my hands up and protect myself properly. The last day of camp is normally the Friday before fight week so that I could jump straight on a plane and spend the weekend at home with Christine and the kids before checking into the Europa. This time, for reasons never explained, Shane told me we needed to do our last hard punching session on the Saturday instead. So, I stayed on in London on Friday night and got up early for the gym the next morning. Shane then texted me to say he couldn't make it. That I should go collect the keys from somewhere and do a sprint session on the treadmill. Apparently, there was no need for punching now. He gave no reason for not being able to do the session with me, although I know where he went instead. I interpreted it as a bit of a fuck you Carl, you're not worth the effort any more. I went to the gym on my own. Nobody else was there. I packed all my gear into a suitcase, clearing out everything that was mine, then locked the door and walked away. I knew I'd never be going back. It felt right.

Fight week was shit. There was so much tension in the air. Tension between me and the McGuigans but also in my own home as we dealt with the tax man's visit and demand for nearly 400 grand.

We went to Monkstown Gym as usual for our final sessions. Paul Johnson runs that club and he'd seen us go through the process on many occasions. But this time he could see it was a completely different atmosphere. Normally they'd all be around me and supporting me through all the sessions cutting weight. These are the worst moments for a fighter, and he needs all the moral support he can get. But ahead of Gutierrez, they all did their own thing while I sweated away, training with a sweatsuit on in the sauna. Shane even told Paul he had no interest in training me anymore because my heart was no longer in it. He hadn't said that to my face, but it was clear from the camp that's how he felt. The weight wasn't coming off and Shane finally said, that's enough. It's not a title fight, he continued, so no point killing yourself to make championship weight. Let's pay Gutierrez a few quid to keep him sweet and fight at the weight I can make. We headed back to the hotel, but on the way they talked me into having one last stab at losing the pounds by taking a hot bath with salts. I went along with it, delaying the weigh-in as a result. I was in such a bad state, they wouldn't even let Christine see me when she came to the room with some drawings the kids had done for me. I'd missed weight, something I'd never done before and would never do again. The bottom line is, it's unprofessional and it's unfair on your opponent. Really, I should have been ashamed and embarrassed, but the truth is I didn't care. I was mentally in such a bad place at that time that I just didn't care anymore.

Then that evening, things got even crazier. Blain pulled me to one side on the first floor of the Europa and told me Gutierrez fell in the shower. He said that he was pretty badly banged up and it looked like the fight was off. I couldn't believe it. No matter what else is going on, if you've prepared for three months, stepped on a scale, done your final head-to-head with your opponent, you're ready to rumble. To then be told you are not is devastating. But this was the McGuigan show so, rather than any concern for me, Blain was just whining about them losing money. I said, surely you've got insurance that'll cover your losses and he fired back, quick as a flash, that they couldn't get insured because of my injury. This is my minor ear injury from the first Kiko fight, four years prior. The same injury I'd had since then in every camp and fight. I'm thinking, if you can't get a boxing event insured because a fighter on the bill has at one time or another suffered an injury, then no boxing event anywhere on the planet would ever be insured. But fuck it, it's not even worth it. I left him and the rest of them to sort it out. My da called it a blessing in disguise. He knew I wasn't right mentally. Christine, as always, was blunter. She said she was expecting me to get beat and pulled me to one side after the weigh-in to say as much and that this was my entire career at risk here.

It was shambolic after the show was cancelled. My da had done his usual and sold tens of thousands of pounds worth of tickets for the McGuigans. They were now saying to some punters to go to their point of sale for a refund. Obviously, my da no longer had the money, though. He'd transferred it to whatever bank account he'd been told to. People are chasing him for their dough and it was stressful. It was his reputation, our family name, on the line. My da got two separate messages from people who were so angry with how he was being thrown under the bus that they offered to go down and fill Barry in. They were deadly serious offers. The night I should have been fighting, I went on the drink. I got a few voicemails from Barry in which he was pleading for me to answer his calls or phone him back. I never did. The following day I blocked all their numbers and handed things to the solicitors.

***

People ask me why it took me so long to see the truth. How I could have been so naive. Like, how the hell could I not have seen what was going on while it was happening all around me. I'm not sure I have a good answer for that, and it embarrasses me to think about things and admit that. All I can say is that they got me on day one when I hadn't a clue about life in general and certainly no idea how the business of boxing worked. Then they treated me well and gained my absolute trust. They created an environment in which I was certain we were all one team, when in fact everyone else in the line-up was united against me. And they were all on me constantly, quick to stamp out any semblance of resistance from me, all trotting out lines that now seem pre-prepared and coordinated. It was a world in which I had nowhere to turn, even when the penny started to drop and I began to ask a few questions. The standard situation in boxing is when you doubt your promoter, you speak to your manager. If you doubt your manager, you speak to your advisor. If you have queries about money, you can bring your own accountant in for a look. Maybe you have a commercial agent getting you sponsorship deals, so he's a separate independent voice. Your trainer is normally his own man, so he's another person you can rely on for an impartial point of view. I had nowhere and no one to turn to. It was one family most of the time. Anyone else I had access to was part of their business circle. I don't know what the hell happened. I felt smothered.

Maybe they noticed a weakness in my character early on. I am, or certainly I was, too trusting of people and their intentions. I made similar mistakes with other people too. A former friend put me on to a solicitor once to help me buy a house and it turned out he was up to no good, stealing stamp duty. The McGuigans possibly saw that naivety or gullibility or whatever you'd call it and exploited it. Others with stronger or more combative personalities handled them differently. I remember they tried to start charging Josh Taylor rent to use the gym. Madness obviously, but had they slipped it in on me in my early years with them I probably would have ended up listening to some ridiculous justification and paid it. Josh said no chance, and then had his own solicitor go through his contract with a fine-tooth comb and he found they'd tried to sneak it in there anyway. I'm not going to be too hard on myself, however. It does embarrass me, but I was the victim. And I was confident when I had my day in court that the truth would be revealed.

CHAPTER SEVEN

FRAMPTON REBORN

The McGuigans may not have thought so, but the rest of the boxing world knew I still had a lot to offer. Plenty reached out either directly or indirectly with a view to managing or promoting me. Strangely enough, there was no one proposing to do both of those very distinct and conflicting roles simultaneously. I flew to Las Vegas at the end of August to attend the Mayweather versus McGregor circus, and while I was there I met with a few of the interested parties. Luis de Cubas was at the front of the queue. He obviously knew me from the Haymon advisory arrangement and the Santa Cruz fights. De Cubas' big carrot was the promise of delivering the decider against Leo if I signed with him. He also expressed delight at finally being able to speak business directly with me, saying how shocked his side had been that I was never involved in any of the meetings they had with Cyclone regarding my career.

Next up was MTK. I sat down with Matthew Macklin and his pitch was pretty simple. If I was a free agent his company wanted to manage me, and they wouldn't charge me a penny. It sounded too good to be true, but then he explained it from MTK's point of view. Basically, having my face on their website, or their logo on my gear, was great publicity for them and would help the company grow and later attract more big names to their stable. And this was a stable that already included superstars like Tyson Fury and Michael Conlan and established world champions like Billy Joe Saunders and Liam Smith. Macklin said I was the type of clean-cut personality with crossover appeal he was looking for. MTK were a proven entity with a great track record. And they had boxers with nearly every top promotional outfit you could think of so it was good to know they could pick up the phone to anyone and shop around on my behalf. Fighters I knew couldn't speak highly enough about them. I was told it was transparent with them. What you see is what you get, and you don't need to be worrying about anything else going on behind the scenes. Also, with Macklin being Irish himself, there was always a big focus on driving forward Irish boxers and Irish boxing. My mate Paddy Barnes was signed to them, as well as top Belfast fighters like Jamie Conlan, Tyrone McKenna and Lewis Crocker. I knew those boys were naturals for my undercards and that would encourage MTK to push for big nights in Belfast for me. It was all music to my ears, and the kicker of a 0 per cent management fee made it a no-brainer. I'd been used to losing at least 40 per cent to Barry, Shane and Blain straight off the bat. Then, up to eighty grand's worth of expenses for things I had zero control over. Then, if I was lucky, a mystery amount hit my account six months later. To be told, you get all the money, and you handle your own expenses and fees yourself was a godsend. So simple, so transparent and I'd be so much better off at the end of the day. I signed with MTK, and it was one of the best decisions of my boxing career. I used to laugh at the bit of grief I'd get in the gutter press or muppets on social media, stuff about Frampton's gone to MTK for the dough and then the innuendos about where that dough originated. It was funny because anyone with the slightest knowledge of professional boxing understands how the money flows. MTK don't pay their fighters. It's the other way around. Their fighters pay them. Promoters get the cash from

TV, sponsors and gate receipts and then pay boxers. Boxers then dole out the cuts to managers and trainers, etc. All MTK ever did for me and other fighters I know of is drive the hardest bargains they could to maximise the amount a promoter was willing to pay for a fight.

The next step was to choose one of those promoters. Again, we weren't short of options. I had two priorities. The first was to fight in Belfast as often as possible and for one of those fights to be at the home of Northern Irish football, Windsor Park. The second was to earn as much money as I could, as fast as I could. I make no apologies for that second factor. No fighter ever should but given the fact I now knew I'd been robbed of big paydays and should have had a lot more in the bank than I did, I was determined to be more direct in what I wanted from the final years of my career. Finally, I was speaking up and demanding to fight as often as is sensible, for the biggest purses possible, and to know exactly what I'm getting before I sign anything. We decided a UK promoter made more sense for the initial comeback fights and that meant there were only two to choose from: my old pal Eddie Hearn or Frank Warren. MTK were extremely close with both men, so it was easy to negotiate on the front foot. In the end, it came down to two things – money and profile. When Frank offered more dough and said he'd make me the face of boxing on BT Sport, my mind was made up.

The final part of the puzzle before I could begin this new chapter in my career was to secure a trainer. I originally narrowed it down in my own mind to three; Adam Booth, Pete Taylor and Ismael Salas. My plan was to do a week with each to see how I liked their gym and coaching style. At the last minute, my da suggested Jamie Moore. Jamie hadn't really been on my radar at that point. He'd been working alongside Oliver Harrison in Manchester, and as Oliver's health deteriorated Jamie took over a lot of his boys. At that time, I think his main fighters were Tommy Coyle, Rocky

Fielding, Martin Murray and Stevie Ward, whom I knew from back home. I didn't know much about Jamie or his style of training, but I added him to the list and Salford became the first stop on the tour. A few days later, it became the last stop as well. I told myself on the flight over, don't get too attached to any gym too quickly. Go and spend time in each and then go home and make the decision calmly. But there was something about the atmosphere in Jamie's gym that made me feel at home straight away. BBC Northern Ireland had gone over to do a piece with me, and while the camera was rolling and the journalist was interviewing me Tommy Coyle unleashed with a fire extinguisher. He covered us and the camera in powder and the BBC fella was raging, telling us how expensive the kit was and all. Tommy and everyone else are pissing themselves laughing and I remember thinking, this place is mad, I'll have a bit of this! It could have gone the other way, I guess. The Welsh middleweight Liam Williams came to try out the gym before he opted for Dominic Ingle. As soon as he walked through the door, Jamie Moore's number two, Nigel Travis, debagged him and his cock fell out in front of everyone. Liam didn't even know who Nigel was. He kind of laughed it off and tried to take it well, but you could see it wasn't his type of thing. He left that day and never came back! It is undoubtedly weird behaviour, but I must admit I loved it from day one. I loved all the boys in the gym there because they were all my sort of people, all from a similar background to me. I enjoyed that feeling of being one of the lads again in a true team atmosphere in which someone is always up to something. Perhaps most importantly, it was the polar opposite of the environment I'd just left behind. I was now somewhere that felt like home. Christine used to say I acted differently when I came back from a camp in London with the McGuigans. Like I'd changed in certain ways she didn't like. But with the characters and personalities of Jamie and Nigel and their fighters, there was no chance of me changing at all from my true self. Sharing a flat with two lads from Northern Ireland in Stevie and Conrad helped in that regard as well. We get on very well and we were able to support each other through camps, in and out of the gym. The bottom line was, I immediately felt happy there. After so long being unhappy at work, that was an amazing sense of relief. It's always incredibly hard to kiss my wife and kids goodbye and fly to another country for a training camp, but if I had to do it three times a year, I'd rather spend that time with good people who I actually enjoyed being around. Me and Tommy in particular have become great pals. After one of my defeats he flew over to Belfast on his own just to see me in person and make sure I was all right. He's up there as one of the most genuine and generous people I've ever met.

So that was that. Jamie became my trainer. I didn't even do a day with the other three. That is no reflection on Adam, Pete and Ismael, whose records speak for themselves. They are top trainers and I'm sure they would have improved me in their own ways. But I was very confident in my decision and there have never been any regrets. And to be honest, there wasn't really time to do a week with four different trainers and then mull things over. I had a fight already lined up for November.

***

They labelled the show 'Frampton Reborn'. It was a comeback, and this was the first page of a new chapter. The hero can't die on page one, so the script was naturally written that I'd win this one and look good doing it. To that end, they offered me a few easy touches. But they were at a level I felt would have been a little bit embarrassing to drop down to. On one hand it's good for boxers to earn their money the easiest way possible in the ring, but people pay to come along and be entertained by us so you can't take the piss. I didn't think we should risk short-changing fans by putting me in with a guy at this stage of my career that wouldn't be competitive in any way. So the selection of the opponent was left up to me, and I hand-picked Horacio Garcia. With a record of 33–3–1, the Mexican was tough, experienced, hit hard and had never been stopped. There was no doubt he would come to fight and come to win, but I was confident I could handle him. I'd sparred him before and, despite his attributes, I'd dealt with him well enough to believe he was the perfect man to get back on the road to the top.

It was a short camp, I think we only had around five weeks to prepare for this one, but I enjoyed it. Jamie had told me at the outset that I already know how to fight so his job was just to refine a few specifics that he believed would make me a better boxer. He also said I'd been overtraining my whole career and advised a major reduction in the amount of sparring and the length of camp. If I stayed in relative shape between camps, then around eight weeks would be enough to get me fit enough and sharp enough to fight. I was used to twelve weeks, so we agreed to split the difference and do ten. But they'd be ten tough weeks, pushing myself as hard as ever. Everyone in Jamie's gym always did. It used to annoy me a little when I'd hear uninformed comments suggesting we were some sort of banter gym, just messing around and having a laugh all the time. Because everything got plastered over social media, some people would see footage of Tommy jabbing someone's neck with a hot spoon or Nigel leaving another poor victim with his bags around his ankles and jump to the conclusion we weren't taking our training seriously. Nonsense. From the start of each camp, when we were running at over 12,000 feet up Mount Teide in Tenerife, until the notorious bar-and-bag sessions in the gym, and everything in between, everyone grafted their balls off every single day I was there.

It was nice to be back fighting in Belfast again. Back to the Jackal's Den in the Odyssey Arena. Avalos, nearly three years previous, had been my last appearance there. I must confess, there were some lingering doubts in my mind about how the public would welcome me back. Barry was once the hero of everyone in Northern Ireland and I'd just had a very visible falling out with him and his family. Maybe everyone would side with Barry. Maybe all the people who had bought tickets to watch me previously were only doing so because of the relationship with him. These thoughts went through my head, but I needn't have worried. The place sold out as fast as ever. Perhaps the reputation Barry had within Irish boxing circles was beginning to seep into the public consciousness as well. A no-smoke-without-fire-type thing. Whatever the reason, it gave me a massive boost to know the people of Belfast had my back and were still behind me 100 per cent.

It was great to be getting properly paid as well. My base purse was over one hundred grand more than the Avalos fight in the same venue with the same ticketing revenue. Against Avalos I was a reigning world champion making a title defence. This time I was doing a ten-round comeback, coming off a loss. Yet I still got paid way more. Avalos had had a cheap seven-fight undercard, with Denton Vassell versus Viktor Plotnikov acting as the co-main event. This time, eleven other guys got the opportunity to fight on the undercard – including two world-title fights and another twelve-rounder. Yet I still got paid way more. And that's before taking into account the enormous difference in my fight expenses and fees now I was in control of the purse strings. Plus, the normal 10 per cent commission on your own ticket sales returned. The McGuigans had given me that industry standard at the outset, but it had disappeared in recent times. It was also nice that so many Irish lads got out on the bill. That's how boxing works and how you develop the talent coming through in each area. Just as me and many others got on McCloskey cards back in the day, the new generation were eagerly awaiting my nights in the Odyssey so they could have that same experience. Despite Warren being an English promoter with a large English stable of fighters, nine of the eleven undercard bouts involved an Irish fighter. Barry is an Irish promoter but against Avalos only four local boys benefitted from such a massive night for Irish boxing.

Like I said, I chose Garcia because I wanted to be pushed in a competitive fight that would help me get back to where I wanted to be and give the fans decent value for money. But it's fair to say he turned out to be tougher than I'd anticipated. I couldn't believe it when he stepped on the scales at the weigh-in. Who the fuck is this beast, I was thinking. This isn't the same fella I'd had my way with in sparring a few years before. This was a different guy, a bigger, fitter, stronger-looking athlete. It was also clear he had come to win. You could tell that by his demeanour and that of his team, the famed Reynoso father-and-son combination. When the biggest star in boxing, Canelo Alvarez, then flew in to sit ringside for the fight, I knew for sure they intended to leave Belfast victorious.

I had to start well, and I did. When you've been out of the ring for a long time there is always the danger of ring rust, but I didn't feel any in the first three rounds. My footwork was too good for him and allowed me to get in and out of range, landing a variety of shots almost at will. He'd move back in straight lines at times, thinking he was out of range, and my feet got me to him before he knew I was there. I punched him back onto the ropes more than once. In the third I landed a massive right hand absolutely flush, but in fairness he took it well. He's Mexican so he was born with a chin most boxers would pay to have.

The first signs that the fight could get competitive appeared in the fourth round. I spent a second longer on the ropes than I should have, and he didn't need a second invitation to let fly. I caught almost everything he threw at me on the gloves and then fired back with more accurate shots, but I could tell he'd taken a bit of encouragement from the exchanges. I sharpened my movement again to ensure I won the fifth a little easier, but a clash of heads opened a small nick above my right eye. He may have won the sixth as he landed enough to get Canelo up out of his seat and roaring his fellow countryman on. I sat down with a bit of damage close to my left eye as well, but again it was nothing to worry about. The seventh was the infamous knockdown round. Something on the centre logo in the ring had got slippy, and my left leg went from under me when I put my weight on it. I was already on my way onto my hole before he even started his punch, but it partly landed before my arse hit the canvas and so the ref, Victor Loughlin, gave the knockdown. I looked up at Victor and said, you can't seriously be counting here, but he kind of gave a slight smile and kept going. It was never in a million years a legitimate knockdown in the sense that the punch had zero influence on me ending up sat on the floor. But they seem to be given so long as your opponent's glove touches you on the way down so I can't be too hard on the ref. The judges probably all felt obliged to score the round 10–8 in Garcia's favour because of it, but that's boxing.

I must admit I was feeling it now. After ten months out of the ring and only getting a five-week camp, what did I expect? I was also starting to slightly regret assuming full responsibility for choosing the opponent. Left in the hands of my promoter, trainer and manager, I imagine it would have been an easier night at the office. He was pushing me hard, and at times I had no option but to stand and trade. It's a fight, so that can happen. I always laugh when people later tell me like it's some big revelation that I was winning easy early doors when I was on my toes, boxing and moving. Why didn't I just do that for every second of every round, they'll ask. Because I got fucking tired, is the simple answer! And I had a crazy Mexican all over me trying to make me do anything but that. There are probably people saying to Garcia, you had so much success when you put it on him so why didn't you just do that for the entire fight. Like it's that simple. Like they'd have the engine to fight like that for thirty minutes non-stop. And like I wasn't doing everything in my considerable power to stop him being able to do it.

The fans would have loved the shoot-out feel of the final three rounds. Me and my team less so. But boxing is the entertainment business after all so if I can fight like that and come through unscathed then, in small and controlled doses, that's fine by me. I saw it through comfortably enough and the scorecards reflected that. I was back. Now I wanted to hunt down the big boys.

***

I'd fought in January or February the previous three years, so this time around it was nice to be able to enjoy Christmas properly with the family and then get back into the gym. With Lee Selby and Josh Warrington facing off, and Santa Cruz fighting Abner Mares, I needed to find a different dance partner. The Filipino legend, and nailed-on future Hall of Famer, Nonito Donaire was announced as my opponent, and the WBO Interim world title was on the line. Donaire is obviously a massive name in world boxing, but a few people were talking like he was some old man being rolled out for a last hurrah. That was an extremely lazy assumption. Aside from a hiccup early in his career, he'd only ever lost to Rigondeaux, Nicholas Walters and Jessie Magdaleno – all top fighters. And what Nonito went on to achieve in the coming years against the likes of Naoya Inoue and Nordine Oubaali has proven he certainly still had a place at world level in 2018. The people came out in force to support me once again and the atmosphere inside the Odyssey was as electric as always.

I was switched on from the opening bell. Unlike for Garcia, this time I'd had a full camp with Jamie and we'd had time to prepare specifically for the challenge in front of us. And with Donaire – as well as all the other attributes he has, which had made him a four-weight world champion – that meant a left hook that was ranked as one of the hardest punches pound-for-pound in boxing. If that doesn't focus your attention at the start of a fight, then nothing will. I also thought Nonito had been playing mind games with me throughout the build-up. It was as if he was trying to lull me into a false sense of security with just how nice he was. And not just to me, it seemed like he was winning over everyone in Belfast during fight week. At one point during his open workout in front of the cameras he had a load of local kids in the ring with him and was giving them an impromptu boxing class. Then he starts singing with them and leading a dance routine! I remember thinking at the time that no one could be this nice in real life. That it must be fake. I thought he wants to lessen the hostility from my support on the night and maybe, even subconsciously, make me take him as less of a threat. I've been lucky enough to get to know him and his wife Rachel in the ensuing years, and I can confirm he is genuinely the nicest guy you could ever meet. But back then I didn't let my head get into that space. As far as I was concerned, he was just another rival trying to knock me out.

I chose the song 'So Strong' by Labi Siffre for my ringwalk. It's a song that has a special meaning for Christine and her family because it was her da's favourite. When he was dying, one of his old mates found out Dennis didn't have long left but had no way to track him down. So, he had 'So Strong' played every day on a local radio station with a message asking listeners to help him find Dennis Dorrian so he could say goodbye before it was too late. And it worked; the two men got to see each other one last time. I hadn't told anyone at all that it was going to be the song, but I knew as soon as they heard it they would all understand. There is also a line in it which resonated with me and what I was going through then.

'You squander wealth that's mine. My light will shine. So bright, it will blind you.' All in all, it was probably the only time in my career that the music I'd picked to walk me to the ring really meant something quite deep to me. So when I'm stood on the platform waiting to go and Macklemore's 'Can't Hold Us' started blasting out, you can imagine I wasn't best pleased. I turned to Jamie and said, 'That's the wrong song.' He turns to Ralph the whip who is coordinating the whole thing and tells him, wrong song, get it fixed quick. People start sweating, running around in a panic, trying to change the track. But of course, it was too late for that. They told me, sorry Carl, you just have to go. My head went. 'It's the wrong fucking song,' I said again. 'You need to fucking change it.' I stood then and waited, but I knew I'd have to go sooner or later. This was live on TV, and everyone is by now wondering what I'm playing at by stalling. Turning my back on everyone I let out this massive roar. I just screamed fuck, and then started walking. But I was all over the place. It was so off-putting. I was actually thinking, see if I lose this fucking fight because of that. That's the type of mad thing that goes through your head. But once I was in the ring, and I saw Donaire in the opposite corner, I quickly realised there was no time to dwell on it. The guy who dropped the ball was Ian Ritchie who worked for MTK at the time, and I still wind him up to this day. Had I lost, it was all on him. He's lucky he's one of the good guys or I would probably have never spoken to him again. I got a little revenge when we went to Ibrox together and I told him we're in the posh corporate box, so he needs to dress to the nines. When he arrived in a three-piece suit with a long coat, I just laughed and gave him his ticket to sit in a normal seat surrounded by regular fans in Rangers' tops and tracksuits.

There wasn't much in the opening round. It wasn't a question of us showing each other too much respect, but when elite fighters meet it's normal both will want three minutes to take a look at what they're facing. In the second, I wanted to show him that I was the stronger, more physical man and I forced him into a corner and landed hard enough to cause a substantial welt under his left eye. But the plan for this one was never to win via physicality. I was going to win by boxing clever. And by the third round I was in full flow and feeling comfortable. Not comfortable in the sense that it was an easy night, but comfortable that I knew what I had to do and I was successfully doing it. I'd had great sparring for this one, mostly with Stephen Fulton – then a top, unbeaten prospect out of the US. He's still unbeaten, but now he's the unified super bantamweight champion of the world. That sparring was serving me well and it got even better in the fourth. I spent the first two minutes frustrating Donaire with my footwork. Little half steps and stutter steps allowing me to get in and out of range, to hit and not get hit. Then in the final minute I bullied him, keeping him pinned to the ropes or in the corner and landing heavy shots. Although there's not an awful lot between us height-wise, Nonito fights very upright while I was spending a lot of time crouched and keeping low to exaggerate the difference. That allowed me to stick close to him when I wanted and smother his work while, with my more compact style, I could get my own shots off from those close quarters. He came back at me in the next two rounds, landing a couple of uppercuts and reminding me of his class and danger. But over the course of the three minutes, the majority of the quality work was coming from my gloves, and I felt like I was six-nil up.

I'd faded a little down the stretch against Garcia, so there were people wondering if the same would happen against Donaire. No chance. I'd had a full camp for this one and felt great. This was a twelve-rounder as well, but I had no doubts there was enough gas in the tank. Midway through the seventh he landed two huge uppercuts flush. They had me momentarily buzzed, but a second later I was firing back. They were eye-catching shots from him,

Becoming unified champion after beating Scott Quigg in Manchester in 2016. It wasn't the greatest fight of my career, but the atmosphere that night was absolutely electric. © PA Images/Alamy Stock Photo

All smiles between myself and Scott Quigg post-fight, with Eddie Hearn looking less than pleased in the background. © PA Images/Alamy Stock Photo

Beating Leo Santa Cruz in Brooklyn in 2016 as a massive underdog was probably the highlight of my career. It meant that I became the first two-division world champion in the history of Northern Ireland.

A selfie with my fans during a civic reception at Belfast City Hall following the win over Santa Cruz. © INPHO/Presseye/Kelvin Boyes

Me and Josh Warrington at the Manchester Arena in 2019. A great fight for the neutrals, but not so much for me. To be fair, he really surprised me with his power. © PA Images/ Alamy Stock Photo

All of Team Frampton in Gallagher's Steakhouse restaurant in Las Vegas in 2019, ahead of my fight with Tyler McCreary. I'm fond of everyone in this picture.

With my beautiful wife, Christine, on our wedding day in 2013. Punching above my weight? Most definitely.

A treasured picture with my firstborn, Carla. Also visible is the tattoo that still haunts me to this day. Getting tattoos of our first names sounded like a good idea to me and two of my mates at the age of 15.

Receiving my MBE from Prince William on 15 March 2016. I genuinely always thought he was standing on a step, giving him the added height advantage. I guess not.

Carla, Christine and me with 'Iron' Mike Tyson at the McGuigans' gym in Battersea around the time that Freddie Flintoff was preparing for his one and only boxing match.

Tyson Fury and Carla in the Europa Hotel in 2018, ahead of my successful title defence against Luke Jackson in front of 23,000 people at Windsor Park. Fury was on the undercard that same night. He could not have been nicer, reaching into his pocket and handing over a £20 note to a delighted Carla. I'll always remember that.

My hands were full in the changing room after my fight with Santa Cruz in Brooklyn – Carla, Rossa and the world featherweight title.

And to the left, me holding the latest addition to the Frampton family, Mila, another smasher!

Carla, Rossa and baby Mila, along with Claudia the cat, a stray we brought in after our wee dog, Manny, sadly died.

At the Belfast High Court in November 2020, one of the many days in court during the Frampton vs McGuigan case. On the final day, I walked out and said to Mark Simpson from the BBC that I was 'very, very happy with the terms of the settlement'. © Pacemaker

Looking relaxed and feeling happy in the gym in Manchester – a place which holds great memories for me. © Mark Robinson

but again I was doing the better stuff throughout the other two minutes and fifty seconds, so I sat down on my stool happy that another one was in the bag. Happy, but with another reminder of this guy's impressive one-punch power. I fought the next three rounds with a renewed focus and sharpness. It was time to get up on the balls of my feet and box my way home. I made those rounds easy for myself and I could sense Nonito's frustration now. He knew he was a million points down on the cards and all he could do was keep stalking and hope I walked into one of his lights-out left hooks. He nearly got it as well in the closing seconds of the eleventh. I felt an uppercut on the inside which started the sequence before a wide, swinging left hook landed flush on my chin. Five seconds later he repeated the trick. Until that point of my career, that was the hardest I'd been hit. It was so hard, even the crowd fell quiet. I'm not going to pretend it had no effect on me, but after the initial shock of it reverberating around my brain I was clear-headed enough to move around the ring and take no more punishment until I heard the bell. I'd taken the feared Donaire left hook and lived to tell the tale.

That was Nonito's moment and there was no chance I was going to give him another. I could have run round the ring in the twelfth and final round to close the show completely risk free, but when 9,000 are chanting 'there's only one Carl Frampton' in unison, it's hard to be that negative. I went out and won the round, ending it with a final barrage as he lay on the ropes. We gave each other a big hug as soon as the final bell sounded. On top of the respect you earn from one another through sharing thirty-six tough minutes like that, there was already genuine affection between us. He's a great fighter and a great man as well. It was an honour to fight him, and I was extremely proud of my performance. I was more disciplined than I'd ever been before, following our gameplan to the letter. The blip in the eleventh when he caught me aside, I didn't put a foot wrong against an elite fighter. I still had a few years left, but when my career was said and done, I could only rank my performance in the first Santa Cruz fight above this one.

***

Fighting at Windsor Park was never a childhood dream of mine. What boxer in their right mind grows up seriously thinking about filling their national football stadium? That's beyond the wildest dreams of even the most optimistic young fighter. It wasn't until talk began about bringing Kiko to Belfast for my first world-title shot that the idea took hold in my head. The Odyssey was the biggest arena we had and the 9,000 seats inside it were being filled easily when I fought there. I believed I could sell close to triple that if it was a big enough fight. And that meant going to Windsor. It was a shame it never materialised during the run I was on when I was with the McGuigans, but I'd made it a condition of signing with Warren and he delivered it for me.

Luke Jackson was flown in as the opponent. He captained the Australian boxing team at the 2012 Olympics and had made it to 16–0 as a professional, so he looked the part on paper. In reality, I always knew I was a few levels above Luke. With hindsight, the ideal scenario would have been Jackson for the second fight and Nonito for the big night at Windsor. The build-up was civil enough until his team got a bit mouthy about their chances and I snapped back that this isn't about Luke Jackson. That he'd been chosen, but it could have been anyone. That this was all about me and Windsor Park. No one in the featherweight division was beating me on that pitch. It was also about teeing me up for my next fight if we're all being honest. Josh Warrington had shocked Lee Selby a few months earlier to claim the IBF featherweight title. He had massive support in Leeds and was also a Warren fighter. From the first press conference with Jackson, Frank wasn't hiding the fact that a deal had already been done for me to fight Warrington at the end of the year and he had him sitting next to him on the front row at Windsor. As far as domestic match-ups go, this was near the top of everyone's wish list. You're setting yourself up for a huge fall by planning ahead like that in boxing. The example of James DeGale losing to Caleb Truax when he had a big domestic showdown with Billy Joe Saunders in the works was one given to prove the point. And I had to admit I'd been guilty of overlooking an opponent before when I fought Gonzalez in Texas. But that first-round experience in El Paso was horrific enough to ensure I'd never make the same mistake again. First and foremost, I was fully focused on beating Jackson.

It was another strong undercard, with eight Irish lads getting an opportunity. But two fights, or certainly one fight and one name, jumped out. The fight was my old mate Paddy Barnes going for the WBC world flyweight title in just his sixth professional fight. Lomachenko aside, challenging for a world title so early in a career is pretty much unheard of. He was up against Cristofer Rosales, who was fresh off winning the belt by knocking out the previously unbeaten Japanese Daigo Higa in Yokohama. It was a massive ask but, after such a long and successful amateur career, Paddy was determined not to hang about as a pro. I think he deserves a lot of credit for that. He could have milked it for eight or ten fights, picking up purses and easy wins as he built his record. So fair play to him for accepting the challenge as soon as the opportunity arose. I would have liked to have been ringside cheering him on, but I had to make do with sticking my head out the tunnel every now and again and watching bits of it on the big screen. He was doing very well the parts of the fight I watched, but Rosales had obviously heard of his biscuit-ribs reputation and stopped him with a body shot in the fourth round. I was back in the dressing room when I heard the news. He was ringside for my fight but then felt lightheaded and got taken away on a stretcher. I was none the wiser at the time, but to be honest I wouldn't have been worried anyway. I know how big a hypochondriac he is, and who the hell collapses half an hour after taking a body shot! He was grand and his missus Mari later joked that he was concussed from a dig in the ribs.

Paddy's was the fight, but the name which jumped out was Tyson Fury. The big man was two fights into a comeback that would see him regain the heavyweight lineal title and become the biggest star in boxing. He was also just a fight away from his first meeting with Deontay Wilder, and the American champion was in town to get that promotional ball rolling. Wilder actually came into my dressing room as I was nearly ready to go, TV cameras in tow of course. He's a larger-than-life character, and he has that sense of American razzmatazz that makes everything seem like an over-the-top performance when the cameras are rolling. We're slightly more understated in Tiger's Bay so it made for an awkward interaction. Wilder was in full hype mode, telling me it's my time and all that. It may have worked better had I been getting ready to face a Warrington or an Oscar Valdez, but it fell a little flat when it was Luke Jackson waiting for me. I mumbled something about doing my best, and he roars back with a 'you've got this baby!!' or something along those lines. I was scundered.

It was a night I'll never forget. Jamie was great. He knew this was something special for me, so he told me to soak the ringwalk in. Usually, you leave the dressing room already in the zone, but he said to take it all in and enjoy it, that we'd flip the switch once I was in the ring. It was absolutely lashing as I stood on the platform, and they played 'Belfast Child' by Simple Minds. 'Freed from Desire' then kicked in and the 23,000 crowd went ballistic. I walked to the ring with a massive grin on my face, doing my best to look around and appreciate the situation. It was an unreal experience. I still get goosebumps when I see a clip of it today. I was delighted David Healy agreed to be a part of it with me. I'd spent thirteen years going to watch him bang in the goals for our country on that pitch and had become good pals with him in recent times. He's the king of Windsor Park as far as I'm concerned so it was a real honour to have him there as part of the team. He also came in handy for the celebrations later when he emerged from the bowels of the stadium with a crate of beer he'd commandeered from an office somewhere!

There wasn't much action in terms of punches thrown or landed in the first round. Instead, I went out and dominated with my feet. My footwork alone was enough to demonstrate that there are levels to boxing, and Luke had found himself one or two above where he was comfortable. It was my job to keep him uncomfortable, so I didn't want to give him any time at all to settle or gain any confidence or find his own rhythm. I didn't throw much in those opening three minutes, but everything I did was enough to keep him wary and moving away behind his high guard. I already had him where I wanted. Round by round, I then gradually stepped up the pressure and the attack. He was marked up early around the eyes and looked a little more battered and a little more forlorn each time he sat back down on his stool. But credit to Luke, he got up for the next round each time and gave it a go despite getting so little reward for his efforts. In the sixth he delivered his best punch of the fight, a right hand that landed flush. I didn't even blink. That just confirmed what I already knew, the hundred-to-one shot of him landing a Hail Mary and knocking me out was as big an impossibility as him outboxing me. The knowledge allowed me to go forward more aggressively and walk him down. In the eighth, I landed a short, left uppercut to the head to move his elbow, and then drove one into his solar plexus. He dropped in serious pain but, credit again, he got up and survived the rest of the round. When we rose for the next, I knew it would be the last round. I targeted the body again, this time a right hand crunched into his ribs and left him in agony. He stumbled backwards onto the ropes, a left hand to the head helping him on his way. He then kind of put his arms out in exasperation and his corner obliged by throwing in the towel before it got a lot worse for Luke. I think it's fair to say he did well to last that long. Jackson was a good amateur and a decent pro, but he'd never mixed it at my level before and it showed from the off. I could have gone through the gears and got him out of there a lot earlier, but I was patient and precise with my work. Despite the grandeur and significance of the stage, the fight was more just a case of job done – now let's announce Warrington.

***

Back to Manchester and back to face an English champ, but the build-up to my fight with Josh Warrington was never going to be laced with the same antagonism as the Quigg fight had been. I'd always had respect for Josh, and I think he reciprocated that. Steve Wood manages Josh, and he also owns the gym which Jamie Moore operated in to train all his fighters. Jamie had to have a bit of an awkward conversation with him where he said, I know the whole building and business is yours Steve, but neither you nor your son can come in here while I'm training Carl for this one. Steve's another gentleman so there was no issue there. It would have been tough for any promoter to manufacture any needle between the two camps but it was a big enough fight between two of the best ticket sellers in the UK, so no bad blood was required.

I was most people's pick going into this one. I reckon I was a stronger favourite against Josh than I was against Quigg. Josh was coming off a fantastic win against Selby, but there was a narrative that it was really the weight cut that beat Selby. The Welshman immediately jumped up two divisions to lightweight as if to emphasise he'd killed himself to make 126. I didn't get sucked into that version of events though. Josh was brilliant against Selby and deserved the win. And I was fully expecting an even better version to turn up against me. I knew I was in for a long, tough night against a world-level fighter who was always super fit, very physically strong, had fast hands, threw a lot of shots and was capable of taking a lot of punishment. I was under no illusions of the task at hand, but at the same time I was full of confidence. A lot of that confidence was based on the fact I believed he couldn't hurt me. There was nothing in his performances throughout his career to make me worry about his power. I think he only had six stoppages on his record. He wore Winnings gloves, a known non-puncher brand. I thought everything he threw would bounce off me. I wasn't complacent – but if you truly believe your opponent can't knock you out, you approach a fight differently. Against a Kiko, a Donaire or even an Avalos, the mindset is altered. If you have that fear that one punch could turn your lights off, you're more focused and alert to that danger. You want to avoid taking one flush from guys with high knockout ratios at all costs. Against Josh, however, I went in prepared and expecting to take a few to land mine. I believed that the risk was acceptable. It never entered my head that he could rattle me early and it could be all over. I was sure I was okay taking one from Josh, right up until I took one from Josh.

Josh's da and trainer, Sean O'Hagan, approached Jamie on fight night and said they weren't going to bother sending anyone to our changing room to watch me having my hands wrapped. I guess it was a bit of a we're-all-mates-here-so-we-trust-you type thing. It put Jamie in an awkward spot as if we sent someone in it was like we'd be saying, cheers but we don't trust you. So, we didn't either and that never sat right with me. I always like having someone in to watch and I always expect to have a member of my opponent's team checking mine. On top of everything else, I like to get a report back on what the mood is in the other dressing room. Did they seem nervous, confident, happy, angry, etc. It was strange to say the least.

It took barely a minute. A right hook which caught me on the temple started it all off. It buzzed me enough for the reptilian part of the brain take over. That's the part which in situations of extreme stress determines whether your body's response is fight, flight or freeze. I'm a fighter so there was only ever going to be one result. I planted my feet and swung with him. Had I landed the next big one it may have been a different story, but I didn't. Josh did and he sent me careering backwards, my legs stiffening with each step. Even then though, I instinctively stood my ground and swung with him again. And again, Josh's winging hooks landed a split second before my efforts did. My legs gradually came back, but my head wasn't completely clear. I saw the final minute out with not too much drama, but it was a horrendous opening round for me. And unfortunately, the worst was still to come. The second was almost a carbon copy as the opening minute passed by relatively uneventfully before the fireworks began. I then got caught flush on the chin with a right hook and was all over the place. Then, as the animal in me made me stand and trade, Josh unleashed around forty punches – all with very bad intentions. Plenty landed and plenty hurt, while my wild replies seemed to have little or no impact on Josh. It took me a long time to rewatch the fight, but when I did it was hard to believe I survived that spell and even harder to believe I reacted the way I did. My legs were shaky so getting on my bike wasn't really a viable option, but I could have held on. Just grab him and hold on like grim death. Hug him and don't let go until the ref, Steve Gray, physically prised my arms from around him. If that didn't buy me enough time to recover, then just take a knee. You're automatically losing the round 10–8 but fuck it. Give the opponent the two-point advantage and give yourself the opportunity to regain your senses. In the long run, a 10–8 would have served me much better than the

10–9 battering which took so much out of me, but the heat of the moment doesn't allow you such clarity of thought.

I badly needed to steady the ship, and I did so to a large extent in the third and fourth rounds. I won at least one of them and lost neither. Standing in the danger zone and swinging from the hip had obviously not been what I'd spent ten weeks preparing for, so it was vital I got back to our gameplan. I needed to start dictating the pace and rhythm of the fight with my box-and-move style. I needed to get up on my toes and win it with my footwork. I felt I was beginning to do that now, but when I sat on my stool at the end of the fourth, I had a shooting pain in my right thigh. About six weeks before the fight, Josh and I both did a thing with our sponsors, 32 Red. He went to Leeds United, and I went to Glasgow Rangers, and we spent the day with a few of the players, doing different football and boxing challenges. In one of those challenges, someone was firing me the ball and I had to try and volley it at a target. I must have repeated the same strike about sixty times and finished the day with a torn muscle in my lower leg. It meant no running for around three weeks and a lot of physiotherapy at the Manchester Institute of Health and Performance. Instead of running, I ended up doing a lot on the bikes inside their altitude chamber. But as well as concerns over cardio fitness, it also hampered me in my favoured style of fighting. For a long time, I couldn't get up on my toes and move about the ring as I would have liked. The leg felt all right by fight night, but in one of our exchanges in the fourth round, Josh's knee must have smashed into the inside of my leg and caused some damage. I felt it immediately and it steadily got worse, preventing me pushing off the back foot effectively and generally hindering my movement. I didn't say anything publicly after the fight, as you don't want to be the guy making all the excuses, but the next day the entire inside of my thigh was turning a blackish purple colour. When I was waiting to get checked over in the hospital it buckled underneath me, and everyone rushed over in a panic. They thought it was a head injury or something, but it was just the damaged leg unable to support my weight now the adrenalin had worn off. The mad thing is, I didn't even say anything about it at the time to Jamie in my corner. He always asks if I'm okay between rounds, but this time I kept my mouth shut. My rationale was that he might interpret it as me asking him to stop the fight without actually having to say it out loud. Christine thinks I'm an absolute eejit for not saying anything. That maybe with that key information we could have improvised and come up with a different gameplan – but again, when you're in the middle of a firefight in which you're coming out second best in most of the exchanges, common sense kind of deserts you.

I tried to fight the way I was supposed to, but the leg wouldn't allow me to sustain it for the full three minutes of the round. The fight then fell into a pattern of each round being divided in three. In one of those minutes, not much happened and it was pretty even. In another, I was getting in and out of range while landing enough scoring punches to deserve the nod. And in the remaining minute, Josh would pour it on me and invariably land two or three heavy ones. I was never in trouble to the extent I was in the first and second rounds but the bigger shots tend to be the ones which catch the judges' eyes, so I knew I was probably struggling on the scorecards. Barry Jones was scoring it live as part of the BT Sports' commentary team and he had it very close after eight or nine rounds, but in truth it didn't feel so close to me in the ring. I had some success in those middle rounds but, if I'm being honest, I never thought while it was all happening that I was going to come back and win the fight. All I was thinking was, don't get stopped. I don't mean I was thinking, just go into your shell and survive. I was still going out and having a go. But it was more a question of gritting it out rather than fighting to win. I was just determined not to get stopped. By the championship rounds, I was physically shattered while Josh was still bouncing around the ring. It took a lot of strength, mental as much as physical, to keep my head up and keep going. I'll always be proud that I heard the final bell.

The changing room was a pretty sombre place afterwards. It's the worst feeling in boxing. It's awkward for a lot of people as they don't know exactly what to say or how to act. And generally there isn't really anything you can say to a fighter at that moment to make things any better. Tommy Coyle was crying his eyes out but pulled it together long enough to give a lovely speech. I saw MTK's media guy Isaac wipe away a tear too. Only one person didn't read the mood in the room and that was our mate, Stacey. She was acting the eejit doing cartwheels or handstands or something! Neither the time nor the place Stacey and my da, who never says boo to a goose, was the one to say get her out to fuck!

I said it in the ring immediately after, Josh won fair and square. He was the fitter, stronger man. More importantly, he was a smarter fighter than he'd previously been given credit for and can punch a lot harder than I'd anticipated. I got a little emotional when asked what, if anything, was next for me in boxing. I mentioned my wife and kids at home and gave the standard response of sitting down with my team to discuss next steps. But to be honest, already in my head I was retired. I was nearly thirty-two years old and it had been a long, hard career. I'd made decent money in the final eighteen months of that career, and it felt like the end of the road. I looked in the mirror and saw my head was in bits, with bumps and lumps all over the place. A lot of attention is now on Josh's style of fighting and in particular how he leads with his head. The fights against Mauricio Lara and Kiko Martinez shone a bit of a spotlight on his tactics. But I can assure people he's always fought like that. It is a dirty style, but I always say that you do whatever you can get away with in the ring. Refs should have been jumping on him from day one over it. Instead, they've always let him crack on with the headbutts so why wouldn't he keep doing it?

Mentally as well I was in a bad way. This defeat really hurt, and I had a tough couple of weeks trying to digest and process it. Christine was desperate for me to retire, and the kids wanted their daddy at home more, so my mind was made up. But hanging up the gloves for good is incredibly tough for a fighter, and when the dust settled I began to think about everything. Leg injury aside, camp had gone well. I'd sparred less but it went great, and I felt as strong and fit as ever. I took early shots I shouldn't be taking and was playing catch-up from then on in against Josh, but I believed I could beat him. That was his night, but why shouldn't I have a few more nights of my own yet? You look at examples like Manny Pacquiao. He'd just lost to Jeff Horn in a major surprise and people wrote him off. He came back to destroy Lucas Matthysse and claim another world title. He then beat Adrien Broner and Keith Thurman in the six months after I fought Josh. I thought about the weight class. I could make feather, but it seemed like I wasn't bringing my punching power from sparring into the fight. All my sparring partners got out of the ring saying I'm heavy-handed, but the only featherweight I'd stopped was Luke Jackson. Maybe I needed to move up again. It also left a sour taste in the mouth ending a great career that way, with a performance I was disappointed in. I felt like I had more left to give in the ring. I began to wonder if everything happens for a reason. Like getting dropped in El Paso making it easier to finally secure nights against Quigg and Santa Cruz. The big names would not be frightened to face me after watching Warrington do a job on me. And it was big fights I was interested in. I didn't have the stomach or the time for a long rebuilding project. I wanted a quick route to another world-title shot against a champion I knew I could get beat. There was no chance of me taking a pay cheque just to get beaten up, but I truly believed I had another world title in me. Early in the new year, MTK told me Top Rank were interested. MTK had a very close relationship with Bob Arum and a lot of leverage due to Tyson Fury. They used that and got me an offer that was impossible to turn down. The money alone was fantastic, a six-fight deal starting off at $1m and increasing each fight, but it was more than that which made me sign and continue fighting. I could see a path towards an opportunity to make history. I was to move up to super featherweight, get one quick win under my belt in the new division and then challenge Jamel Herring for his WBO belt. It was a chance to become the first ever Irish three-weight world champion and stake my claim as my country's greatest ever fighter.

***

Step one, my debut at 130lb, was scheduled for Philadelphia in August 2019 against a Mexican named Emmanuel Dominguez. He looked the perfect opponent considering I was coming off a damaging defeat and debuting at a new weight. Not much of a threat, but hopefully he'd give me a few rounds. My ring return had already been delayed by some messing around in court, of which I'll say more later, so by the time fight week arrived I couldn't wait to get back under the lights. I checked into the Renaissance Hotel on the outskirts of Philly, and on Monday morning was waiting in the lobby to get picked up for some ESPN media stuff in a nearby gym. I was on my phone when next thing I know something crashes down, grazing my shoulder on the way, and smashes my left hand off the table. It was an eight-foot ornamental stone pillar that the hotel had placed in the lobby, and it must have weighed around fifty or sixty kilos. Jamie had come into the lobby with a bag over his shoulder and, in sneaking between the see-through lace curtains, he'd inadvertently knocked the pillar over. There was the shock and a sharp pain in my hand. It swelled up pretty quick and, although I prayed it was just badly bruised, deep down I knew something was seriously wrong. An X-ray at the local hospital soon confirmed my worst fears. I'd suffered a fracture of the fifth metacarpal bone. That's the bone that extends from your wee finger through your hand. I wouldn't be punching anybody or anything for a while. I was devastated. I just couldn't believe it. So much time and money and effort for absolutely nothing. All the camp expenses, the month in Philadelphia, the flights for me and others. The sacrifices and time away from home and from family. All down the drain. I was raging. And I directed some of that anger at Jamie as well at first. Why did he have to sneak through the curtains like that? Why couldn't he have just walked around like everyone else? I even wondered if this was one of their pranks that had gone wrong. But I soon saw how genuinely upset Jamie was. This wasn't a joke. He was as gutted as I was and angrier at himself than I could ever be. It was just a freak accident. There was all sorts of nonsense on social media. The usual conspiracy stories or accusations of something else going on, and it was all fake. And as usual, none of the theories made any sense whatsoever. I switched off social media and booked a flight home for the following day to lick my wounds and heal up as fast as possible.

We rushed the comeback. It happens in boxing. When television and promoters are dictating the dates, sometimes you need to take what you are given or else you could find yourself at the back of a long queue. End of November in Vegas was what was on offer, this time against the unbeaten American Tyler McCreary. I was being treated by two top orthopaedic hand surgeons, Michael Eames when I was home and Mike Hayton when I returned to Manchester. Dr Hayton is one of the best in the UK for sports injuries, and he told me that the crack in the bone was still not completely healed and that in an ideal world I'd have another month out. But he conceded that it had healed to a degree that if I made sure it's always wrapped up well and I used the biggest, most padded gloves I could find then I might get away with it. I had no choice. I had to risk it. I didn't punch many skulls that camp. There was a lot of body sparring, which is easier on the hands. I also wore these massive Everlast gloves that were so soft my sparring partners didn't feel a thing. Where normally I'd land a few big ones early doors to make them think twice about just bombing in at me, with these pillows on my paws they were happy marching forward for the entire spar. It would have been perfect preparation if I was up against a pressure fighter.

In Vegas, I trained out of the UFC Performance Institute there. I wasn't exactly slumming it at Manchester's version, but this was another world: facilities like you've never seen before. Despite that, something went wrong with the weight cut and I ended up with seven pounds still to lose on the morning of the weigh-in. It wasn't easy, but I did it and we headed to the venue. Once there, however, I was made to hang around for hours before being allowed on the scales. In the UK, especially if you're the main event, you just arrive and get weighed immediately. You want it done and dusted as soon as possible so you can start rehydrating and refuelling. But not there that day, and as the minutes turned to hours I started feeling terrible. I saw the doctor for the standard pre-fight check and he actually told me that if I didn't make the weight at the first attempt, he wouldn't allow me to try to lose any more ounces. I was struggling now, dry retching and all. A fighter tries to put a brave face on things at a weigh-in to give the impression the cut was no bother regardless of the amount of torture you've just endured. But I couldn't even muster a façade. I lay on the floor in front of everyone and then Jamie and Nigel guided me into a disabled toilet where there was space to lie on the cold, tiled floor. Luckily, I made weight first time of asking. We headed straight for food, but had to stop the car a couple of times so I could be sick. It was the worst one

of my whole career. Worse even than El Paso. All I can think is that
the type of water I used to do the water-loading cut played a part.
Rather than normal water, I was guzzling this pH Alkaline water
which has additional minerals in it. I think it has salt, the very thing
I'm trying to get rid of. It was a nightmare all round, but would be
far from my biggest physical issue going into the fight.

I also used the Top Rank Gym in Vegas, and it was there I did
my final spar of the camp. We were a week out from the fight and
Jamie said four rounds would do me as we were tapering everything
down. I said, sure I'll do six, it's no bother. Famous last words.
Midway through that final round, I felt something in my hand
and knew straight away it was gone. A scan in the hospital later
confirmed it. Broken again in the same place. You start to wonder
if you're cursed, or the universe is trying to tell you something at
this point. But I was fighting no matter what. It never entered my
head to withdraw this time. People had paid up to fly over. A lot
of time and effort and money had gone into everything. I did it in
Philly, but not this time. My hand could fall off and I'd still glove up
the bloody stump and give it a go. Once my team understood that,
it was all about how we make the best of the situation. Dr Hayton
had previously contacted the Nevada State Athletic Commission
that governs boxing in Vegas to find out their rules on painkilling
injections before combat. He did that without mentioning my name
and was told the amount of cortisone you're allowed to inject. Even
before I broke it for a second time, Mike was telling me I'll want
to be taking the biggest dose permissible. Now, that cortisone had
become even more vital. But when we went through the motions
with the Commission, the main man there, Bob Bennett, suddenly
said it wasn't allowed. No cortisone injections whatsoever. Instead,
they gave me some sort of topical cream to rub into the skin.
I've a fucking broken bone in my hand and they're giving me a
numbing cream used when getting a tattoo. It was bullshit and it

was pointless, but I rubbed a couple of tubes' worth in for the sake of it. Needless to say, it was no help whatsoever.

Luckily, I could have beat McCreary with one hand. In fact, towards the end, I had to beat him with no hands. I think it was around the seventh that I felt something strange, this time in my right hand. X-rays would later reveal a fracture at the base of my third metacarpal. It's not much fun punching someone with broken hands. It's just pain, a real severe pain. I found that if I jabbed with an open hand, it wasn't as sore as with a closed fist, but you can't really do that when throwing a power shot. So, the body became the focus. I dropped him in the sixth with a body shot and then again in the ninth with a lovely double left hook to the liver. They were probably the highlights of what was one-way traffic from the first bell to the last. McCreary had nothing that could trouble me. He was much taller and had more than an eight-inch reach advantage, but he had no clue how to maximise that. I fought well, winning every round. The only thing McCreary had the upper hand in was trash talking. I don't get into that sort of thing during the fight, but this kid loved it. I didn't know what he was saying half the time, but I remember when I crunched him with a body shot early, he started shaking his head and saying, no, no, no. Soon after, I whacked him again and he couldn't hide wincing in pain. Seizing on my opportunity I went in close and blurted out, 'what do you think of that one you wee fruit!' It's hard to get more Belfast than that. Old school too. I'm not sure where Tyler is from, but I doubt he's ever been called a wee fruit before. I said it without thinking, and when I stepped back I caught myself on and started smiling.

It was all smiles at the end as well when Herring got into the ring and we posed either side of Arum. You tend to size a future rival up when you meet them for the first time but given he had me by what seemed like a foot, I thought it best to make a little joke out of the height difference. The plan was to do the fight as soon as it was warm and dry enough in Belfast. Insert your own joke here. The promoters knew I'd guarantee north of 30,000 ticket sales for this one. A farewell and a shot at history all rolled into one. But then out of nowhere, the Covid pandemic hit and the world was turned upside down. It caused millions of deaths and untold suffering across the globe, so I'm not going to sit here moaning about a boxing match getting delayed. Boxing, like all sport, ground to a halt for a period. And when it restarted a few months later, it was with some major restrictions. It was clear neither of us would be getting permission for cross-Atlantic travel, and we didn't know for how long that would stay the case. Although neither of us wanted to, the sensible option was to have an interim fight and wait for the worst of the pandemic to pass by. It was frustrating, especially as the freak hand injury had already delayed things by four months at a time in my career in which four months was a long time. I would have loved to have had an immediate crack at Herring rather than the McCreary fight, but after the loss to Warrington I needed to register a ten-round win against someone before the WBO would approve me to challenge for their world title. This now looked like another six or maybe twelve months being added on again. But like I say, in the grand scheme of the suffering going on around the world, sometimes you need to put your own problems into perspective.

My interim fight was in August against the Scottish fighter Darren Traynor. Traynor came in last minute to replace an Armenian called Vahram Vardanyan, who couldn't secure a visa to enter the UK in time. It took place under boxing lockdown conditions in York Hall, making it all pretty grim. York Hall is an iconic small-hall boxing arena, and when it's packed to the rafters for a domestic level fight it is absolutely brilliant. But in the cold light of day, it's a dirty, pokey old place and a far cry from the arenas I'd grown used to in the second half of my career. No fans were allowed in to watch it. Even when I was an amateur fighting in the Crues' Club, 500 would squeeze in and make a racket – so this was just surreal. The whole build-up and fight week and everything was flat. It took going through the motions to a whole new level. I ended up agreeing to fight at lightweight and felt like a fat mess when I stood on the scales. I didn't even feel in fighting shape physically, never mind mentally. On fight night I thought it would be funny to walk out to that 'Oh So Quiet' song by Björk. But that fell as flat as the non-existent atmosphere, and I felt embarrassed walking to the ring. The only thing flatter was my performance in the fight. I kept telling myself not to get complacent, but I wasn't able to trick my own mind which knew this was a gift. Traynor hit me on the arm early on and that confirmed he had no power to trouble me. That's the only tiny doubt that would have existed so, without that fear, complacency was inevitable. I don't mean to be disrespectful to Darren at all, but like everything in life there are levels and he operated on one much lower than I did. You probably had to go back to my Commonwealth title days to find a comparable opponent. In a weird way, fighting well below what you're used to creates its own little problems. As well as the lack of focus and urgency and switching off mentally, he was not capable of mounting the type of attack I'd just spent the past four or five years training to defend myself against. The only risk now was he did something so badly it caught me unawares. But even if that happened, his lack of power would render it little more than an irritant. I dropped Traynor in the sixth and finished him in the seventh round of a very pedestrian performance. Alarm bells should have rung really. In my prime I would have stopped Darren inside two rounds and not taken a single punch for my trouble. I told myself it was just the situation that caused the drop in standards, but there was probably more to it than that. The fact it was a body shot that did it was one of the few upsides of the night. It was a part of my attack I rarely worked on when I was with the McGuigans. I think Parodi was the only guy I hurt with a body shot while I was with them. Jamie spotted early how I'd neglected that very fundamental weapon, and we worked on it a lot in the gym and during sparring. After doing the same to Jackson and McCreary, this was three victories out of five with Jamie in which I had folded guys with a body attack.

A month later, Herring finally had his own keep-busy bout against Jonathan Oquendo after a couple of postponements due to the champ contracting the coronavirus. It was an ugly, scrappy fight with Oquendo headbutting as much as he punched. The ending was bizarre, with Jamel eventually succumbing in round eight to an eye injury caused by what was ruled a deliberate headbutt in round five. The rules meant the ref could call it as a win for Herring via the disqualification of his opponent. The whole thing was confusing, but all that mattered to me was that he'd kept his title and I'd finally get my shot at it. Before that, however, I faced an altogether different type of battle. One that would play out in Belfast High Court.

CHAPTER EIGHT

FRAMPTON VS McGUIGAN

I couldn't wait for this fight to begin. Carl Frampton versus Finbar Patrick McGuigan, Sandra McGuigan and Cyclone Promotions (UK) Limited in the Belfast High Court of Justice. Their side had delayed and delayed but finally, after three years, I was going to have the opportunity to have everything revealed in court. My only regret was that no members of the public were allowed in the gallery due to the pandemic restrictions in operation at the time. The place would have been packed to the rafters every day!

I had a small, but very strong legal team on my side. My friend Jim Conlon introduced me to John Finucane and, after giving him my side of the story, he was happy to become my solicitor. John works closely with a barrister by the name of Peter Girvan, who just so happens to be married to Barney Eastwood's granddaughter. Obviously, Peter was there on merit as a great lawyer – but knowing how superstitious Barry is, the Eastwood connection was an added bonus. A little later, Seamus McIlroy also came on board to work alongside Peter. In the early days of attempted mediation, a barrister from Manchester was helping out, but when it came time to litigate John and Peter both suggested Gavin Millar QC. Gavin had worked on plenty of high-profile cases on behalf of the likes of the BBC and *The Guardian*, so it was clear I'd be in safe hands with him. He is also one of the most intelligent people I've ever met. To the point that conversations with him are a little weird because his brain is operating on a totally different level than mine! The way it worked though, I went through John for most things, and he liaised with the barristers.

Our side of the story was very straightforward. I signed up to being managed by Barry McGuigan and I put my trust in him fulfilling the obligations of that role. But when it became clear there was a lot of money to be made from my career, Barry moved to be my promoter as well. He turned me against other promoters and kept me within the McGuigan circle, smothering me with other McGuigan family members to keep me under control and pushing me towards their own accountants to deny me any semblance of independent advice or counsel. He had me sign a contract to ensure I was their property for the most lucrative period of my career. Money that was earned from the shows I headlined and the sponsorships I attracted was then used to enrich the entire McGuigan family. All the while, I was being assured the shows made no money. Then when I grew too big for Cyclone events, Barry replaced the show income with my purses from third-party promoters. The actual size of the purses was often kept from me, expenses were always inflated and payment was often delayed so that there continued to be plenty on top of what I was paid to fund the McGuigan family. For the second Santa Cruz fight, I never received my full purse at all. The judge in a previous hearing over jurisdiction summed it up quite well when he wrote:

'The obligation which lies at the heart of this case is the obligation owed by McGuigan as Frampton's manager and agent to ensure that Frampton received his share (in the widest possible sense) and that sums were not syphoned off or diverted into bank accounts controlled by the Cyclone connection as Frampton alleges.'

I knew our case to be the true version of events, and I knew there was a wealth of evidence to prove each point. I just needed my legal team to present and prove it.

My QC Millar's style was to go about his business in a very clinical and measured manner. He seemed the polar opposite of the McGuigans' QC, Liam McCollum, who was more combative in his cross examinations. I was very happy with my guy and the way he approached everything. It felt to me like Millar was happy to focus on simply presenting facts. In his opening statement he sought to lay out the framework of how we were going to prove our case. Step one was to take a look at the management contract I signed with Barry and to highlight the clauses indicating the role he was contractually obligated to perform. The headlines here were the requirements for Barry to avoid conflicts of interest and secure for me all due and proper profit and reward. Also, there was nothing specifying that money I was due couldn't go directly to me, but when it didn't Barry had to promptly pay me what I was owed. I could sense my old manager already squirming in his seat. Millar went on to emphasise the fundamental fiduciary responsibility Barry had towards me as my licensed and contracted manager. At the centre of it was the need for a single-minded loyalty which ensures a fiduciary acts in good faith, makes no profit out of the trust put in him, cannot place himself in a position where duty and interest conflict and must not act for his own benefit or that of a third party without my informed consent. I'm sitting there listening and ticking off each point one by one – he breached that, breached that, breached that, breached that. Millar was going through all of this to make clear what Barry should have been doing before he began detailing what he actually did.

We used the aftermath of beating Kiko the first time as the starting point. That was the moment when I became box office and my value skyrocketed. Finally, Barry had within his grasp the fighter who ticked all the boxes to become both his star and his cash cow.

'*It was at that point*', Millar said, '*that Barry McGuigan's ambitions to become a successful and no doubt he hoped wealthy promoter himself came to the fore.*'

Millar detailed the steps Barry then took to achieve his goal. These seven phases, all of which constituted flagrant breaches of his duty as my manager, had been laid out in our opening written submission to the court, and I think it's helpful to repeat them here in full:

a) Dissuading Frampton from having an accountant independent of them/Cyclone during the Cyclone era and from implementing an arrangement where the monies from his career came to him/his company/his accountant before payment of commission and expenses. This was directly contrary to Frampton's interests and intended to ensure that they could have control over those monies without proper/professional scrutiny.

b) Dissuading Frampton from continuing the promotional arrangement with Matchroom/Hearn in May 2013 when his interests would have been better served by this arrangement which was with an experienced promoter and carried no risk of a conflict of interest. They did this in order to become promoters themselves and to be able to profit secretly from their position as promoters, as Frampton's career took off, as described below.

c) Persuading him that he would be a trusted partner in the Cyclone promotional venture after 2013, receiving 30% of the profits from the promotion of his career, when they neither intended for this to happen nor did it happen. This is why they sought to persuade him that his fights were not profitable and to conceal the true profitability of his career. They did this in order to become the sole promoters themselves and to be able to profit secretly from their position as such, as Frampton's career took off, as described below.

d) Failing to provide him with information and documentation relating to their operation/use of Cyclone Promotions Ltd and its bank accounts as vehicles for them to receive and benefit from monies from the promotion of his career.

e) Promoting Frampton bouts and obtaining sponsorship from which they derived income/profits without providing him with relevant documentation or budgets/accounts relating to the same. In some instances, documents were deliberately withheld/concealed from him. They did this in order to enable them to profit from their position as promoters without Frampton knowing.

f) Obtaining for themselves and their sons income/benefits from the promotion of Frampton's bouts and wider career (such as ticket/sponsorship monies and promoter commissions, and travel/hotels/meals) without accounting for these to Frampton. These appear to have included the monies referred to at 6.11 in the ASM trial report though the amounts and form of the payments to these recipients remain obscure even at this stage in these proceedings.

g) When Frampton's success enabled him to start fighting opponents provided by US promoters and/or in the US, they set up a 'shadow' corporate structure to enable them to derive income and profits from this stage in his career without Frampton knowing. This involved setting up the Cyclone Promotions (UK) companies without him knowing and setting up bank accounts for those companies without him knowing (to receive the income and profits). It also involved getting him to sign an agreement on trust (the IPA) [International Promotional Agreement] which enabled them do deals in this phase of his career and to receive the income/profits from the same in the name of the undisclosed CPUK companies. These receipts were concealed from Frampton.

Millar then went on to summarise five key points he felt it important to highlight to the court which we'd demonstrate and evidence throughout the trial. The first was that there was zero transparency within the Cyclone business as far as it related to my career. I received precious little in terms of financial or contractual information. I was never shown budgets or post-fight reconciliations, while agreements entered into with third parties for broadcasting rights, sponsorships, ticket sales, etc. all happened behind my back. I was rarely aware of their existence, never mind the detail of the deals. The second point was that I was led to believe that events like the Cazares and Kiko fights were not profitable. Our investigations had proven that to be a lie but, as Millar stated, it was obvious they made money as 'common sense will tell you, given they were effectively all sell-outs in Belfast'. The third point was that 'income flows from these promotions were used to remunerate the McGuigan family and financially benefit them in other ways that were kept secret from Mr Frampton'. Millar explained how multiple bank accounts and multiple companies I didn't know existed were involved in this, as well as there being a lot of cash floating about. The fourth point was the fact that I was the only director of Cyclone Promotions Ltd who was not a signatory of the company's bank account. Barry, Sandra, Blain, Jake and Nelson all had access to the account, but I did not. That meant I had no way to know of the money going into the account or, just as important, the money going out. Monthly wages to Blain, Jake and Shane, which no one told me about at the outset, came out of this account, for example. This is also when the first mention of the infamous expenses was made with Millar flagging that this account was used for vet's bills, dining out in restaurants, petrol purchases, supermarket shopping, cash withdrawals and many more transactions that had absolutely nothing to do with my career. There'd be a lot more examples of rogue expenses throughout the trial. The final point Millar wanted to make was that throughout this time, I was not once involved in a Board meeting or a directors' meeting or in any meaningful conversations or discussions on the business of the company whatsoever.

From here, Millar jumped forward to what happened at the end of the BoxNation deal when I was now a world champion needing purpose-built outdoor arenas because there was no indoor venue big enough to satisfy demand to watch me perform at home. My value was clear for all to see, and interest in working with me would have been extremely high from major promoters in the UK and beyond. It was then that 'two strange twists in the tale', as Millar termed it, happened. Firstly, a company called Cyclone Promotions (UK) Ltd was established without my knowledge. An incredibly similar name to Cyclone Promotions Ltd, which I was a director of and which was understood to be the vehicle through which my career was driven. In this new company, only Barry and Sandra were directors. And better still, they set up the first of what would eventually be at least three bank accounts with Coutts using this new company's name. Again, I was kept oblivious to all of this. Secondly, Millar described the signing of the infamous International Promotional Agreement (IPA) when I was pulled into the gym's office while training for Avalos and basically told, sign here. No emails or any evidence of any discussion on the contract have ever been found or disclosed. That is because none ever existed. Cyclone would normally, as you would expect, engage with lawyers to draft and execute contracts. But for this one, Blain did it himself with the help of a German matchmaker. Big Olaf was a nice man, but he was certainly not a legal professional. Millar was clearly not impressed with Blain and Olaf's ham-fisted attempt to be lawyers and declared that a genuine lawyer would find it hard to keep a straight face while drafting it. He then quoted Barry from his own book by calling it a slave contract, one in which I signed away everything and received almost nothing in return.

'*It was an appalling breach of his duties as a manager to get a boxer to sit down and sign a document such as this,*' said Millar. '*Though perhaps it is not so strange if what was happening here was that Barry McGuigan was trying to tie Mr Frampton into a long-term promotional arrangement benefitting him, Barry McGuigan, without actually appearing on the face of the document to be the counterparty with the promoter himself.*'

This IPA was, of course, simply a means to lock me down and prevent me being able to speak or sign with any other promoter. It served no other purpose. As Millar said, at no point going forward did Barry call me as my manager and say we need to negotiate your purse now under clause 2.3 of the IPA. In fact, the document was never mentioned to me again until 2017, when our relationship had broken down and they frantically looked for a basis to sue me.

Millar then took the opportunity to quickly run through a bit of a timeline of what happened and how the boxer–manager relationship disintegrated. The mysterious Cyclone Promotions LLC company set up in Texas around the time I fought Gonzalez there, which no one can explain. The witnessing of personal expenses being put on the Cyclone account at the Quigg fight. Needing Sean to chase for my Quigg money and only getting it ten months after Matchroom had paid the McGuigans. Large, undocumented or poorly documented deductions being taken from that purse. Being told the Santa Cruz I purse was $1.5m when there was actually $1.665m in the pot. Again, needing Sean to chase for my money and only receiving it six months after the McGuigans got it into their Coutts account – once more, with huge and dubious deductions for camp expenses. The VAT issue, which appeared out of nowhere. Meetings in October 2016 and the spring of 2017 which resolved nothing and left more questions than answers. The original Cyclone Promotions company posting massive losses while the UK version was dissolved and then reappearing after an off-the-shelf company was purchased and had its name changed to the same name as that of the dissolved company. Finding out the real number paid by Richard Schaefer for Santa Cruz II was $1.948m and I only received £518k. Then learning that for the purposes of suing me they concocted deductions to arrive at the conclusion that I was actually overpaid despite receiving barely a third of the total amount! Millar described that as:

'... *no doubt an audacious and sadly predictable attempt to legitimise after the event secret dealings with Schaefer and the promoter in America which we discovered from our own investigation*'.

He then posed the question whether, without litigation, '*would any of this have been revealed to him? It seems highly unlikely*'.

The next stage of our opening statement was to address the forensic accountants' evidence. Barry had instructed Grant Thornton to act on his behalf while ASM were on my team. Obviously, ASM had to rely on figures and information provided by the McGuigans' side. These were self-serving figures and information they pulled together after litigation began in an attempt to reconcile and justify everything. But even with those numbers, ASM calculated that the income they declared for the fights from Parodi through Santa Cruz II was light to the tune of £1.5m! In fact, ASM discovered that every single one of the eight events had been profitable. The major caveat they attached was that:

'*Our review is limited to the information available to us and there may be additional income that was earned in relation to Mr Frampton's fights that we have not yet identified.*'

This was not just a standard qualification they arbitrarily add to every investigation they undertake, and to prove that they went on to give the specific examples of '*income from complimentary ticket sales, or additional sponsorship income, or income that has been allocated to non-Frampton fights that relates to Mr Frampton's fights*'. Millar then flagged a few more of ASM's comments and concerns. There was the '*income from sales by Cyclone of large volumes of complimentary tickets*' which they hadn't accounted for. Plus '*the fact that bank statements discovered in these proceedings have shown monies from ticket sales being paid into different bank accounts for different fights, that is, accounts other than the one we looked at, the Cyclone Promotions Ltd account for the NI company*'. ASM raised the '*problems thrown up by Cyclone claiming as fight expenses large figures as deductible expenses, as cash expenses and as subsistence travel costs, including in the periods after fights and sometimes for days and weeks after fights*'. And they lamented the fact that the schedules they had to work from were '*effectively self-serving*'. They were '*calculations prepared by the Cyclone side for these proceedings*'. ASM '*questioned the completeness and accuracy of the figures advanced in those self-serving schedules*'. Last, but not least, Millar highlighted that when Barry had been ordered to disclose what he, his wife and his kids had been paid from the monies my career generated, they arrived at a figure of £1.27m. This amount was provided '*with no supporting details or documentation for the form or indeed the rationale of those payments*'. It's a big enough number but it still made zero sense in light of the fact that what they said Barry earned was substantially less than the '*£990,000 in manager fees [which] had been claimed from Mr Frampton over the period of the eight bouts and deducted from his bout fees*'. Not much about their numbers made sense. The McGuigans were supposed to have gone away and produced the necessary evidence to reconcile income and expenses with the accounts they had already filed at Companies House. Surely the official accounts they signed off on and submitted were accurate and correct?

'*One is tempted to say at this stage,*' Millar concluded, '*why would they produce self-serving calculations through their accountant which don't reconcile to those filed statements?*'

Millar was nearing the end of his opening now. He'd meticulously laid everything out in a very precise way, so it was time to summarise a little and give the facts a little context:

'*The court should focus on the realities of the arrangements put in place by Mr McGuigan during the period 2013 to 2017. He was the prime player in this. That's clear from the facts from the outset from 2012. He was the one who was experienced in the boxing industry. There are other people involved in the case obviously, Mr Frampton as a young boxer and [McGuigan's] sons and so on, but he was the one at the heart of it and he was the one at the start of it. He was the one who had been in the boxing industry all that time and assumed the obligation of manager and agent. According to those arrangements that he put in place not only, as I have said, was he a manager and an agent and a fiduciary throughout; he also sought whenever he could to act personally as the promoter of Mr Frampton, to occupy that dual role as manager and promoter. He also sought to ensure that the income streams which resulted from those fights and indeed the other activities of Mr Frampton, appearances and so on and so forth, came directly to him and his family, and to ensure that that happened in ways that Mr Frampton was simply not informed about. This involved him repeatedly putting himself in a position where he was almost by definition not respecting his overarching duty of single-minded loyalty to Mr Frampton. He had made it effectively impossible for him to do that in the arrangements that he set up. It was just not going to happen. He was not acting in good faith and with complete transparency towards his principal, because Mr Frampton wouldn't have persisted with those arrangements if he had known what was going on.*'

There then followed a lot about the law and relevant legal principles, looking at cases relating to breaches of contract and discharge by breach. It was pretty dry stuff but presumably meant something to the judge and lawyers in the room, and it culminated in Millar emphasising why Barry didn't have a leg to stand on:

'*Carl Frampton was not fully informed of the full facts in the way he should have been. Quite the opposite. He was kept in the dark. So necessarily Barry McGuigan was almost at each turn failing Frampton as his manager and agent. He was not serving his interests properly, and I have to say if he were … he would never have set up the unexplained arrangements that he did to benefit himself, his family, or if he wanted to, if he wanted to be that promoter and do all those things, he should have relinquished the manager role and made sure that Mr Frampton had an independent boxing manager and … a lawyer to advise him as to what was in his best interests independently in real time as his career was developing. That's what's fatal about what was arranged here, that he persisted in doing both functions and it was an impossibility to achieve compliance with his duties as a fiduciary under those arrangements. There are so many points in the story where his failings are apparent. No doubt more will emerge in the course of the evidence. It is almost impossible to list them all.*'

The only other thing Millar needed to do at this stage was address the counterclaims by Barry and Blain against me. Both were looking for fantasy numbers for supposed future earnings they'd lost out on by saying I was the one that breached the management and promotional contracts with them. They were so frivolous and irrelevant that it wasn't something our side was in the least bit concerned about, and we didn't waste much time or energy on them. It didn't take Millar long at all to highlight them for what they were.

'*Mr Frampton was entitled to treat the management and promotional arrangements as discharged for breach in August 2017 whoever or whichever company in addition to Barry McGuigan had an interest in promoting his fights in the future at that stage, and we suggest respectfully the court should see for what they are, should see the reality of the IPA. It was a discreditable and inept attempt to conceal Barry McGuigan's conflict of interest and to tie Mr Frampton into a long-term disadvantageous promotional arrangement, and the court should see for what they are the claims against him in these proceedings. They are tactical claims to obscure the indefensible nature of the McGuigans' position in August 2017 and their obvious liability on the main claim.'*

By the time Millar had concluded his opening statement and sat down, I half expected McCollum to wave a white flag. We hadn't even called a witness yet. We hadn't even put Barry and Blain and Jake on the stand to hammer them yet. We hadn't even started going yet and they were languishing on the ropes. I couldn't imagine what the three of them were thinking that night when they went to bed and envisioned getting cross-examined in the coming days and weeks. I was loving the whole thing, and when it came to my time to speak I had no fear and no nerves. People kept asking me if I was nervous, but I couldn't see what I had to be nervous about. I hadn't done anything wrong, and I didn't have anything to hide. My conscience was completely clear. All I needed to do was tell the truth and let the facts speak for themselves. I actually couldn't believe that the McGuigans were happy to let it all get this far. The examination-in-chief by Millar was straightforward. It started towards the end of day one and lasted through to near the end of day two. That's your first opportunity to tell your story and your barrister guides you along the way, so it went smoothly. But with a little bit of time left before we adjourned, they let McCollum start his cross-examination. That worked out well because his aggressiveness did take me by surprise. It was good he had less than an hour to work with before I went home and I could come back for a full day better prepared for how he'd come at me. Not that I hadn't been warned about his style and the importance of me staying calm throughout. I could not let myself fall into the trap of losing my cool and acting like some sort of hothead. Being cross-examined is a really strange and unnatural experience. It is totally removed from the real world, where it is extremely rare to be involved in such aggressive exchanges. I think everyone who has ever taken the stand has struggled to bite their tongue while being provoked. It was also so repetitive with a lot of irrelevant tripe thrown in for good measure. He called me a liar a few times. If I ever countered a little, he'd say he asks the questions here not me. If I got my retort in in time he'd say, don't you worry Mr Frampton, we'll come back to that. We never did come back to those points but that was his way of airily dismissing my successful effort at wrecking his argument. At one point there was a bit of a debate on a previous point and when I was proved right and McCollum wrong I couldn't resist asking who is lying now. I was out of order, though, and the judge immediately let me know it. Sorry my Lord was all I could say! Nerves is not the right word, but it's certainly stressful being on the stand for a prolonged length of time under cross-examination. It seemed they had a definite strategy to keep me there as long as possible and it wasn't until day six that I stood down. It felt a lot longer. My team kept saying it's nearly over, but on it dragged. The judge was a nice man but maybe a little placid by nature and I wondered if the likes of Justice Horner or Justice Colton, who had presided over the previous hearings, would have moved things along a lot quicker. I don't think I ate a proper meal throughout that whole period as you're always a little on edge and thinking about what you've said and what's around the corner. I remember necking full bags of wine gums just to get some sustenance into me before going again. It would have been a great way to cut weight ahead of a title fight. It was a great feeling when I finally sat down, knowing I could now just sit back and enjoy the show.

***

In days six, seven, eight and nine of the trial we called our witnesses. Each was another nail in the McGuigans' coffin. My accountant Sean McCrory was first up. I've already talked about what he did for me in terms of chasing what was owed and trying in vain to get some clarity on everything, and that's what he ran through again in court. When he was talking about the lengths it took to recover my outstanding appearance-fee money another penny dropped on how naive I'd been. I sat there thinking to myself, why were these bastards taking anything at all. Benchmark, my talent agency, did all the work sourcing and scheduling the work. They then received the money and deducted their fee – which was fair enough, they'd earned it. Why didn't I just get paid the rest then? Why did it go to the McGuigans? Why were they taking any percentage of it? And why the hell did the remainder sit in their accounts for months on end while Sean begged for it? It's mad looking back now that I allowed arrangements like that to be put in place. There were a few times in Sean's evidence when he described himself as being shocked or flabbergasted by what he found. Barry taking cheques addressed to me out of my hands in dressing rooms and ripping them up. Me not knowing what the deductions for expenses related to when I did finally receive some money. Seeing on Companies House that Cyclone Promotions Ltd was apparently insolvent to the tune of £545,000 when he knew they'd recently received £1.2m. He described their filed accounts, necessarily signed off by the Board, as being 'materially inaccurate'. Hounding him to reissue historical VAT invoices was another point he could never get his head around because they would never provide him with any information or evidence as to why my company should have to do that. In actual fact, all the evidence he found suggested the complete opposite. My company was not registered for VAT during that period. Lermer, the McGuigans' man, had also decided it didn't need to be. When an early purse I was paid did have a VAT element attached, Lermer actually wrote to Barry to tell him VAT should not be included going forward. The next purse after that, there's an email from Sandra specifying it is net of VAT as it should have been. The BBBofC's own standard bout contract also stipulates that bout agreements are exclusive of VAT. They were chancing it, and Sean wasn't playing ball.

Paul Johnstone, who runs the Monkstown Boxing Club where I'd train during fight week in Belfast, was up next. He'd seen us all together during the good times early on and said ahead of the doomed Gutierrez fight it was clear that everything had changed for the worse. Where before they'd have been all around me helping as I shed those final pounds, now Barry was doing his own weight session while Shane wrestled with his mate John Connors, an S&C guy. Paul also recalled a conversation he had with Shane in his office at the gym while I was outside in a sweatsuit killing myself to make weight:

'*He said that he was finished. He said that, at best he has one more fight in him. And that he didn't really want Carl to be a Ricky Hatton and retire and spend his money and come back. That he wasn't going to train a bum essentially.*'

That's my trainer, speaking about me to someone he barely knows just before a major fight. Unreal.

Cherri Norman then took the stand, and she was very good. She had been Barry's PA from 2007 until 2015, working across all their various companies on a wide range of tasks. From Barry's own TV work and appearances, through all of their property dealings and everything in between, Cherri had been involved in the lot. There were offshore companies set up in the Bahamas and Isle of Man to house their assets. There were properties in Canterbury rented out to students. She talked about various company-name changes that I struggled to keep up with. Then original accountants being dismissed due to a dispute over unpaid invoices and Lermer arriving on the scene. When asked how she would describe the financial record keeping she answered, *'pretty shambolic'*. There was mention then of a tax investigation into the McGuigans' business, which led them to want to ringfence some properties. Yet another new company was opened, and a few months later the two companies switched names. I had no clue what was going on, but it all seemed weird. It also seemed like Barry and Sandra opened and closed companies as often as the rest of us change our socks. I was interested to learn from Cherri's evidence about the original guys whom Barry had had fund everything. Until then, I never knew of their existence – but it seems like that tried-and-tested method was in place from the start. Paul Dunkley and David Hammond were wealthy businessmen who liked boxing, so Barry had them stump up the cash to embark on his management career via Barry McGuigan Enterprises Ltd. Towards the end of 2013, when I was European champion and had just headlined my first Cyclone show, that company was suddenly shut down. Cherri explained why:

'He was concerned that it be shut down properly in case Paul Dunkley or David Hammond came back at any point to pursue a financial recompense for having started Carl's career at the beginning.'

Getting Cherri's inside take on the end of the Matchroom affair was also enlightening. She said Matchroom:

'... could agree Carl's purse and what Carl needed, [but] they couldn't agree on what Barry wanted'. That *'it came to an end in short because Barry was pushing for too much in terms of his own arrangement financially'*. She said it was the *'only time I have seen him a little bit panicked, and he was worried he may have done something quite bad for Carl's career. I think Matchroom could see that there was a conflict between Barry's role as manager and what he was trying to obviously get for himself.'*

Cherri was also unequivocal in her evidence that they were all very aware of the direct conflict of interest between being manager and promoter, and that they discussed how they'd navigate that issue. When they talked about Barry becoming promoter as well as manager:

'... *they were conscious of the fact that there would be a conflict of interest. They discussed using Blain McGuigan as the promoter instead, so that there was a degree of separation between the management and the promotion.*'

All this is obvious to anyone with any knowledge of the whole situation, but it was great that here was someone on the stand who had been there in person witnessing it all in real time. Cherri was also able to confirm that they'd invoice Warren for more on top of what was being invoiced for my purse. Remember, they took their cuts out of my purse, but apparently they had a side agreement to get even more without my knowledge. Regarding the time when I first instructed my own accountants in Belfast to look after my affairs, Cherri described Sandra as being:

'*very agitated by that and [she] made it clear that that wasn't going to happen, and she did say repeatedly that he had to move to Jeff Lermer's*'.

When Millar asked Cherri why Sandra was so adamant on the point, her answer cut to the core of everything:

'*Because his accountants would want to see full transparency on the monies coming in and all of Cyclone's financials and that there was no way that was going to happen.*'

Millar then asked why most of the McGuigan family were appointed as directors of Cyclone Promotions when the original company was set up:

'*Blain and Jake wanted to be involved, they needed jobs. Barry and Sandra very much wanted to help them financially and set them up so they could obviously have mortgages. Blain in particular I remember Sandra saying that he was getting to an age where he may want to settle down and have a family and he would need a mortgage. He didn't have a job therefore he didn't have a wage and he couldn't get a mortgage. So, by giving them directorships it guaranteed them an income.'*

It's difficult to explain my emotions listening to evidence like this. It's a mixture of anger, disbelief and pity I suppose. Anger that I was the mug paying those two. Disbelief that it was all so cold and calculated. And pity that two grown men still needed support from their parents.

Cherri wasn't on the stand for long, but nearly everything she said was a damning indictment of how the McGuigans operated. Although nothing at all had been disclosed in evidence despite court orders, Cherri confirmed that there most certainly were budgets and post-fight reconciliations compiled relating to my shows. She would have sat alongside Sandra doing many of them. They were, Cherri said, confusing because there were always multiple sets of figures floating about. Using the Parodi fight as an example she said:

'there was a profit of, in one set of figures, for about £130,000 but we sent it into the BBBofC at a loss of £2,000 for that fight'.

As time went on, however, Cherri was eased out. Despite having always had access to everything across all the businesses, she was kept completely away from the Cyclone emails. Then, when she came back from maternity leave, she was told the office had moved to London and everything would now go through the Cyclone arm of their businesses. Cherri couldn't understand how that would work as there were a lot of different revenue streams, not just the Cyclone events which the company was formed to run. That didn't matter, she was told. Barry is the sole shareholder and so any profit is his entirely.

There followed a couple of brief appearances by witnesses who gave an idea of the amount of cash that floated about the shows. A guy called Conor Robb worked in the Money Store in Belfast city centre and recalled separate occasions when Nelson, Barry and Sandra came in with bags of notes. Around £70,000 or

£80,000 he reckoned. Enough that they had to close and lock up the shop in order to deal with the quantity safely. The Belfast boxing promoter and manager Mark Dunlop then recounted the time he met with Barry in a car park to give him a grand in exchange for two of Dunlop's fighters being allowed onto my undercard. It was important for us to highlight the fact there was so much cash passing from hand to hand, above and beyond anything that would have been documented via bank records. It was all money I was generating. All money I should have been aware of and should have received my share of.

Our final witness was Ger Murphy. The McGuigans brought him on board in early 2015, originally as operations manager. As he'd done with other companies in the past, Ger was going to improve the internal systems and make the business more efficient. But he said that role never came to fruition. All of his suggestions or attempts to enhance how Cyclone operated day-to-day were shot down. No one wanted to change, he said. When asked to describe how the operations of the company were run, his answer was similar to that given by Cherri the day before: 'pretty chaotic'. In truth, Ger said, the majority of his time was spent putting creditors desperately seeking what they were owed on the long finger. He was also heavily involved in the ticketing for each of my fights. Sandra controlled all of the ringside seats and pushed hard to get as much as she could for them. Face value may have been between £400 and £800, but she had crazy aspirations of getting up to £10,000 a pop as if my fights were the reincarnation of Ali versus Frazier or something. She also put tickets on third-party vendor sites like StubHub, simply because that's what Matchroom did. But in Ger's experience, she never got anywhere near what she was hoping for. He's not sure any of the tickets put on StubHub for the Quigg fight were even sold at all because they were so overpriced. He said a lot of the best seats often ended up unsold because Sandra wouldn't accept face value for them. Ger could never get his head around the McGuigans' approach to comps for VIPs either. He'd spent years working in the music business, organising big festivals and concerts, and he explained how a VIP guestlist was standard. Having a few stars at your event was free and great publicity. When he saw Sandra was charging the likes of Rory McIlroy and Snow Patrol for their seats, he couldn't believe it but was told boxing is different. I now know that's complete bollocks. McIlroy sat ringside for my comeback against Garcia on a Warren promotion, and I know for a fact he wasn't charged a penny for the pleasure!

Ger is an IT guy as well. He was a computer programmer by qualification and when he was young he delivered a massive project for Halifax Bank, which earned him enough dough to do what he wanted for a decade. That turned out to be volunteering for Oxfam, which in turn led him to the events industry. His computer skills made him a good man to comment on the infamous email migration which the McGuigans claimed caused them to lose access to all of their emails for the period in question. Before I go on, I'm conscious that with the expenses deducted from my purses, the IPA I signed and now the missing emails, that's three separate issues I've described as infamous in a short space of time. That probably seems like a lot of infamy for a single story but you're going to have to live with it because they all qualify fully for the moniker! The emails were of importance to us for a number of obvious reasons. First and foremost, I knew I was telling the truth and all I wanted was everyone else to be forced to do the same. I had no idea what they'd all been emailing each other over the years, but I knew that I wanted absolutely everything disclosed for the court to review. I knew, for example, that there would be plenty of emails proving Barry was acting as a promoter and a manager. And on the flipside that Blain most certainly was not a genuine promoter, leading negotiations and deals on little more than a few undercard bouts. I knew that there would be correspondence which would shed light on the Matchroom fallout. Likewise, I knew there'd be emails from other promoters expressing an interest in me and giving us a better idea of my true value. Bottom line, I believed the emails could only help my case while at the same time undermining the McGuigans'. And that's why we didn't for a single second believe the cock-and-bull story about everything being lost. Ger's testimony when asked if he was aware of any problems with the migration is therefore worth repeating here:

'No, there were definitely ... no problems. It's very hard for a migration like that to go wrong because you are copying data over. So even if it fails the first time, the data still exists in the previous, so when you are copying over to Microsoft it still exists on Google until you say I don't need it anymore. The system doesn't allow you to accidentally cut it and paste it, rather than cutting and pasting, it has to be copy and paste.'

No further questions on that one, your honour!

*＊＊

We were so far up on points right now that the other corner really should have thrown in the towel. But that was the last thing I wanted them to do at this stage. I was enjoying myself. It was time for Barry to take the stand and I knew the mauling he was in for. It had been going terribly for the McGuigans from day one of the trial, but things were about to get a whole lot worse. Their QC did the best he could, teeing Barry up with questions and guiding him to the answers they had obviously practised. It was embarrassing stuff, but they'd created such a fantasy version of events that even while in the safe hands of his own barrister, it was easy to catch him out on a few points. At one stage he claimed that if a promoter allowed his fighter to fight on another promoter's show, the fighter would be expected to pay his promoter *'at least 50%'* of his purse. Absolute nonsense. It would be a standard 80–20 per cent split in most promotional contracts and, if you had a good manager negotiating on your behalf, you'd try to limit it even more. Blain even testified as much a few days later when he said it would be anywhere from 10 to 20 per cent and that 15 per cent is the usual. Barry also swore that me getting £145,000 to fight Kiko for the world title was great money, much more than he received when he fought for his world title in 1985. £90,000, he said he was paid. Which with inflation was actually worth over £200,000 in 2014 when I beat Kiko the second time. So no, Barry. It wasn't great money, mate. You got around sixty grand more than me and I bet you the Loftus Road show wasn't heavily funded by the government either!

Barry also slipped up while McCollum was trying to create a world whereby no other promoter was interested in me and that signing the IPA with Cyclone was both a fantastic career move and my only option at the time. Not once, but twice he named the American promoters Golden Boy as an example of a big gun not wanting to sign me. *'They didn't show any interest in him'*, and later, *'there was absolutely no interest in him from them'*. Absolutely no interest. No interest, that is, apart from the formal written offer and contracts received from Golden Boy's attorney in 2014, which I was never made aware of. They came via email to Barry and Jake. Note that Blain was nowhere to be seen. The attorney wrote that he had been advised on *'the parameters of a promotional agreement between Golden Boy, Carl Frampton and Cyclone Boxing'*. That he had *'reviewed the document that you sent in which you set forth your vision for Mr. Frampton going forward'*. I wonder what that vision was. And that, surprise surprise, *'Golden Boy is interested in pursuing a deal whereby Golden Boy would promote Mr. Frampton and remit payments to Cyclone each time he fights.'* Note the strange way it expressly confirms no money will go directly to me, the fighter. Finally, Golden Boy had '*drafted and attached a Letter Agreement between Cyclone and Golden Boy and a Promotional Agreement between Golden Boy and Mr. Frampton*'. Note the two separate agreements on the table. One for me, and the rest for the McGuigans, on top of the percentages they'd take from my purse. It was Barry – my manager, remember – who led the way in responding with an email to the team, minus myself, the next day:

'*We are not handing everything over to them, (they'll put us down as co-promoters)!! But "they" have complete control of World wide [sic] TV rights, gate receipts etc!! Are they serious?*' he ranted.

I'm still trying to figure out why my manager would care about any of that.

'*If we sign this, we've all worked for four and a half years for nothing,*' he continued. '*Based on the demand for tickets Carl will sell out Ravenhill 20-000, or better still the outside arena at the Kings Hall where we could erect a teared [sic] seating arena that could hold 15-000 people and we could control pouring rights, food merchandise and every person who comes through the gate.*'

Getting me the most money and best opportunities doesn't seem to be part of anyone's thinking here.

'*It has long been our ambition to not only make Carl a World Champion but to also have an ongoing Broadcasting deal with a substantial TV Network, this deal scuppers that objective, so we can't have that.*'

And there you have it, folks. The true goal of my manager!

Millar versus Barry was about as competitive as me versus Istvan Szabo. It's hard to put into words the extent of the battering Barry took. It's why I'm still gutted people couldn't sit in the court gallery and watch it all happen in real time. Or better still, that the whole extravaganza wasn't broadcast live like the OJ trial or something. And it's impossible in a book this size to detail every punch that landed. But I'll do my best to recall a selection of the exchanges to give a flavour of what unfolded during the five days he spent giving evidence.

We opened up asking about the mysteriously irretrievable emails. Millar read an email from June 2017 in which Rupert Phillips says, '*Stuart has now completed the data migration moving Gmail to the new Microsoft Office licenses and transferring the data.*' Basically, job done, no issues to report.

'*I am going to put to you that the email migration exercise appears to have been successful, do you agree or disagree?*' Millar asked.

'*If you tell me so,*' answered Barry.

We were only five minutes in and to my mind he was coming across as extremely nervous. When pushed on anything he kept repeating the same rehearsed dopey line. He must have churned it out dozens of times. It was always a variation of:

'*My business was to be in the gym managing the fighters, making sure they trained correctly and getting them into great condition, picking their opponents, getting them the best purse they could get.*'

Over and over again he relied on this defence. It was an obvious tactic, to act like he was just a simple, humble boxing man – used to the spit and sawdust of the gym, but incapable of opening an email. His instinct was to deny everything. Even the most basic question like, are you familiar with the BBBofC's management contract? This is a two-pager he's signed numerous times.

'No,' he replied. '*I wouldn't say I'm familiar with it.*'

Thirty seconds of probing later, '*I was familiar with it, of course, yes.*'

It was truly surreal stuff. Everyone already knew the lost-emails excuse was pure fantasy, but it's a court case so you need to labour the point to eliminate all doubt. So Millar asked – rhetorically, basically – whether Barry was planning to call the IT company Eipsys as a witness. They did the migration, so would be able to testify that it had somehow gone horribly wrong and all data had vanished. Needless to say, there was no plan for us to hear from Eipsys at any point in the trial. Then Millar threw in a query as to how the hell they had managed to find an email from Jake's Cyclone address whilst Mark Dunlop was on the stand in order to use it against him in cross-examination that same day. Good going considering it should have been irretrievable. Barry also had his own personal email address he used, and unfortunately for him Cherri Norman once had access and would send emails from it. She'd provided one from that address for her own evidence, which is what alerted us to its existence. Millar asked Barry whether, as part of the disclosure exercise, he'd been told by his solicitors to do a word search on those emails for the name, Carl Frampton. The question was again virtually rhetorical, and the answer, that he didn't do the search, was just as predictable.

Next up was a brief look at the performance of the myriad companies Barry and Sandra had set up and dissolved over the years. The first one mentioned was Barranda, which collapsed with debts of £80,000 in the mid-nineties. The pair of them were declared unfit to be directors of a company and picked up five-year bans after they admitted allegations made by the Department of Economic Development that they had misappropriated company funds. In other words, spending company money on their own personal expenses. They had never told me about any of that before. The second was Barry McGuigan Enterprises Ltd, the company which signed me and which Dunkley and Hammond funded with at least £200,000 by Barry's own estimation. It reported losses of £224,000 in 2009, £123,000 in 2010 and £365,000 in 2011 before being dissolved in 2013. In 2010, Barry McGuigan Boxing Academy Ltd was set up and subsequently reported losses every year from 2010 through 2015. Square Ring Ltd appeared in 2012, reported losses in 2014 and 2015, and was dissolved in 2017. In 2013, McGuigan's Gym Ltd was established. True to form, it also reported losses in

2014, 2015 and 2016. The last company mentioned was Cyclone Promotions Ltd, also founded in 2013. Its losses rose steadily from day one and in 2016 a massive £555,000 loss was filed at Companies House. Every set of accounts we could find for every company Barry was involved in had reported a loss. Then, however, the litigation began. Then, my forensic accountants started doing a bit of digging. And then, as if by magic, a profit was finally reported. Millar pounced.

'*And it's obvious, isn't it Mr McGuigan, that the reason that happened was that we had caught you out ... as somebody who serially filed company accounts for sports management companies, reporting losses; we caught you out, didn't we?*'

'*I don't accept that.*'

'*And you and your accountants and your lawyers presumably had to decide what to do about that and you decided to account for that next financial year in a completely different way to the way you had always accounted before and report a profit?*'

'*Mm-hmm.*'

We took a quick look at the original contracts I signed. As usual, nothing was straightforward. Barry didn't actually have a BBBofC managerial licence at the time, so Barry Hearn was officially my manager. What I signed with McGuigan was an agreement that he would promote or co-promote my first sixteen fights. It was also agreed that after a year he would have his managerial licence in place, and he would then take over from Hearn and effectively become my manager and my promoter. That's the very thing the world of boxing, for obvious reasons, tries very hard to avoid. The very thing that the US actually has in place a federal law named the Ali Act to prohibit.

'*From the outset your intention was to manage and promote him,*' Millar accused.

This time, even Barry couldn't act dumb.

'*Yes,*' he said. '*In this agreement, yes, that's right.*'

There is an entire section on page one of the standard BBBofC Boxer/Manager Agreement entitled, 'Possible Conflicts of Interest'. The first clause in it regards scenarios where the manager will also be the promoter and the second addresses scenarios in which the manager has any connection to a promoter which '*might reasonably be thought to affect the manager's ability to act independently in the best interest of the boxer*'. The BBBofC has created a form, Form 36A, which the manager must complete and deliver to the boxer to flag the conflict when it arises. In reality, it's all a bit of a joke and Form 36A makes the whole situation worse. It essentially legitimises a conflict of interest detrimental to a fighter that would otherwise be regarded as a straightforward breach of the Boxer/Management Agreement. But anyway, that's boxing. Millar asked Barry whether he thought either of the two conflict clauses ever applied to him throughout my career. He had the gall to answer that they didn't. He'd just admitted that his intention from the outset was to manage and promote me! And even if we believed the fantasy that he was only my manager, his case was that his own son was promoting me on behalf of a company Barry was a shareholder and director of and yet he still couldn't admit that fell within potential conflict of interests. Better still, he confirmed he'd sent me Form 36A – which is explicitly for conflicts of interest. All we needed to do was give him a spade and he kept digging a deeper hole for himself every time he opened his mouth. And it teed Millar up perfectly to quote from Barry's own 1992 memoir, in which he made his views on conflicts of interest crystal clear:

'*One thing that must, simply must, be done away with is this crazy situation where a manager can also be a promoter. The Board tried to abolish this practice in 1989, but all that happened was that a manager would get his son or a friend or a business associate to be the promoter of record and the whole charade continued exactly as before.*'

'There should never be any financial connection whatsoever, either directly or indirectly, between any manager and any promoter. Even a blind man can see that when you have the one person wearing two hats – or having someone else wear one for him – then that is an obvious conflict of interest.'

No amount of semantics or moral gymnastics could get him out of that one. That he had such forthright views on the whole issue was important for a number of reasons. It proved that he didn't stumble into this situation where he unwittingly found himself wearing both hats. He strode in with his eyes wide open. It also blew through this façade of naivety and simple innocence Barry was attempting to portray. In reality, this is a man who has been through extensive legal battles pertaining to the management and promotion of his own boxing career. He has been in the business of boxing all his life. He knows it inside out. He has been a vocal and public advocate for fighters having more rights and more of a say and more control over their own careers. He is well read and well educated on the subject. In his own book he went into some depth on the deficiencies of contracts and business arrangements in boxing:

'To read the standard contract you would think that the manager owned the fighter when, in fact, it is the boxer who employs a manager to carry out certain functions and duties for him.'

'... as far as not knowing anything about managing their careers, they could hardly be any worse off; as it stands most of them know nothing about it because their managers won't tell them.'

'The management/boxer contract should be for no more than twelve or, at an absolute maximum, eighteen months. Right now, it is little more than a slave contract.'

'... his relationship with his manager ... has to be a relationship built on trust and faith, and once you've lost that the relationship is over.'

Barry even attempted to establish a trade union for boxers and campaign for their rights against managers:

'We encourage boxers to play an active part in their careers and learn to handle their financial affairs in conjunction with their managers – let them know they are entitled to see all the records and all the financial papers relating to them.'

For the man who has done all this, and to have had his own experience of a legal dispute, to claim ignorance is implausible to say the least.

More damning evidence followed relating to the brief moment in time when I had my own independent accountants, Flannigan, Edmunds & Bannon, in Belfast to act on my behalf. They spoke to Sandra and then emailed Barry with a proposed cashflow structure allowing me to receive my purses directly and then pay out my expenses. They requested a meeting with Barry to discuss. An email from Sandra to their own accountant Lermer at the time was then read out, including the line, '*Barry is not getting involved with the meeting.*' It also said he'd spoken to me about Jeff being the man to look after boxers. It was all there in black and white – so Millar got to work, emphasising that Barry didn't want independent accountants anywhere near me:

'*You and Sandra spoke to him to persuade not to stay with them, but to go with Mr Lermer, your accountant, didn't you?*'

'*Yeah, that's what it seems like in the letter, yeah.*'

'*I'm putting it to you that you arranged for him to meet Mr Lermer at the Butcher & Grill restaurant with Sandra present?*'

'*Mm-hmm.*'

'*And persuaded him that Mr Lermer was the accountant who should act for him, rather than the Belfast accountants, do you remember that meeting?*'

'*I accept that.*'

It was a deliberate strategy, Millar said, put into effect as soon as my own accountants proposed that my purses were paid to me before anyone else had a chance to take their cut.

We then moved on to post-Kiko I and the lack of effort to secure me a deal with another promoter. Eddie Hearn had emailed Matchroom's offer to Jake because Barry had been ill. Email evidence was then produced to prove Cherri knew about it and Barry had spoken to the lawyers about it. It seemed like everyone knew about this offer except me. Barry claimed he showed me the email but made a fool of himself again when pressed on it. He couldn't explain why it wasn't just forwarded to me, the regular way you'd share an email with someone. And he couldn't articulate how exactly I was supposed to have physically seen this email if it hadn't been forwarded to me.

'Why', Millar asked, '*is there never a document, a letter or an email to support your account of things with him?*'

The delusion levels continued to rise ever higher when Millar challenged Barry on his contention that, off my own bat, I had gone to him and said, let's forget about Hearn and Warren and all the other established and successful promoters with years of proven success in building fighters. I don't want any of them, I want you Barry who's done a couple of shows in the Ulster Hall. And let's get your unemployed musician son involved too please.

'*Tell me what he said? What was his proposal?*' Millar asked him.

'*I want you to do it, I want you to manage and promote me because, you know, you done a great job in the two Ulster Hall shows and I believe that you can do, you can bring me to the world championship.*'

'*Who is "you" in that sentence?*'

'*As in me.*'

'*Barry McGuigan personally?*'

'*In conjunction with Jake and Shane.*'

'Oh he said that, did he?'

'Yes, he did. He said if you, you know, with your promotional abilities and you have done it before.'

Barry's second day under cross-examination was just as damaging for his side's chances of salvaging anything from the trial. Our quotes from the Steve Wellings' articles in which Barry and I spoke about the new Cyclone set-up were read out – confirming again that, contrary to what the McGuigans subsequently argued, everyone was publicly projecting the understanding that I was part of the new Cyclone promotional outfit. Then the contract signed with Warren to get the whole thing rolling was presented, including the line, *'This is an agreement for a four-fight deal with Carl Frampton, who is promoted by Barry McGuigan.'* Just more evidence Barry was acting as my promoter regardless of what he was claiming about being my manager only. He was very on edge on the stand now, often appearing on the brink of losing his temper. He kept jumping in and trying to respond before full questions were asked or giving whatever answer he had prepared in his head without actually addressing what had been put to him. The judge had to warn him a few times about that.

Barry got even more worked up when it came to discussing the set-up of Cyclone Promotions Ltd. He played the humble boxer card again, professing to have zero knowledge of how a business is run. At one point an exasperated Millar asked him why the hell he was both a director and the sole shareholder then! Barry's mood got worse as the evidence continued to stack up against him. Not a single shred of paper to show I took part in a meeting or decision regarding Cyclone business, despite Barry's claims I was involved in everything. The revelation that I was the only director without access to the company bank account. Confirmation that Blain, Jake and Shane were all on about three grand a month as directors, while I got nothing. Director's loans popped up too. Apparently, everyone else was taking advantage of that happy benefit of being a director except me. Best of all, though, was our first look at some of the expenses that the McGuigans were charging to the Cyclone account. Expenses which needed to be directly related to the promotion of my boxing career to be considered genuine and appropriate business costs.

'4th of November 2013, £197.23 spent at the Whitstable Oyster Company in Whitstable?'

'Yes.'

'What's the Whitstable Oyster Company?'

'The Whitstable Oyster Company, I believe, is a restaurant.'

'It is an expensive restaurant on the beach near your home in Kent, isn't it?'

'Yes, it is an expensive restaurant, yes.'

'So why was this company paying for a meal at that restaurant?'

'I don't know the answer to that.'

'26th of November 2013, somebody used this company to spend £365 at Marks & Spencer in Canterbury. But why was this company spending £365 in Marks & Spencer in Canterbury?'

'Again, I can't answer that.'

'This is a boxing promotion company for my client's career, isn't it?'

'Mm-hmm.'

'So there has to be some explanation of how that relates to his career, doesn't there, and the promotion of his career?'

'Yes.'

'So, what is it?'

'I can't answer that.'

'24th of December 2013, Christmas Eve. £48 spent in the Tandoori, the Kashmir Tandoori in Canterbury on Christmas Eve?'

'Yes.'

'What's that got to do with the promotion of my client's boxing career?'

'I can't answer that either, I'm afraid.'

'It's got nothing to do with it, has it? These are McGuigan family expenses, personal expenses being paid out of this account, aren't they?'

'It appears so, yes.'

'Entry for 6th of January 2014, now in the beginning of 2014.'

'Yes.'

'Somebody is spending £374.00 at the Whitstable Oyster Company?'

'Mm-hmm.'

'It's got nothing to do with my client's career, has it?'

'I don't know, I can't answer that.'

'It's a lot of money to spend on a meal, isn't it? 27th of January 2014 at the bottom, somebody's shopping in Waitrose in Canterbury using funds from this company; do you know what that's about?'

'No. I didn't do, I don't do the shopping.'

'14th of April 2014, seven entries down on that page.'

'Mm-hmm.'

'Somebody is spending £270 in Branching Out in Canterbury. Do you know what Branching Out is in Canterbury?'

'No idea.'

'Can I put it to you it is an antiques store –'

'Oh right.'

'– in Canterbury, does that ring any bells?'

'No idea.'

'Do you know why somebody would be paying money to an antiques store in Canterbury from this account?'

'No.'

'Do you know who was doing that?'

'I have no idea.'

'29th of April, there is a payment of £262.00 to a veterinary surgeon in Whitstable. Do you have a pet in your family?'

'*I'm currently minding my son's two Bulldogs, yes.*'

'*Did you have a pet in 2014?*'

'*Oh we would have done, yes.*'

'*Was your vet in Whitstable?*'

'*We have a vet in Whitstable, correct, yes.*'

'*11th of July 2014, somebody spent £4.29 in a McDonald's in Billingsgate using this company account. Why was that a permissible use of this account?*'

'*Again, I don't want to dispute any of this with you because I don't know where the accounts came from, or I don't know who was responsible for popping into McDonald's.*'

'*3rd of November £250 in Fenwick's in Canterbury. Was personal clothes shopping permitted on this? £350.00 spent at David Linley & Co. in London, do you see that?*'

'*I'm not there yet. I see that, yes.*'

'*Do you know what David Linley & Co. is?*'

'*No idea.*'

'*It's a luxury furniture maker in Belgravia, in Pimlico in London.*'

'*Okay.*'

'*Can you help as to why somebody was spending money on this account in David Linley & Co.?*'

'*No, I can't tell you.*'

'*You see the truth is you were, this was just being used as a McGuigan family account, wasn't it, when convenient, for personal expenses?*'

'*It looks like we were using it for some personal expenses, correct, yes.*'

'*This was exactly what you and Sandra had been disqualified for as company directors in Northern Ireland in 1996, wasn't it?*'

'*I think it was, yes.*'

Those were just a few of the hundreds of examples my team picked out. But there was plenty more to come as Barry's nightmare in the dock continued. Millar listed three separate Cyclone bank accounts which were set up and which we only became aware of after the McGuigan's own side discovered transaction statements during these proceedings. Barry played dumb and Millar put it to him that he was:

'*... pleading ignorance about these bank accounts because you don't want to answer my questions about them*'.

There didn't seem to be any justification for this constant opening of different bank accounts, just like it was difficult to find good reason for them establishing new companies on a continual basis or changing names back and forth. But it all pointed towards one strategy:

'*Fragmenting income and expenditure for a company between different company bank accounts makes it more difficult for people to follow the money, doesn't it?*'

'*I'm sure that all of the money for the tickets and everything else was reconciled. I can be sure about that.*'

'*Just as it is the practice, your practice to have lots of different companies to do business through, it's your practice to have lots of different bank accounts to do business through, isn't it, Mr McGuigan?*'

'*I didn't do the accounts and therefore I don't know and can't answer that.*'

Our point well and truly made, Millar left it at that and moved on. We challenged the contention that Blain, a twenty-nine-year-old jobbing musician, could on any planet be regarded as qualified to be the promoter of major boxing events with budgets running into hundreds of thousands, or later millions, of pounds. Then we challenged the weakness and cheapness of undercards, all done to maximise the McGuigans' profits. Barry was adamant that the structure of the undercards had nothing to do with him. That Blain was the only man to speak to about them. So why didn't you say that to Mark Dunlop when he dealt with you to place his fighters then? I loved that Millar was too clever for him and was always sharp enough to catch him out. Barry changed tack and acted mortified that the undercards could be described as weak. It was an insult to the fighters he said. For the record, it was not at all insulting to the fighters involved to say they were weak undercards. Whether weak or strong, it was not a reflection on their ability or their potential. You could fill an undercard with ten future superstars and it would still clearly be weak because they'd all be doing four- or six-rounders, against uncompetitive opponents, for a few grand each. Boxing fans accept a few of those to open up each show, but then they want evenly matched contests featuring experienced high-level operators or established names. As I've said before, just look at the difference in terms of strength in depth when Warren was promoting me in the same venues.

Barry would tie himself in knots when grilled on why his side had not managed to produce during the disclosure exercise a single contemporary document to evidence pre-fight budgets or post-fight reconciliations. According to him, they definitely existed, and they were definitely shared with me – so I definitely knew exactly what was going on. But at the same time, he definitely didn't see them and wasn't involved in them because he was in the gym with me and the other fighters all the time. He struggled then when Millar asked him how he could be fulfilling his fiduciary duty towards me and ensuring I was getting the best purse possible if he had no knowledge of the overall income and what the show was forecast to make.

Tickets followed. Again, Barry had produced zero documents to evidence how many tickets Cyclone took from the venue, how many they sold, what they sold them for or who they sold them to. The majority were cash transactions so there were no bank statements either. We went to Ticketmaster ourselves and they disclosed how many complimentary tickets the McGuigans took for each fight: 1,103 tickets for the Parodi fight, 1,535 for the Cazares fight and 1,374 for the Avalos fight. Huge quantities for a venue with less than 9,000 seats by anyone's measure. To give a bit of perspective, Ticketmaster disclosed that Matchroom had taken 594 tickets for themselves when I fought Kiko at the same venue. Our forensic accountants had specifically requested information on where the money received for these thousands of tickets went and the only answer they ever got from Barry's forensic accountants was, 'records not maintained'.

Moving on, an email from Barry to Sampson Lewkowicz, arranging Kiko II, then led to an interesting exchange:

'December 2013. And you are trying to negotiate with Sampson Boxing, a bout with Martinez, a second bout with Martinez, correct?'

'Okay, yes.'

'And it is from your Barry McGuigan [personal] email address?'

'Mm-hmm.'

'Not from your Cyclone Promotions email address. So, in what capacity were you doing this, manager or promoter, for my client?'

'I was the manager, obviously.'

'As the manager?'

'Yes, can you give me time to read it and then ask me the questions?'

'Sure.'

'Okay. Sorry I'm so slow, my Lord, this is just a small magnifying glass. Yes?'

'All right, so that email is you acting as promoter for the potential fight against Martinez, isn't it?'

'Well, I'm sure myself and my son would have drawn, or would have drawn that up.'

'It's not from your son, it's from you?'

'It's from me, yes'

'To him?'

'*To him, correct.*'

'*It's a direct approach by you as a promoter to try and set up a fight, isn't it?*'

'*Yes.*'

'*It's the sort of communication I was putting to you yesterday we hadn't received in your discovery in this case from the CyclonePromotions.com email address. We have this example because it's from a different email address.*'

The exchange was telling for a number of reasons. It proved once again Barry was more than capable of handling emails and negotiating major deals for my career. He did not actually spend each waking hour in the gymnasium, getting me in good condition, picking my opponents, etc. as he'd like the court to believe. It proved once again Barry was the real promoter and Blain was not doing the job. It hammered home once again our point that if we had their emails from the Cyclone address, we'd be overwhelmed with evidence to back up our case. The exchange was also a template for understanding Barry's tactics and performance on the stand. Step one was the '*Mm-hmm*', which would appear when he knew he was being led down a path which was only going to end badly for him. Then he'd get tetchy, like the snapped '*Can you give me time to read it and then ask me the questions?*' when he's on the edge of losing his cool. Step three, the '*Sorry I'm so slow, my Lord, this is just a small magnifying glass*' is the attempt to garner sympathy for the respectful and humble old boxing man who can barely see and is just mystified by everything that's happening to him. This, despite the fact that there are articles online in which Barry claims to have 20/20 vision after undergoing laser eye surgery. I think the magnifying glass he was using on the stand had actually been left out as a bit of a laugh more than anything else. And then there'd be denial, here trying to rope his son in as if maybe he drafted the email and sent it from his old man's address. Finally, when there were no more outs, there'd be a resigned acceptance of what Millar was putting to him. I could read him like a book by this point!

There was still time for us to land a few more blows before the judge rang the final bell on day eleven. Barry kept trying to downplay the size of the crowd that attended Kiko II at the Titanic Slipway. He said it was all a PR stunt claiming it was 16,000 and in actual fact was closer to 12,000. The idea here was obviously to reduce the actual gate they had to declare and therefore under-report the profit made. It didn't take long for Millar to make a mockery of Barry's claim. Firstly, he reminded Barry that he'd told his own forensic accountants that the crowd was 13,500. So, we're already 1,500 up on 12,000 and it appears Barry is plucking numbers from thin air. Our side didn't need to pluck numbers from anywhere. We'd gone to Ticketmaster, who controlled the tickets, and Eventsec, who controlled the seats which were installed. Ticketmaster confirmed there were 15,886 tickets and we had the signed contract with Eventsec which was for 15,900 seats. Strikingly similar numbers which tied in with everything reported at the time. There was another amusing moment when Barry claimed that Eventsec had removed thousands of seats ahead of the fight.

'Where is the evidence of that, Mr McGuigan?' Millar asked.

'You'd need to get the guy from Eventsec to come along and –'

'Yes, you do, don't you?'

'Yes.'

'So will you do that, will you?'

'I don't think so, no.'

Another one of those classic courtroom-drama, no-further-questions-your-honour moments!

Barry's third day of cross-examination was as bad for his case and as good for mine as days one and two. The Quigg expenses were up first. A nice round £75,000 is what they'd calculated. When litigation began, they had been forced to provide some evidence as to how they arrived at this figure, so finally I got a bit of a breakdown. It was hilarious. The Midland Hotel, where we stayed, was a big number. Apparently, I needed forty-one rooms on the night of the fight for my team! Millar concluded that they started at what I was paid and worked backwards on the expenses to try and justify the number I received. From Quigg we jumped to Santa Cruz I. Barry denied ripping up my cheque in the changing room but admitted taking it from me and handing it back to the guy who'd given me it. Why do that, Millar asked. Why not let me have it and wait for the rest to be wired? When Barry wasn't able to provide a sensible explanation, Millar did it for him:

'You wanted to receive the money as Cyclone so you could control the money.'

Millar shared the contract detailing the pot for Santa Cruz I was actually $1.665m and that one of the mystery Coutts accounts got the money before transferring most of it into a second, equally mysterious, Coutts account. Three facts I was never made aware of, and Millar wanted to emphasise that to the court:

'You were concealing the amounts and you were concealing the accounts into which the money was paid.'

We then looked at the answers Barry provided via his solicitor to Sean when we were chasing for my money. Even at this stage they were being very sleeked about when they received my dough and how much they had. Millar then hammered Barry on his boxer waiting nearly six months to be paid after he himself already had the money sitting there in his own account:

'What was it that entitled you to sit on his share of the money for five and a half months?'

'All I can say is that I pressed them to pay him as quickly as possible.'

'But why did you have to press, who are "them"?'

'That would have been Blain and Jake and Rupert.'

'*But the money came into a bank account, the Coutts dollar account, it went out of that account in the way we have just seen –*'

'*Yes.*'

'*– to another Coutts dollar account?*'

'*Mm-hmm.*'

[Here we go with the template – step one is the *Mm-hmm*]

'*Both in the name of Cyclone Promotions (UK) Limited?*'

'*Mm-hmm.*'

'*Which was a company of which you and Sandra were the directors and shareholders?*'

'*Correct, yes.*'

[The abrupt answer of step two – trying to keep his cool]

'*Why did you need to ask anybody else to ensure that he was paid, you had the money.*'

'*I accept that, my Lord, but I didn't do that side of the business and therefore I wasn't involved in those things. Obviously, I insisted that Carl get paid as quickly as possible, but I didn't actually handle the accounts.*'

[Step three addressing 'my Lord' – looking for sympathy]

'*When you said: "I accept that" in your answer to the last question, what do you accept? Do you accept that you were in a position to ensure he was paid because the money came into that bank account?*'

'*That's a fair question, my Lord, and I didn't, I didn't handle that side of things and I understand that it sounds like I could have, but I didn't. I didn't do that, so.*'

[Step four – denial]

'*You could have ensured he was paid?*'

'*I could have ensured that he was paid quicker, I suppose, but I tried my best.*'

'*But why did you have to try, this is what I'm putting to you, the money came into a bank account of a company that was your*' *company, what's the difficulty? Why do you have to try and get other people to pay him?'*

'*Yes, I can't answer that question.'*

[Step five – resigned acceptance]

The expenses breakdown for Santa Cruz I was even better than the Quigg list. Once again, it was only provided when litigation was ongoing and it had to be. A cool £77,000 this time, broken down into £55,000 of direct costs and an estimated £22,000 of legal, advisory and accountancy fees – whatever the hell they were. The expenses kept coming out of my pocket until 15 August. I'd fought on 30 July. Seems a little strange until you remember the McGuigan clan stayed on in New York for a holiday. My forensic accountants asked for supporting documentation and the business rationale for the expenses, and were told by Barry's side that '*the request is too wide-ranging'.* Millar plucked one out to see if we'd have any luck getting the business rationale from Barry for these camp costs. He opted for the £343.71 spent in the high-end women's shoe shop Stuart Weitzman on 11 August, twelve days after my fight was finished:

'*Do you want to expand on that answer that we received from McEvoys [solicitors acting for McGuigan], as to why those items are camp and promotional costs?'*

'*No.'*

'*They are clearly not costs of a boxing camp or a promotion of a fight, are they?'*

'*I can't answer that.'*

'*So, this is an inflated schedule, the schedule of £77,000 in expenses, isn't it, covering lots of items that are not legitimate expenses of the fight.'*

Millar went for Weitzman's but there were loads to choose from. Could have been the £180 spent at Oscar de la Renta, or the £170 at Bloomingdale's. Or why not the £153 spent on designer labels at Club Monaco or the £110 on shoes at Tani NYC? I personally would have picked the £24 someone blew at Sunspan Tanning!

Millar next quizzed Barry on a few of the many companies, of which he was director and shareholder, which would appear, be dissolved, reappear, change name, etc. It was hard for me to follow it all, but I guess that was the point. The first was Cyclone Promotions (UK) Limited, which was dissolved in 2016 having never submitted any accounts. Sandra applied to have it reinstated in 2019 and they needed to submit accounts to do so. She only did this because when the proceedings began, my team started investigating the status of this entity and its finances. Looking at them, however, they showed a company with no assets and no trading. Millar stated the obvious to Barry:

'*But we have seen the bank accounts of the company with all the money going through, going in and out, the Coutts bank accounts over these years, why are the accounts presented in this way?*'

'*I can't answer that question.*'

We found out about another company called Cyclone Promotions (UK) Limited in our research. This one had originally been called Wheelhouse Sports Management Limited but changed its name to Cyclone the month after the original Cyclone Promotions (UK) Limited was dissolved. Barry, his missus, his three boys and Rupert were the shareholders. All very strange and when Millar asked what was going on, Barry played the not-my-domain card again. Millar had had enough of his nonsense:

'*This is not true, is it, Mr McGuigan? You know full well about these companies, about their establishment.*'

'*No, I don't. I didn't do those.*'

'*You are just claiming not to know anything about it because we have been pursuing them in these proceedings as secretive companies into which monies were paid relating to my client's career that he was never told about.*'

'*That's not true, my Lord. Absolutely not. I didn't do any of that stuff. I wasn't involved in that accountancy-type thing.*'

'*And you are just choosing to pass off responsibility for these companies and their dealings by feigning ignorance.*'

We'd gotten to Santa Cruz II now. Once litigation was underway, I finally found out that the purse for that one was a minimum of $1.85m with the potential to rise to $2.2m. That was documented in a co-promotion agreement which I did not know existed as all I'd been shown to sign was a bout contract with the promoter, Ringstar Sports. Millar looked at Ringstar Sports' head honcho Richard Schaefer's email then, detailing that he had paid a total of $1,948,143 to our side. Remember, all I knew about was the $653,000 I had received directly from Ringstar. Millar asked Barry why I didn't know about the rest of the money and after Barry's fumbled answer about not being involved in that sort of thing – that sort of thing being my manager paying me my money! – Millar gave the correct answer to his own question:

'*It was because you and Cyclone didn't want Mr Frampton to know about these figures and these arrangements, wasn't it? You didn't want him to know that money was being paid into the dollar account for a company that he didn't know about.*'

When Sean was chasing for the rest of my Santa Cruz II money, I was still only aware of the $1.75m I'd been told by Jake was the total amount. So that's the figure Sean was asking for in August 2017 and neither Barry nor any of the rest of them felt the need to correct him on that when their solicitors, CRS, responded. Another open goal for Millar:

'*Why in your responses didn't you instruct CRS to say: No, no, you have misunderstood that, we were a co-promoter and there was a pot agreed of upwards of $1.85m for this fight. Why didn't you specify that in the answer?*'

'*I don't know.*'

'*In other words, to correct his misunderstanding that that was the fee, $1.75 million. You don't know why you didn't correct that misunderstanding?*'

'No.'

'*Why didn't you say $850,000 has been paid into a Coutts dollar account in the name of Cyclone Promotions (UK) Limited as of the 1st of June and we have had that money since the 1st of June, why didn't you say that?*'

'*I don't know.*'

'*Why didn't you mention that figure that appears in the Ringstar documentation of $1.98m as the total monies paid by Ringstar?*'

'*I don't know.*'

Instead, they replied to Sean that they were in the process of negotiating with various stakeholders in order to agree the figures. Open goal number two for Millar:

'*That's misleading, isn't it?*'

'*I don't know, my Lord. I can't answer that question.*'

'*Because the calculation has been done and the payment was made on the 1st of June, we have seen that in the Ringstar documentation. What was left to discuss?*'

'*I don't know the answer to that.*'

Sean was never given the truth, but in a document produced as part of the disclosure exercise Cyclone broke down how I was paid for Santa Cruz II. It started well enough with confirmation that Ringstar paid a total of just under $2,000,000. But then it went downhill as far as my bank balance was concerned. Around $400,000 apparently went straight to Cyclone as their 20 per cent share of 55 per cent of the promotion. Whatever that means. No contract or agreement was produced to back up that little arrangement. It then identifies my purse as $1,000,000. This was the official amount put down on the bout contract to limit the sanctioning fees, but certainly not what I was told I'd get paid as the champion, taking my belt into the challenger's back yard. The document then deducted all my camp expenses, more on those shortly, and concluded that I was not due another cent above the $653,000 I had received. In fact, by their calculations, I had already been overpaid by around ten grand! It was beyond belief, even by their standards. In black and white, and now on the stand under oath with a straight face, Team Cyclone were saying I had been overpaid by receiving under 33 per cent of the money.

We just about had enough time for a comedy interlude before moving on to the next point, so Millar ran through a few of the camp expenses I incurred for that one:

'*20th of January. Beach Bunny Swimwear, Las Vegas, £117. It's not a fight expense, is it?*'

'*No.*'

'*Below that. European Wax Centre, Las Vegas. That's not a fight expense, is it?*'

'*I wouldn't imagine, no.*'

'*23rd of January. Pink Lotus Nails, Las Vegas, £125. That's not a fight expense, is it?*'

'*I wouldn't imagine so, no.*'

'*This is an inflated list of expenses, isn't it, to try and justify the amount you are claiming is due to Mr Frampton for this fight, isn't it?*'

'*I don't accept that, no.*'

He doesn't accept it. It was unreal. £96,000 they reckoned my camp expenses were for Santa Cruz II. And with thousands of dollars spent in shops with names like Tadashi, Shoe Palace, Bebe and Guess, it appeared I was spending a chunk of my wages on women's fashion. It was the quantity of clearly female expenses on the list that made us all presume the fight-week trips to tanning salons were down to the girls too. But an email discovered from Barry to himself while in Vegas casts a bit of doubt on that theory. At the end of a to-do list for the following day, which in fairness was all fight related up the final point, Barry reminds himself of '*Sunbed session*'! You couldn't make this stuff up.

Millar grilled him a bit on all that extra dough they got from Schaefer and where it went and where it is now. They'd shifted it from one Coutts account to another for some reason. Barry, true to form, denied all knowledge so Millar put it on him a little:

'*The entire arrangement, sequence of events in relation to Santa Cruz II demonstrates that what your objective was, was to keep that money for yourself.*'

'*No, that's not true, my Lord. I didn't want to fall out with anybody, that's not my style.*'

'*And to conceal it and the movement of that money from my client and our side in this case?*'

'*Not true.*'

'*The only reason we found out about all of this was because of the documentation we obtained from Ringstar in the discovery process in this case.*'

'*That's not true.*'

'*Mr Frampton wouldn't have known about any of that otherwise, would he?*'

We were nearing the end of day twelve of the trial now, but there was still time to land a few more blows on Barry. First, Millar undermined his justification for the fact that my purse for the proposed Gutierrez fight was dependent on ticket sales. Okay, I was coming off a loss. But a majority-decision loss in a world-title fight, headlining Vegas, against a pound-for-pound ranked fighter, for a seven-figure purse (supposedly). From that to you'll get paid so long as you sell X number of tickets is a hell of a fall from grace. Safe to say, no manager worth his salt and without a conflict of interest to wrestle with would have encouraged me to agree to those terms. Millar then finished things off by probing Barry's own personal tax returns. Barry's case was that he didn't receive most of the management fees that were deducted from my purse. That, in his words, he left it all in the company. That made him a long-term creditor of Cyclone Promotions Northern Ireland Ltd and those amounts were then treated as accruals on the company's books. In lieu of any explanation from Barry on why it was structured like that, Millar moved forward with the most obvious explanation – to avoid personal income tax. By doing it this way, Barry didn't have to declare it as income or pay any tax on what was close to £1,000,000. Millar then highlighted the drawings or withdrawals from the company in favour of Barry and his family. It was listed as a debtor's balance of just under £600,000. In other words, the McGuigan family as a whole owed the company nearly £600,000. Having drawn attention to these massive numbers, Millar walked Barry through his own personal tax returns for the years in question. For the tax year 2014–2015, Kiko II and Avalos fights, Barry declared income of £9,999 as employee of Square Ring Ltd, £7,500 as employee of McGuigan's Gym and £7,900 as director of Cyclone Promotions Ltd. He paid just £3,079 in tax.

'– there are two fights that year in Belfast?'

'Yes.'

'Big fights?'

'Yes.'

'In which you are earning commission as a manager and you are involved as a promoter?'

'Yes, involved in the promotion, yes.'

'So why was no meaningful income declared from this work in that financial year on your tax return?'

'I don't know is the answer.'

'Who prepared this tax return?'

'My wife and my accountant, I would imagine.'

'You signed it?'

'Yes.'

'*It is not an accurate representation of your income for that year, is it?*'

It got better the following year, when Barry declared total income of £10,600 as an employee of Cyclone Promotions and paid zero tax and made zero National Insurance contributions.

'*You are telling the Revenue … there is taxable income but it's not above the threshold.*'

'*Mm-hmm.*'

'*In the year that you were acting as his manager for the Gonzalez and Quigg fights?*'

'*Yes.*'

'*It can't be right, can it?*'

Nope! Because I had 20 per cent deducted in the name of Barry McGuigan from my two seven-figure purses that year. The next year didn't make much prettier reading as far as Barry was concerned, with a paltry £1,188 paid in tax and nothing in National Insurance contributions for a declared income of £11,000 from Cyclone Promotions. Millar decided to sum it up and end his misery:

'*So, coming back to the earlier cross-examination about the accruals and the loans in the accounts and how they were treated it is right, isn't it, that that was in order to ensure that you didn't have to pay income tax?*'

'*I don't know and I can't argue that rightly or wrongly, my Lord.*'

Barry came back the next day and we looked briefly at his own claims he was making against me. I say briefly because they didn't need or deserve much recognition. The first, that he was due 20 per cent of £250,000 for the Gutierrez fight that never happened, was dealt with in about five seconds. As soon as Barry accepted that the fight did not take place through no fault of mine, he was left with no grounds to claim anything there. His second claim was even more ridiculous. He wanted another 20 per cent of £250,000 for the rearranged Gutierrez fight. Spoiler alert: I never fought Gutierrez.

But here was Barry simultaneously claiming twice for what amounted to the same thing. He was on a hiding to nothing on both. His final claim was for 20 per cent of £500,000 for a hypothetical fight I would have had in Belfast after beating Gutierrez. Barry had never paid as much as half of that for fighting in Belfast, even when I was world champion, but apparently now that was easy money to secure for me. Millar pointed out the obvious: that it was pretty wild speculation based on everything being as favourable as possible for Barry's calculations. Barry was adamant that it wasn't speculation, that it was a sure thing. He then started ranting about fighting for a world title, fighting Santa Cruz, fighting at Windsor Park or New York or Vegas. It was like he was deliberately teeing it up for Millar to smash it out of the park!

'*Well, this is what you would have tried to do, but it's speculation and we can see it's speculation because you postulated, even in your own evidence, three possible venues ... and two possible different opponents.*'

That just about did it for Barry. The judge asked him a few clarifying questions and he fumbled through them and was then dismissed, presumably scurrying straight back to a gymnasium with his magnifying glass to manage fighters, make sure they were training correctly, get them into great condition, pick their opponents and get them the best purses he could. There was a break for a couple of weeks and then it was Blain's turn.

***

Blain's cross-examination was a kind of Barry-lite. We'd been through nearly everything with his da and it was a case of rattling through it again and watching the eldest son squirm now. I almost had a bit of sympathy for him before it began. While he was an integral part in the whole deception, it was obvious he'd been placed there by his parents rather than being a ringleader at the outset. But any tiny seedling of sympathy that may have been embedded in my mind vanished almost as soon as he opened his mouth on the stand. While Barry had opted for the poor-me-I-wouldn't-know-anything-about-that-my-Lord approach, Blain went in a totally different direction and came across as unbelievably smug and arrogant. I guess it was a more honest approach, but it was never going to pay off for him in the long run.

We decided to knock off the irretrievable-email charade first. Ger's evidence, their reluctance to call the IT guy as a witness and Rupert's email saying everything was hunky-dory with the email migration had undermined their original lie, so Blain changed tack and now said the emails had been deliberately deleted. That seems the type of thing you probably would have remembered and described as such rather than calling them irretrievable emails, but maybe that's just me. According to Blain, the IT guy had said to Rupert and Rupert had said to the McGuigans, why not go ahead and delete all your irrelevant emails. When questioned on what constituted an irrelevant email, Blain answered that it meant anything at all from a past show or fight. He said he searched all his emails by the name of a show or fight and then deleted everything in sight! It was all so ridiculously unbelievable, but Millar had to go through the motions to highlight how fanciful it was. Space requirements was one of Blain's justifications for adhering to a process in which you're encouraged to delete all email correspondence when a fight or show ends. They were moving to fucking Microsoft Office – you can literally save millions of emails on that platform, no problem! When Millar asked him what happens if there is a dispute and you need to refer back to correspondence, Blain said he didn't anticipate any disputes. He said that confidently while currently under oath in a courtroom giving evidence in a legal dispute! At the moment he said he deleted his emails, we were already in dispute over Quigg money, Santa Cruz money, appearance fees, expenses, VAT invoices and Christ knows what else. Six years is a rule of thumb some companies use before they consider deleting anything as six years is the limitation period for legal claims. Not the McGuigans, though. Blain testified he deleted everything just a couple of months after some shows! There was another easy win in challenging him on the discovery of the email about Dunlop getting his fighters on the Parodi undercard. Blain said Jake found it and his brother would have done the same deletion exercise as he did.

'Well, we'll ask Jake how he did his deletion, the level of detail that he descended to when he decided what to delete and what not.'

That was most likely the moment Jake had second thoughts about his trip to the witness box!

The next highlight in Blain's cross-examination was a look at the miraculous turnaround in the financial performance of Cyclone Promotions once litigation had begun. As per the accounts filed at Companies House at the time remember, Cyclone lost £367,418 in 2015 and £545,441 in 2016. When Millar put those losses to him, Blain confirmed, several times, under oath, that they were accurate representations of the company's finances. That contradicted his own side's case that they were not accurate, which was why they had provided new figures adjusting the losses in 2015 and 2016 and transforming the bottom line in each year to be a profit of £305,000 and £994,000 respectively. I'll do the maths for you – an extra £672,418 and £1,539,441 had magically appeared from down the back of the McGuigan family sofa. The new accounts detailing these adjustments were filed a mere month after the jurisdiction hearing we had in 2018, in which my side strongly questioned the apparent loss-making nature of Cyclone Promotions. Blain's position was that was just a coincidence and completely unrelated.

We spent a little time on his own tax returns. Like his old man, he was declaring minimal amounts and some years not paying any tax at all by claiming a lot of his income was in the form of director's loans. Again, it was highlighted that I was the only mug not benefitting from director's loans or a salary from the company despite being a director just like Blain and the rest. I don't know, maybe I'm just a neanderthal when it comes to money, but when I listened to how they went about things all I thought was, am I the only mug round here paying my fair share of taxes?

A common thread throughout Blain's evidence was him claiming something was done and Millar then asking where the proof was. Is there an email, is there an agreement, is there a budget, is there a reconciliation, is there a contract, etc. Essentially, can you provide this court with a single contemporaneous document to evidence anything you are claiming? The answer was invariably no. The other theme of his evidence was that although he was making a great show of acting like he was the promoter and the main man in a lot of the business and dealings around the events, over and over again we saw his da's or younger brother's name attached to what was being done. Over and over again he'd answer that his ma did that part, or his ma would have recorded that or his ma told him how something was done. I don't doubt that to be true, but it was clearly a strategy Barry and Blain had devised. Sandra wasn't going to appear at all throughout this case in which she was a joint defendant. I was gutted about that because there was no doubt in my mind that she was aware of a lot of what went on in the businesses. She should have been on the stand. I was told we could wait for her, but their side had delayed so much already that I just wanted to get on with it. We fired ahead without her and that allowed Barry and Blain to use their wife or mother as a kind of human shield to get out of many of the holes they found themselves digging deeper and deeper into during cross-examination. I suppose it gave them a bit of temporary relief when Millar had them struggling, but the judge would have seen through it. Blain couldn't answer simple questions you'd expect him to know, like why did the company you were a director of have multiple bank accounts set up? Overall, he just came across as a frontman put in place while his parents ran the show.

The danger of immersing yourself in a multi-person web of deceit was laid bare at the end of the day when Millar questioned Blain on £63,000 that had been almost immediately transferred to his da once they got the $858,000 in from Schaefer after Santa Cruz II.

'*Most probably my father's commission,*' Blain reckoned.

'*Your understanding is that he took his commission out of that money and paid it into a bank account in his name?*'

'Yes.'

'*But I thought he dealt with all his commission through the Northern Irish company, and indeed it's regarded as an accrual to the Northern Irish company?*'

Oh-oh – rumbled!

'*That's what I meant. I'm looking at this and thinking that's probably what it was, but I don't know for sure that's what it was. All I do know is that Carl Frampton received all of the money into his account.*'

'*You don't know what it was?*'

'*I am looking at that and thinking that might have been for his commission.*'

'*But you don't know. So, you are a promoter of a fight in America, you give an instruction for the proceeds of that fight to be paid into this account?*'

'*Mm-hmm.*'

'*A large chunk of it is immediately paid out to a personal account of your parents and you don't know why?*'

'*I would assume that was for his commission, yes.*'

'*But you don't know?*'

'*That would be my, that would be what I think it would be, yes, it would be his commission. But hold on, the most important thing is that Carl received all the money into his account.*'

Ha ha! Nice attempt to deflect! But Millar wasn't about to let him off the hook just yet:

'*No, no, the most important thing is that your case here on the manager's commissions is that they are all accounted for through the Northern Irish company, that he didn't actually take the commissions, but they are accounted for as accruals to the Northern Irish companies.*'

Way to throw your old man under the bus, Blain!

Blain fought on bravely during his final day on the stand. But the thing which struck me most that day was the level of delusion he; his family; and, I have to confess, myself as well operated under back in those days. He was being questioned on the purse deductions I suffered for camp fees each fight and there was a lot of back and forth about the lack of information or documentation provided to me to back up the expenses. That seemed to be the focus as Blain confidently stated that £75,000 of camp expenses are what you'd expect for a twelve-week camp to fight Scott Quigg. I completed a lot of fight camps once I was free from the McGuigans and not one came close to that amount. Since my eyes have been opened, I've spoken to a lot of world-level fighters and not one said they had ever spent anywhere in the vicinity of £75,000 on a camp. When you think about what a fighter needs, it is literally impossible to reach those type of figures. So, for me, debates on invoices and receipts were a welcome sideshow for the McGuigans. It distracted from the real issue. They were blatantly using my purse to pay for things that should have never been my financial responsibility. And I don't mean the comical ones like high-heel shoes or pedicures. These people were taking the piss on a much higher level and had been doing so from the off. They did it in a way that led me to think what they were doing was perfectly normal and legitimate. It was only when I was being managed by MTK that I could really see how crazy my set-up with the McGuigans had been.

This idea that a squad of McGuigans, and at times their partners, were with me overseas ahead of fights and that their flights, accommodation, food and everything else came out of my purse was crazy. MTK had plenty of staff that helped in my career, and I'm sure a lot of them had wives and girlfriends. But when I fought in the US or Dubai, a load of them didn't jump on the plane and enjoy a week or two at my expense. I discovered that the industry standard is that you should include your manager, him or her alone, as part of your team and their expenses are covered by the promoter whose promotion you are fighting on. The promoter will say he'll pay for fighter plus five for five nights, for example. Then you work within those parameters. If someone else wants to come along, no problem – but they pay for it themselves. This idea that the wages of Cyclone staff should come out of my purse was also crazy. That the salaries of a Cyclone operations manager or PR person, or social media person or S&C guy should be my responsibility. MTK had staff doing all those roles. I'd interact with plenty of them and see them around my fights. But MTK obviously paid them their wages – they didn't pull me to one side after a fight and say, so-and-so did a fair bit towards that show Carl so we're going to give them three grand from your purse! This idea that the normal way of things was for the fight purse to go to the manager first and the fighter had to patiently wait for the deductions to be made before he got his share was crazy as well. For my post-McGuigan fights, I got all the dough and then made bank transfers to trainers etc. as required. I could go on with more examples, but I'd only depress myself further putting them down in black and white.

Day seventeen drew to a close with Blain claiming I was perfectly happy waiting half a year to be paid and that dissolved companies reappearing with the same name a few months later was completely normal behaviour. He was committed to his cause, I'll give him that much. That was a Thursday afternoon and we adjourned with the expectation of completing his cross examination the following morning. After Blain, Jake was up. That was going to be very interesting. Rupert was then scheduled to be put through the wringer too, and I couldn't wait for that public massacre either. Finally, someone who couldn't shirk responsibility on the numbers. But unfortunately, I never got to see that pair squirm under questioning. Because day seventeen was the day the irretrievable emails became miraculously retrievable.

Out of nowhere, thousands upon thousands of Cyclone-Promotions.com emails emerged from their hiding place. A few hundred were Rupert's. Barry, who'd have the court believe he could barely switch on a computer, had a thousand or so. Blain had around 2,600. Sandra, double that. And Jake apparently had so many they didn't count them. All in all, there were over 10,000 emails to deal with. Instead of a day in court, the legal teams spent Friday sifting through this new information. They toiled through the weekend, and by the time we appeared before the judge again on Monday they'd still not broken the back of the work required before we could move forward. It was a pretty wild situation, and Millar made sure he highlighted that to Justice Huddleston. He detailed the background to the emails, how we'd flagged from day one that we felt the McGuigans were withholding vital info. Now we had it, but in a deluge that made it a logistical nightmare to assess and digest. It is apparently a well-known tactic called a document dump. We'd made a repeated song and dance about emails not being disclosed, so when they finally had to do so they did it in a manner that made it as difficult as possible to review. Millar drew attention to the fact that a defendant's solicitor has a responsibility to work hand-in-hand with their clients on discovery issues. They are supposed to be there every step of the way when it comes to how documents are searched for and then what is chosen for disclosure. We had serious concerns about how the entire discovery process was conducted and so Millar requested the court order the McGuigans' solicitor to swear an affidavit covering four vital points. Firstly, why these emails were presented as being irretrievable when the argument soon became that they were deliberately deleted? Secondly, why did they not respond to our pre-trial letter expressing concerns and seeking clarity on the issue? Thirdly, when, how and by whom were the emails eventually found? And fourthly, how was discovery of these emails now being conducted in terms of determining what was relevant to the case? McCollum seemed shellshocked. The emails were found on a Thursday. This was now Monday. And yet all he could say to the judge was, '*I haven't got to the bottom of the reasons why this has occurred so late.*' They had Thursday, Friday, Saturday and Sunday to get their story straight! The judge sent us on our way to sort out the emails, saying he expected the affidavit explaining what the fuck had just happened by the end of the day. As far as I know, Huddleston never got that explanation. We went back briefly the next day to update him and confirm the plan to return to Blain's cross-examination before then calling Jake. A day later, we'd settled.

It all happened very quickly. My team told me the McGuigans had made a move to settle. My initial reaction was, no, fuck off. We've come this far, they're out on their feet, now let's finish them. But my team was split on what to do. Peter also wanted to keep going. John kind of sat on the fence in the middle. And Gavin clearly thought we should just settle. I was undecided what to do myself but when advised that I could be waiting years for a judgment, I weighed it all up and decided to settle.

Had I not a world-title fight to prepare for, I probably would have kept going. Had I not had Christine and the kids to think about, I definitely would have kept going. It was a great settlement, but I wanted that definitive judgment made and read out against them. To be sat near them in the courtroom when that happened.

I wanted to see Jake and Rupert on the stand sweating it the way Barry and Blain had. I wanted every last drop of info squeezed out of them all so we could have the whole truth laid bare.

I also wanted to keep going because I was enjoying it. And not just the one-way traffic as they were all cross-examined. There were lots of little interactions outside the court which I found hilarious. The way John and I would dander through the city centre to get to court each day from his office, while the McGuigans jumped out of a blacked-out van parked on double yellows with two security guards as if they were Jay-Z and Beyoncé. This was during Covid too, remember, so there was nobody about even if they had been superstars dodging paparazzi! Trips to the bathroom during recess tended to involve a bit of craic with the other side too. Walking Christine to the ladies one day just after Barry had had a particularly rough ride on the stand, he actually smirked at us. 'Ohhh Barry, you were getting it a bit tight this morning,' I said as I walked straight through them. 'I wouldn't be smirking if I was you.' His face just dropped. Barry muttering something less than complimentary at John as they passed each other in the toilets. On another occasion the security guard outside the bathroom telling me, 'them two are in there', as I approached. He meant Barry and Blain. 'I couldn't give a fuck,' I said and proceeded to take my piss in the urinal between the pair of them. When Barry finished, he just hung about as if I was going to attack his son or something! There was the day I came across Jake and his solicitor outside just after the evidence about them putting tickets for sale on StubHub. They'd always been so anti-StubHub to me. Slabbering about Matchroom doing it and saying how it robs the fans etc. 'Fucking StubHub, Jake?' I said to him, and he replied with a 'is that all you've got, Carl?' When I fired back, telling him he wished that's all we had because they were getting fucking mauled, his solicitor squealed on me and I ended up getting reprimanded!

Reprimands got handed out to both sides, though. One day just before we started, some judge came out of the chambers, walked past me, and started chatting away to Barry acting all pally. Me and my team were all looking at each other like what the hell is going on here. Turned out that judge was Barry's junior barrister during the Eastwood trial. It was bizarre to say the least, but a complaint went in and there was widespread shock across the board at that judge's behaviour.

But settling was the sensible decision to make and so I made it. Maybe it was a little bittersweet, but the overwhelming feeling was one of victory and a weight being lifted off my shoulders. I stood beside John in front of the TV cameras outside the court with a massive smile on my face. While I was telling Mark Simpson from the BBC that I was 'very, very happy with the terms of the settlement', the McGuigans were scurrying away without speaking to the press. The best they could muster was a written statement later saying a settlement had been reached and no judgment had been issued. Factually true but not offering much context. We'd been in litigation for over three years by this stage. They'd been confident and bullish and refused to give an inch throughout. Within days of the emails we'd been desperate to see being disclosed, they were reaching out for a settlement before we had a chance to use the info we now had. I was then on the evening news with a big grin on my face while they went to ground. So yes, an official judgment may not have been issued, but I think the world drew their own conclusion in terms of the outcome of the case. I enjoyed a glass of champagne that night and slept easy.

CHAPTER NINE

HAPPILY EVER AFTER

There were plenty of times when I thought I'd never face Jamel Herring. It felt like the fight was cursed, the number of obstacles that kept appearing and wrecking plans. There was the pandemic, my hand injuries, Jamel getting Covid, my court case. One thing after another arose and kept pushing our meeting further and further away. Then, in the middle of everything, Shakur Stevenson was made mandatory for Jamel's WBO world title and that was another complication thrown into the mix. He didn't have the patience to wait around, and his manager was lobbying hard to get the fight announced. Being only a voluntary defence for Jamel, I was on shaky ground – and I have to thank MTK again for keeping us on track. They made a bit of a power move in signing Herring in order to maintain as much control over the whole situation as they could. And of course, it helped that Jamel was desperate to fight me before he had to go anywhere near Stevenson.

The final and, as is invariably the case in boxing, biggest hurdle to overcome was who was going to fork out to pay for it all. Bob Arum and Frank Warren had been all for it pre-Covid, when their eyes lit up at the prospect of me selling 25,000 tickets for them. But now, under pandemic conditions, they were suddenly not as enthusiastic. I understand the business, so it is what it is. Promoters aren't running charities and will only ever make a fight when they see a guaranteed financial uplift for themselves. I don't hold that against them, it's just all part of the shitty boxing system. The hard, cold truth is that promoters don't really give a fuck about fighters any more than any businessperson cares about their assets. Fighters need to get their head around that fact early and go through their careers accordingly. A boxer is an asset with a value for a very limited amount of time. Arum grinned in the ring between Jamel and I like a Cheshire cat after I beat McCreary, but the bottom line is he couldn't care less about either of us once it was clear the pandemic prevented us fighting in a packed arena with a multimillion-dollar gate attached. We were two guys in the twilight of our careers. Someone like Shakur is the new star coming through. A promoter can live comfortably for the next five or six years off the money Shakur will generate in the ring during his prime so the priority would have been to keep him happy. And then as soon as he looks to be over the hill, focus will immediately switch to the next blue-chip asset in the stable.

MTK fought hard to keep the fight on. And one night I had to make a call to Arum as part of that campaign. He's in Vegas so it was late my time and I phoned him while already in bed beside Christine. I basically had to massage his ego and lick his arse for ten minutes. Thanking him profusely and promising him a full house in Windsor when I immediately faced Shakur after beating Jamel. When I hung up Christine was looking over, absolutely disgusted with me. She couldn't believe I'd just degraded myself like that. But it's all part of the game, unfortunately. It's all egos and smoke and mirrors. Christine knew that win, lose or draw against Herring, I was retired so it was all bullshit I was spouting into Arum's ear. But she was still horrified I had to kiss an old guy's ass like that just to keep him from scrapping my fight.

The whole saga dragged on and on. The exact timeline and sequence of events confuses me even now. There were fake dates announced in amongst it all. Dates I knew were not going to happen. I felt very sorry for Jamel when I found out he wasn't always in the same loops I was. There was a fear that the fact a date wasn't real would leak out and if Shakur and his manager caught wind of it, they'd easily scupper our fight. So, he's away from home, missing Thanksgiving, holding his weight, investing in camps – and all for nothing. At least I knew enough to only have to pretend to do those things. But I felt awful inside while the charade was going on. It was necessary to get my shot at history, but it just proves how dirty the whole game is that a good guy like Jamel, the champion, could be treated like that. I was even told to fake an injury at one point. A positive Covid test was every promoter's go-to around this time when they wanted to delay something. Just say you got Covid and that does it. But I didn't want to do that because it would impact on Christine and the kids. We'd all be trapped in the house for two weeks or whatever the isolation period was back then. I went with a flare-up of my hand injury instead. Very few people knew I was faking it. I was doing an interview with Chris Lloyd, and he asked me which hand it was. I kind of looked down at my hands thinking, good question, which one is it? I hadn't bothered to think my lie through that far. I randomly said, the right one. Watching it back, I didn't even believe myself. I'm definitely not a good liar!

Finally, we received a legitimate date. We'd fight in Dubai on 3 April. I flew out three weeks early to get settled and acclimatised, and brought Alex Dilmaghani with me to spar. Alex, alongside the likes of Anthony Cacace and Aqib Fiaz, had given me great work throughout camp. My performance against Traynor had been poor and I wanted to spar well against quality fighters to prove to myself that I still had something left. And I did that, barely losing a round against those guys throughout camp. I felt ready and all through the build-up I was confident I could pull it off and win a third world title.

That confidence started to wane as soon as the first bell chimed. In fact, earlier even. I felt shit warming up in the changing room. My timing was off, and I wasn't hitting the pads clean. It was a cramped space and in my head I was blaming the lack of room to move my feet properly, but deep down I probably knew. Deep down I probably even knew that I was kidding myself a little with the sparring as well. It's a funny thing, sparring. Some great fighters are bang average in spars while the other extreme is the gym superstar who can't maintain the same level under the lights when it matters. Sparring well is an indicator of where you are performance-wise, but it shouldn't be relied on 100 per cent as a gauge. You shouldn't let it alone lull you into a false sense of what your true level is. Maybe Traynor wasn't a one-off abomination brought on by the circumstances of a lower-level opponent and a grim, empty venue. Maybe that was my level now.

Grim is the word for that night in York Hall. And while Dubai was a definite improvement, this was still the Covid era and all the associated restrictions were still in place. There couldn't have been more than a hundred socially distanced people in attendance. You can't use venues and atmospheres as excuses because your opponent is dealing with the exact same conditions, but it undoubtedly affects fighters. And it undoubtedly affects some fighters more than others. When this fight was made, I was envisioning close to 30,000 at Windsor or 20,000 inside Madison Square Garden. I was used to the noise and energy that enormous crowds generate. This was a massive fight and it deserved more than the sterile atmosphere of that night in Dubai. Let's just say that it doesn't help you get into the right frame of mind to go to war.

I wasn't shocked by Herring. He battered me, but I didn't feel like he was a monstrous puncher. I wasn't fearful of his power either before or during the fight. I just simply didn't see the punches coming. And it wasn't even as if he had such fast hands, I'd certainly faced quicker fighters. It was all me. My reactions weren't there. The big gloves and the headguard and maybe the drop in intensity from opponents during sparring must have papered over the cracks. I was slow. My footwork wasn't there. My hand speed wasn't what it had been. My reactions were non-existent. My punch resistance had deteriorated beyond all recognition. There's no two ways about it, I was shot. It just wasn't me in there that night in Dubai. And I say that honestly, without wanting to take anything away from Jamel. At thirty-five, he was older than me and probably also past his best. But in boxing terms I was much older. I'd more miles on the clock, most of them put there via excessive sparring during camps at least a month longer than they should have been. Jamel was also five inches taller than me with a seven-inch reach advantage. I couldn't get past those long shots and get into any sort of range that would give me a chance. He controlled the distance and landed at will. It was all a bit of a disaster for me, and yet even within the nightmare you get enough success to keep dreaming. The fourth was my round and I opened up a cut over Jamel's right eye. The same cut that had caused his fight with Oquendo to be stopped. Time to get to work worsening the wound. Maybe the tide is turning. Maybe it was just a slow start and now I've found my rhythm. Maybe the momentum is swinging in my favour. Or maybe that was all just wishful thinking.

I haven't watched the entire fight back and I'm not sure I ever will. People say it makes for very tough viewing. Midway through the fifth, I walked onto a lovely straight left from Jamel which put me on my arse. Then around the same time of the sixth, an uppercut folded me like a deckchair. I've seen that highlight, or lowlight, almost by accident and it made me feel sick. But that night, I didn't even remember it happening. I got up from the uppercut and Jamel set about me, forcing Jamie to throw in the towel. At the time, I actually complained to Jamie. Why'd you stop it? I'm okay here. It was the usual deluded bravado from a fighter in the heat of an onslaught. Jamie was spot on by saving me from further punishment. A little later I was talking to him about the knockdown and he asked, which one? That was the first I realised I'd been down twice. It's scary stuff.

I was completely devastated after this one and I broke down in floods of tears in the dressing room. It felt like others were more upset than me after the Warrington defeat, but this time I was the one in bits. This time it felt so much worse. I knew I was retiring no matter what happened, so that wasn't part of it. I think it was more the feeling that I'd let everyone down and embarrassed myself by getting dropped heavily twice and then stopped before the fight was halfway through. I was thinking of all the work from so many people that had gone into making this night happen, and then I go and get chinned inside six rounds. The final years training with Jamie and Nigel had been the happiest of my career and I would have loved to have given them the world title they deserved. There is a popular revisionist theory that I went downhill after I left Shane. Then cause and effect gets muddled to suggest I went downhill because I left Shane. That ignores great performances like the Donaire fight. It also skips over the fact that I got old in boxing terms a lot younger than I should have. That's down to the excessive sparring, the training when injured and just generally having the life and love of the game sucked out of me over a prolonged period of time. I would have been a world champion no matter who trained me. Jamie and Nigel would have had just as much, if not more, success had they been in my corner for the first three quarters of my career. In fact, maybe I wouldn't have lost the second Santa Cruz fight because they don't have that arrogant trait that can blind a person.

It was hard not having Christine and the kids there either, so that got to me too. Then I guess there was the sense of disappointment that I didn't manage to make history. I thought I was going to be

Ireland's first ever three-weight world champion and be a shoo-in for the Hall of Fame off the back of that achievement. That dream was shattered now. It was a brutal way to end my career, and it took me a long time to get over it. But now I can look back with a bit of perspective. I tried to do something which has never been done before. Let's be honest, I should never have been fighting at 130lbs and I think everyone knows that. It was only the chance to make that history which drove me to try, and I'm proud now that I went out on my shield attempting it. If someone had told me when I turned pro that I would get that close, I would have thought they were mental. Even after I beat Kiko to claim the super bantamweight crown, I still wouldn't have believed it possible. I would have said I'm far too small to ever beat a top guy at super feather. I'm glad I had a go at it because I think if I hadn't there would have been a real risk a couple of years down the line of me being one of the many boxers who get lured into an ill-advised comeback. The fighters who get convinced they still have it and can relive the glory one more time. They rarely can. I'm lucky that urge to give it another go does not exist inside me. I know that part of my life is over for good. I had a fantastic career and even without the third world title I think I deserve to be involved in any conversations on Ireland's greatest ever professional. When you consider the calibre of fighters the country has produced down through the years, I think that's pretty incredible for a midget from Tiger's Bay. I'm proud of everything I achieved in the ring, and prouder still of the support that followed me for every step of the way. I didn't get the fairy-tale ending, but boxing is not a business that hands those out very often. All things considered, I can't have too many complaints. I left with my head held high; a few quid in the bank; friendships I'll keep forever; and, most importantly, I have my health intact.

***

It has been two years since that night in Dubai, and I can honestly say there was only one moment in all that time when the idea of returning to the ring even entered my head. That was when Kiko chinned Kid Galahad. I got up the next morning and for the first time in a long time I put the trainers on and went for a run. I say a run, but it was really just a very slow four-mile jog. By the time I made it back to the house, my groin was hurting and my knee felt in bits. Fuck that, I said. I couldn't think of anything worse than getting ready for a fight again. You might see me back in a few years for one of these charity exhibitions that are all the rage, but that'll be the height of it. The truth is that retirement from boxing has been very good for me. It was nice to begin a new chapter and the transition has been easy. You hear a lot of ex-athletes talking about missing the roar of the crowd or needing to find replacements for the adrenalin rush of competing, but not me. That's not in my character. Maybe I'm just naturally a lazy bastard, but I'm more than comfortable loafing about the house and doing nothing! Not that I have many opportunities to do that either. Christine keeps me busy. It feels like we redecorate the entire gaff every six months. I don't actually do any DIY, but I've to choose and buy the paint or paper for others to crack on. I like cooking so I've taken on that role. I do the school run, driving Rossa to the school gates. I used to take Carla to her bus stop as well until I realised how scundered she was to have her daddy walking her. Recently I've joined a couple of other parents in helping out the official coach of Carla's football team. Training twice a week then a match on a Sunday morning, so that's become our daddy–daughter thing. There's always something to keep me out of trouble.

Things are no less quiet outside the family either. I was lucky enough to walk straight into the punditry job at BT Sport. I really enjoy that, and working on a big fight gives me a bit of a buzz and keeps me excited about boxing. My role there is expanding so

I do some commentary, a few interviews and sometimes scoring the fights as well. The commentating is a lot tougher than being a pundit in the studio as you need to be fully focused on the action for every second and you've no time to consider what to say or how to say it. It all has to flow along with the fighters' punches. The scoring part I don't mind. I think I can score a fight well, and the feedback online tends to be supportive of my cards. It's amazing to me that plenty of people in the game, ex boxers included, haven't a clue how to score a fight. Then there are the judges themselves. Every week there seems to be another controversy. Sometimes I think there is no way we just watched the same fight. I don't believe it's like the movies when brown envelopes are being passed around ahead of the first bell, but there is no doubt that the judges know they're more likely to be invited back if they're generous to the house fighters. I regularly see refs and judges boozing away in the fight hotel the night before, with members of the promotion or fighters' teams milling around the same bar. It's crazy really. But boxing is crazy. It would require another full book to go into everything that is wrong with the sport.

It also must be the bitchiest sport on the planet. It's full of genuinely hard men, but they are hard men with the thinnest skin imaginable. As a pundit now I have to say what I see. If you've fought well, I'll gladly sing your praises. And if you haven't, I feel I should be honest about that as well or else what's the point in me being there. No doubt plenty of fighters will fall out with me because of it, but it is what it is. So long as big John Fury doesn't threaten to knock my pan in again for saying Jake Paul will beat his son, I should be all right. There is regular stick from the anonymous masses on social media as well, but that's life in general today. There is literally nothing I could say on air that would be met with universal approval and agreement. And there will always be someone who'll open his Twitter account and tell me I'm a dickhead who doesn't know what he's talking about. I was vocal recently on a certain fighter who failed two separate drugs tests ahead of a fight and yet his promoter was still trying to push the fight through. Then a few weeks later a sanctioning body comes along and tries to say, nothing to see here, we're happy for everything to go back to the way it was. For all the obvious reasons in an activity in which people try to punch each other unconscious, it's incredible that a harder line is not taken on drugs cheats within boxing. Worse than that, if the fighter in question has commercial value, the sport seems to proactively try to sweep the case under the carpet. It often seems that the lesser lights who fail a test are the only ones ever in danger of having the book thrown at them. My personal view is that performance-enhancing drugs are rampant in boxing and it is getting worse each year. Who knows, I may even have faced opponents who have juiced at some point. It's sad and worrying, but I can sleep easy knowing my conscience is completely clear.

I don't think I'll ever return to boxing as long as I'm happy in the media work. Possibly the management side of things at one point because for me that's the easiest job in boxing, particularly if you're an ex-fighter with connections and respect within the business. I'm happy offering advice to any fighter who asks for it, so I think I could perform a role there. I'd probably be too soft to be honest, giving a handout to every boxer that comes along with a bit of a sob story. I certainly wouldn't take as much as the 20–25 per cent management fees that many do charge their boxer anyway. To me that's a crazy amount in comparison to the work being done. A trainer generally gets 10 per cent and I think they deserve more than managers. The trainers dedicate by far the most time and effort to the fighter, and that's why I can't ever see myself in a coaching role. If you have a gym with five or six of your own boxers, it's essentially a 365-days-of-the-year commitment. And having been around boxers my whole life, I know how difficult they can be. Some need their hands held just to cross the road. If I did ever get tempted back into the gym, I reckon it would be at an amateur club. It must be an amazing feeling to take a young kid and help them develop into a national champion.

I'm probably a bit more outspoken now on certain subjects that I feel strongly about. Part of that comes with age and maturity and taking an interest in the wider world outside of boxing. But it's also true that as a young fighter coming through and trying to bring as many fans as possible along for the ride, I was more likely to stay clear of anything that could cause a controversy. And being from Northern Ireland, that meant remaining pretty quiet on all the usual political stuff. It's not that I was hiding the fact I'm a Prod, but when you put it out there in a more visible way the abuse starts flowing. I don't think I've ever been called an orange bastard so much as when I was sponsored by 32 Red, and they had me doing a few promotional things with Rangers players! So, it was partly a conscious decision not to get involved in any political debates. But much more importantly, I just don't give a fuck about any of that. I didn't decide to go and find a Catholic from west Belfast to marry because I thought it would look good and help me sell more tickets. I fell in love with Christine Dorrian and couldn't give a fiddler's what her religion, nationality, politics or background was. That's the way it should be across the board. I got some grief from hardliners when it became public knowledge that John Finucane is my solicitor. I don't agree with John's political views in the slightest, but he's a good solicitor and that's what I hired him for. The rest is irrelevant to me. The only time I felt uncomfortable with our relationship was when the Shankill bomber, Sean Kelly, was canvassing for Sinn Féin, and therefore for John, in North Belfast ahead of the 2019 general election. It disgusted me that they had him involved. I was absolutely raging and, being honest, had it happened before I'd gotten to know John I wouldn't have chosen him to represent me. However, I'd consider John a friend now. He actually sorted me out to see the Queen lying in state last year when she passed away. Sinn Féin MPs don't even take their seats in Parliament, so it was no surprise they weren't using their tickets for this. I got two and I think Ian Paisley Jr took a couple. That was the day when Beckham got lauded for standing in line for hours while they tried to cancel Phillip Schofield and Holly Willoughby for bunking the queue. My fast-track pass was the way to go, and I actually had a spare so could have sorted Becks out if he'd only asked. In all seriousness, though, I'm glad I had the opportunity to go and pay my respects.

People talk about me getting involved in politics at home. The guy in the mixed marriage who people can relate to and who has support from both sides of the community. But it will never ever happen. I've just left one cesspit in professional boxing so no chance I'd jump straight into another in official politics. But I will speak up more now and I'm happy to advocate on behalf of issues which I genuinely feel strongly about. One such topic is integrated education in Northern Ireland. I know how easy it is to be influenced by people in your own area and how that can warp your views of other people that you have no opportunity to mix with. Boxing helped me, but even today a lot of kids grow up and all they know about the so-called other side is what they're told. Plenty have zero interaction until they're sixteen and go to a college or start working. It's absolutely insane and the rest of the world must look on in disbelief that the vast majority of our schools continue to segregate children according to what faction of Christianity their family nominally believe in. The stats say that around 70 per cent of parents want integrated education now, yet over 90 per cent of schools remain segregated. I'm not saying it's something that can be solved overnight but getting the ball rolling is easy and we should be doing a lot more to push the process forward. My old high school in Glengormley converted to an integrated school and if it can do it whilst surrounded by loyalist estates, then anywhere can. Had you said to me when I was there twenty years ago that there'd be Protestant and Catholic kids attending the same classes I'd have laughed in your face. But it happened, and it's happening across the city. It would be nice if the two main political parties, the Democratic Unionist Party and Sinn Féin, would get behind it but unfortunately their shared reluctance is about the only thing they ever agree on. Both are frightened it would dilute their identity as British or Irish. Both are embarrassing themselves on the world stage with their stance.

In addition to that very NI-specific problem, it's nice to have opportunities to get involved with and support plenty of other causes. I'm working on a documentary with the BBC at the moment which focuses on young men with mental health issues. It's a real eye-opener to see what fellas are struggling with behind the scenes. Christine and I did a thing for the Irish charity Trócaire in Kenya a few years back, and that was another experience that had a major impact on me and put things in perspective. There are so many people that need help, and so many fantastic people and organisations dedicated to providing it. One thing for all you photographers out there, however. Please stop asking me to put my fists up for photos. I was in a hospice recently, chatting to staff and the patients they are delivering end-of-life care to, and the photographer was asking me to pose like I'm about to knock someone out.

So, all in all, I'm in a very good place now. I'm happy and healthy and have plenty going on to keep me busy. And just in case there ever was a risk of getting bored, the Framptons have recently increased by one. Mila Kerry arrived weighing 6lbs and 9oz on 27 January this year. She is the only one of our kids to have a middle name, given to remember Christine's cousin Kerry who passed away not too long ago. Mila is another smasher, the spitting image of her big sister and brother at their age. If there is one thing Christine and I do well, it's producing good-looking children! I hated being away at camp when Carla and Rossa were newborns, so it is an amazing experience to be here to help Christine with all the baby stuff this time. I won't be missing any more of my kids' celebrations or milestones. Whether they like it or not, I'm going to be around for everything from here on in.

ACKNOWLEDGEMENTS

My thanks to my ma and da, Billy McKee RIP, brother Craig and sister Valerie, Joe Farrell RIP, Cooper McClure and all at Midland ABC, Big Lils, Lisa and Ciaran Magennis, Jamie Moore, Travis Nigelson, Gerry Storey Sr, Gerry Storey Jr, Seamus McCann, Paddy Barnes Sr, Paddy Barnes Jr, and all at Holy Family ABC, Paul Johnston, Billy Walsh, Zaur Antia, the McGuigans for time spent and lessons learned, Ben Pilbeam and Benchmark Sport, DJ, Rab Anderson, Stacey Smyth, John Millar, and the rest of my amazing support, John Campbell RIP, Dr Martin Duffy, Hugh Russell, Ian Ritchie, Anto Fitzpatrick, Isaac Robinson, Daryl Richards, Steve Broughton, Steve McGregor, Simon Bitcon, Rachel, Ross and Malcolm from MIHP, MTK Global, Frank Warren and Queensberry Promotions, Top Rank, Eddie and Barry Hearn and Matchroom Sport, Stevie Ward, Tommy Coyle, Conrad Cummings, David Haye, Kerry Kayes, Assam Fiaz, Gavin Millar, John Finucane, Peter Girvan, Seamus McIlroy, Sean McCrory, Ruth Gorman, Drew Walsh, Thomas Kane, David Kelly, Nicky Fullerton, each and every sparring partner, all my sponsors and anybody who played a role, big or small.

I also want to thank the team at Merrion Press: Conor Graham, Patrick O'Donoghue, Wendy Logue, Maeve Convery, Conor Holbrook and Peter O'Connell. Finally, my thanks to Paul D. Gibson, the man who turned my ramblings into something worth reading, if I do say so myself.